When Lawyers Screw Up

When Lawyers Screw Up

IMPROVING ACCESS TO JUSTICE FOR LEGAL MALPRACTICE VICTIMS

Herbert M. Kritzer and Neil Vidmar

University Press of Kansas

Published by the University Press of Kansas (Lawrence, Kansas 66045), which was organized by the Kansas Board of Regents and is operated and funded by Emporia State University, Fort Hays State University, Kansas State University, Pittsburg State University, the University of Kansas, and Wichita State University.

Library of Congress Cataloging-in-Publication Data
Names: Kritzer, Herbert M., 1947– author. | Vidmar, Neil, author.
Title: When lawyers screw up : improving access to justice for legal malpractice victims / Herbert M. Kritzer and Neil Vidmar.
Description: Lawrence [Kansas] : University Press of Kansas, [2018] | Includes index.
Identifiers: LCCN 2017052559 | ISBN 9780700625857 (cloth : alk. paper) | ISBN 9780700625864 (ebook)
Subjects: LCSH: Lawyers—Malpractice—United States. | Attorney and client—United States.
Classification: LCC KF313 .K75 2018 | DDC 347.73/5041—dc23
LC record available at https://lccn.loc.gov/2017052559.

British Library Cataloguing-in-Publication Data is available.

EU Authorised Representative Details: Easy Access System Europe
Mustamäe tee 50, 10621 Tallinn, Estonia
gpsr.requests@easproject.com

In memory of Amelia "Amy" Howe Kritzer (1947–2016),
Bert's beloved wife, partner, and best friend of 47 years

Contents

Tables

Figures

Preface and Acknowledgments

HERBERT "BERT" KRITZER

Sometime during the summer of 2010, Neil Vidmar contacted me to inquire whether I would have any interest in collaborating on a project looking at legal malpractice (we had collaborated on several projects over the prior 20 years). A major focus of Neil's work over the years had been medical malpractice, and a major focus of my work had been legal practice. The project Neil suggested would be a marriage of each of our long-standing areas of research. Neil had done some very preliminary work looking at some legal malpractice cases and had presented a paper at the 2010 annual meeting of the Law and Society Association. Although I had not written anything about legal malpractice, I had, during my research on contingency practice, observed at a firm trying to cure its own error that created a potential legal malpractice claim, and I was attracted to the idea of a project looking at the phenomenon.

Neil and I decided that the initial work should consist of trying to find any existing data that might be relevant and having some conversations with lawyers who handled legal malpractice claims. We both had other active projects at the time, but we began some preliminary work. Based on that preliminary work, I suggested a small-scale jury simulation, carried out through the facilities of the University of Minnesota with funding provided through the University of Minnesota Grant-in-Aid program administered by the university's Office of the Vice President for Research. Chapter 6 briefly discusses the results of that experiment, which we reported in detail in an article published in the *Hofstra Law Review.*

Access to several datasets or case summaries was provided by agencies or companies that collected the data, and we would like to acknowledge both the agencies and the staff persons who assisted us. These include Carol Bernick and Betty Lou Morrow at the Oregon State Bar's Professional Liability Fund; Rachel Crowe at the Missouri Department of Insurance, Financial Institutions, and Professional Registration; and John Kirkton at the Illinois (and Cook County) *Jury Verdict Reporter*.

Nora Freeman Engstrom (Stanford University) read the entire manuscript and provided a variety of helpful comments. Leslie Levin (University of Connecticut Law School), Vincent Johnson (St. Mary's School of Law), and Susan Saab Fortney (Texas A&M University School of Law) provided very helpful comments on several chapters. We are, of course, responsible for any errors that remain. Tom Baker (University of Pennsylvania Law School) and Rick Swedloff (Rutgers School of Law, Camden) responded to several queries drawing on their current research on lawyers' professional liability insurance and shared the data they had compiled from a series of reports by the American Bar Association's Standing Committee on Lawyers' Professional Liability. Rick also served as a reviewer for the University Press of Kansas, and his review provided helpful suggestions for the final revisions.

We presented portions of this project at several venues, twice to the faculty at the University of Minnesota Law School, twice at the annual Conference on Empirical Legal Studies (2014 and 2015), twice at the annual meeting of the Law and Society Association (2012 and 2014), at a conference on legal malpractice at Hofstra Law School (2014), and at a workshop I co-organized at the International Institute for the Sociology of Law in Oñati, Spain (2015). The participants at those venues and conferences provided helpful feedback.

I received significant assistance in my work on this project from Soren Lagaard (JD, University of Minnesota, 2015). Staff at the University of Minnesota Law Library, particularly but not limited to Suzanne Thorpe, Connie Lenz, and Scott Dewey, answered my frequent questions and supervised research by students employed at the library. I received funding for research assistance, purchase of Florida data, and summer research stipends from the University of Minnesota Law School.

Neil received support through the Duke Law School. This included paying for research assistance, help of the staff of the Duke Law Library, and covering the expense of a trip I made to Durham to work out details of the book project.

I want to more generally acknowledge both the University of Wisconsin–Madison (UW), where I spent 30 years as a member of the Department of Political Science with an affiliation with the Law School, and the University of Minnesota (UM) Law School, which I joined as a faculty member in 2009. Like Neil, I am a non-JD teaching in a law school, which came as a major change after 33 years of teaching political science. (Between UW and UM, I spent two years as a faculty member at William Mitchell College of Law.) The supportive interdisciplinary environment in Madison allowed me to pursue interests unusual for a political scientist. The welcoming environment at the University of Minnesota Law School has allowed me to pursue a range of projects, some more reflective of my political science roots and some, such as this book, more aligned with the role of law schools.

—HMK

NEIL VIDMAR

Similarly, as a coauthor on this volume, I am deeply indebted not only to Bert as my colleague and friend but also to the Duke Law School and its faculty for many reasons. The first is the invitation of Professor Donald Horowitz and Dean Paul Carrington to visit Duke Law for the academic year beginning in the fall of 1987. Subsequently, I was offered a full-time faculty position as Russell M. Robinson II Professor of Law at Duke even though I held a PhD only in social psychology (I had previously spent a year as Russell Sage Resident at Yale Law School and a year as a visiting professor at Osgoode Hall Law School in Toronto). Almost all of my research and publications following my year at Yale have focused on either criminal or civil law issues. Additionally, I have occasionally testified about various legal matters arising in the United States, Canada, England, and Australia. These experiences have broadened my perspective on law as well as legal malpractice.

As Bert mentions above, our collaborative relationship literally goes back decades, and although I intend to keep academically active, it is a "coda" to my official retirement from Duke Law in December 2016, when I took emeritus status. Finishing this book with Bert drew me back to a comment by eminent psychologist E. C. Tolman (1886–1959), who, reflecting on his long academic career, wrote, "In the end the only sure criterion is to have fun." I too have had fun!

—NV

CHAPTER 1

Introduction

[Legal malpractice] is not a synonym for undistinguished representation.

—*Judge Richard Posner*[1]

Based on information provided by an informant concerning a potential illegal-drug purchase transaction, Augustus "Pete" Hall was arrested in his home in Lexington County, South Carolina, by Detective Larry Harrison on drug-related charges. At the time of the arrest, police seized $40,000 in cash. Hall retained lawyer David Fedor to defend him, and because of Fedor's efforts, the charges were dropped and the money was returned. Hall then asked Fedor to file a civil suit alleging abuse of process, malicious prosecution, and violation of civil rights against the detective who had arrested him. When Fedor initially declined to file the suit, Hall retained another lawyer who did initiate a claim; Fedor then agreed to be cocounsel in the case. A few days before the trial was scheduled to begin, the defendant's insurer, Insurance Reserve Fund (IRF), offered to settle the case for $10,000. Hall rejected that offer, and in response IRF raised the offer to $30,000. Hall accepted, allegedly upon the urging of Fedor. Not long after accepting the settlement, Hall sued lawyer Fedor, claiming that Fedor had made misrepresentations regarding the proposed settlement. More specifically, Hall claimed that Fedor had told him either that the defendant was not liable or that IRF would refuse to pay but had failed to tell Hall he knew that $250,000 had actually been available for the settlement. Hall also alleged Fedor had breached attorney-client confidentiality by making comments to third parties that "Hall was dealing drugs" and that "Hall was guilty and lucky to avoid jail." Fedor moved for summary judgment, asserting that there was no evidence either that Hall would have won if the civil suit had gone to trial or that if the suit had been successful, the award would have been more than the $30,000 Hall received in the settlement. The motion was granted. Hall then appealed to the South Carolina Court of Appeal, which affirmed the trial court's grant of summary judgment, ending the lawsuit.[2]

Contrast this unhappy result for Hall with the very different result obtained by Texas businessman S. Lavon Evans. Around the year 2000, Evans entered into an agreement with another businessman, Reed Cagle, regarding the creation of an enterprise named Laredo Energy Holdings (LEH) to operate an oil rig in the Gulf of Mexico. Cagle was to contribute $5.6 million in cash, with Evans providing the oil rig. Evans was to own 51 percent of the business and Cagle the remaining 49 percent. Subsequently, Evans charged that rather than making a cash contribution to the joint enterprise, Cagle mortgaged the oil rig without his knowledge or consent. Evans further contended that without his knowledge or consent, Cagle spun off companies from Laredo. In the end, however, the original oil rig and another rig were seized by the sheriff and sold at auction to satisfy debts accrued by LEH.

Evans then sued what was at the time the world's largest law firm, Chicago-based Baker and McKenzie, for legal malpractice, alleging that the Baker and McKenzie lawyers colluded with Cagle to put the oil rig, and a second rig, $7 million in debt. Evans asserted that the firm had in fact been representing him and/or the cross-plaintiff, bankrupt LEH. Evans's complaint listed seven causes of action involving legal malpractice and breach of contract, including breach of fiduciary duty, negligent omission and misstatements of material facts, civil conspiracy, aiding and abetting tortious interference, and breach of duty of good faith and fair dealing. At trial, a Mississippi jury ruled in favor of Evans and LEH, awarding $81 million to Evans and another $22.4 million to LEH.[3]

Not surprisingly, Baker and McKenzie appealed to the Supreme Court of Mississippi, claiming that several errors were made at trial and that the plaintiff's evidence was not credible. In October 2013, that court upheld the original verdict with regard to liability but found that the jury was erroneously instructed with regard to whether the plaintiff had suffered any actual damage ("causation") and, if so, what the proper amount of damages should be. The court remanded the case, ordering a new trial on causation and damages.[4] After the remand, the case settled for an undisclosed amount.[5]

At least in monetary terms, these two cases lie toward the ends of the continuum of claims involving the professional liability of lawyers and law firms, what is generally referred to as *legal malpractice*. One would not expect to see any news reports of Hall's suit against Fedor because it was relatively small and was thrown out of court. However, a case producing a verdict award of $100 million dollars would typically catch the attention of the popular media. Although we were able to find a number of stories about Evans's suit against

Baker and McKenzie in the legal media and in the business press, we could find only two reports in the general press, one of which was in the *Chicago Tribune.*

Imagine if there were a $100 million verdict against a hospital or a physician. That would be widely reported in regional, if not national, news. In fact, the proponents of placing limits on verdicts in medical malpractice cases would probably jump on the case as an example showing why such limits were needed. More broadly, although many books and articles have addressed the topic of medical malpractice, the issue of legal malpractice has received scant attention, either from policy makers or scholars undertaking systematic research on lawyers' professional liability, beyond legal treatises or casebooks.[6]

In many ways, this is surprising given that a quick search of the internet shows that claims of legal malpractice and subsequent litigation are not uncommon. Indeed, thousands of claims are made every year, and some lawyers and law firms specialize in handling legal malpractice claims, either prosecuting those claims or defending them. Legal malpractice claims are brought against mega law firms as well as against solo practitioners. The plaintiffs might be mega corporations or impecunious individuals. The asserted damages might involve relatively small sums or many millions of dollars. The alleged grounds on which the claims are made range from simple errors, such as missing a filing deadline, to charges of major conflicts of interest or even fraud. Many claims are settled without formal litigation. Others involve settlements at various stages along the litigation continuum. Few claims, at least in relative terms, are decided by jury or bench trials.

The lack of scholarly attention to lawyers' professional liability claims is also surprising because legal services are big business in the United States, producing $270.6 billion in revenue in 2012, according to a US Commerce Department report on professional services.[7] In terms of expenditures on professional services, they are surpassed only by physician and clinical services, which, according to the Centers for Medicare and Medicaid Services, totaled $566.6 billion in 2012.[8] The issue of negligence and error in the delivery of medical services is a familiar topic and has long been a prominent public issue, engaging medical professionals and their organizations, policy makers, and legal scholars. In fact, general articles bemoaning medical malpractice litigation can be found at least as far back as the 1930s and even earlier in journals of the medical profession.[9] Over the past 30 years, extensive empirical research has documented the myths and realities of medical malpractice, showing that the incidence of medical negligence is very high although the volume of medical malpractice claims has remained a tiny fraction of the incidence of actual malpractice.[10] In contrast, lawyers' liability for negligence or other harm-causing behavior has received virtually no attention from anyone other than members of the legal profession itself. We do not have good measures of the amounts paid out in connection with lawyers' professional liability, but an indirect indicator is the amount paid by lawyers for insurance to cover that liability: $3.5 billion compared with an estimated $5.6 billion paid by physicians and surgeons.[11] This means liability insurance costs constitute about 1.3 percent of overall revenue for lawyers compared with only 1.0 percent for physicians and surgeons.

The purpose of this book is to provide a portrait of claims concerning lawyers' professional liability (LPL), commonly referred to as legal malpractice, including what gives rise to them, how they are handled, and the nature of outcomes of those claims. Our central argument is that LPL cannot be viewed as a unitary phenomenon. Rather, there are two distinct LPL worlds, one involving claims in the context of legal services for individuals and family businesses and one for claims arising from work on behalf of large corporate entities. The analyses in the following chapters show that these two distinct LPL worlds align with what Heinz and Laumann labeled the "two hemispheres" of the bar. Based on their study of the Chicago bar in 1975, those authors described two distinct segments of legal practitioners, one serving primarily the corporate sector and one serving primarily the personal services sector.[12] At the time of the 1975 study, these two segments each made up roughly half of the legal services produced by private practitioners in Chicago, and hence the metaphor of "hemispheres." That metaphor has continued to be used to distinguish between the two broad sectors of legal practice even though the balance between the two sectors has shifted such that the corporate sector is now substantially greater in terms of both amount of effort[13] and revenue.[14]

THE TWO HEMISPHERES OF LAWYERS' PROFESSIONAL LIABILITY

Based on wide-ranging data and other information assembled for this book, the following chapters show sharp differences in LPL along the corporate/personal services divide: the frequency of LPL claims, the areas of practice producing LPL claims, the kinds of errors or behaviors asserted in claims, the amounts at stake in claims, and the amounts ultimately paid out to resolve claims all differ depending on whether the claim arises from types of legal practices that serve primarily individuals and their small businesses or those that serve large corporations. Fundamentally, this finding reflects the differences in the nature of the legal work conducted on behalf of individuals compared with the work conducted for corporations. Riding on the coattails of Heinz and Laumann, we label this contrast the *two hemispheres of lawyers' professional liability.*

A central difference discussed in Chapters 5 and 6 is that corporate firms appear to face fewer claims, at least as measured on a "per-lawyer" basis. It is likely that this is in part because those firms implicitly or explicitly build in checks of various types to catch errors before these errors cause harm. However, even as corporate firms might be able to limit the frequency of the claims they face, when such a firm does face a claim it is likely to be much more severe in terms of the potential loss involved. For the largest firms, a loss could be many times what one sees as the largest losses in medical malpractice, as illustrated by a $196.1 million verdict in 2015 against the Texas firm Andrews Kurth.[15] As is discussed in Chapter 3, the magnitude of these risks is such that single insurers are generally unwilling to underwrite insurance policies covering those risks.

A key problem posed by the differences between the two hemispheres is the differential ability of clients to obtain redress when the action of a lawyer through negligence or incompetence or other kinds of behavior has caused the client a financial loss. First, although corporate clients are less likely to experience a loss caused by their law firms, when a loss does occur, corporations know that their firms have insurance that can be used to provide compensation for the loss. In contrast, the lawyers used by individuals and/or small businesses have a significant likelihood of not being insured—except in the state of Oregon, where LPL insurance is mandatory. Lawyers experienced in prosecuting legal malpractice cases seldom take on a case if the lawyer-defendant is uninsured, a situation that will be discussed in Chapters 3 and 7. Second, many of the losses experienced by individuals or small businesses are relatively small in relation to the costs of prosecuting a legal malpractice claim even if they are significant from the perspective of the potential claimant. This fact serves to further limit the willingness of knowledgeable lawyers to take on legal malpractice claims.

Thus, there is a real dilemma for the clients served by the personal services sector of the legal profession. They face a greater likelihood of a lawyer making a costly error, and they face greater limitations in securing the kind of assistance needed to prosecute a claim against a negligent lawyer. This is an access to justice problem and a potential image problem for the legal profession. Although there are possible solutions to the access problems, which will be the focus of the concluding chapter, the likelihood that many of those solutions will be implemented is small.

The balance of this chapter consists of a brief discussion of the access to justice challenge and a review of the scant extant empirical research on LPL in the United States. Chapter 2 provides further illustrations of the kinds of LPL claims that arise by presenting selected examples of actual cases. Chapter 3 discusses three foundational issues: the structure and use of LPL insurance, the legal bases for LPL claims, and key legal questions that arise in those claims. Because many of the issues in physicians' liability have been widely discussed, Chapter 3 also includes a discussion of the major differences between physicians' liability and lawyers' liability. Chapters 4 and 5 draw on a range of empirical data; those data come largely either directly or indirectly from LPL insurers: from reports published by the insurers, from reports published by the American Bar Association (ABA) Standing Committee on Lawyers' Professional Liability, and from reports of individual cases to state insurance regulators as required by state law. Chapter 4 focuses on the frequency of claims, the areas of practice producing claims, and the types of errors or behavior alleged in claims, highlighting the contrast between the two hemispheres. Chapter 5 examines the outcome of claims, with respect both to which side prevails and to the amounts paid out when claimants obtain compensation. Here again, the focus is on the difference between the two hemispheres. Chapter 6 looks at what happens when LPL claims reach trial, including the likelihood of getting to trial, who wins, and the size of awards. Because of the small number of LPL trials, it is not possible to delve deeply into variations in outcomes. The data used in Chapter 6 come primarily from studies conducted by the National Center for State Courts for the US Justice Department's Bureau of Justice Statistics, supplemented by LPL verdicts reported by the Illinois *Jury Verdict Reporter* and information appearing in several published reports. Chapter 7 turns to a series of semistructured interviews with representatives of insurers and lawyers who regularly handle LPL cases, some on the plaintiff's side and some who defend LPL claims on behalf of insurers. Detail on specific data sources is provided in the chapter where a particular data source is first used. Chapter 8 concludes with a brief summary and a discussion of changes that would mitigate the access to justice problems facing individuals and small businesses who have grievances against their former lawyers.

THE ACCESS TO JUSTICE CHALLENGE

The challenges aggrieved parties face in obtaining redress are probably as old as human society. The first organized systems to address access to justice issues were charity legal aid organizations.[16] The first such group in the United States was part of an organization founded in New York in 1876 to aid and protect German immigrants. In 1890 this organization became the Legal Aid Society of New York. Two years earlier the Ethical Culture Society of Chicago established the Bureau of Justice, which offered assistance without regard to nationality, ethnicity, race, or sex. Another landmark development was the publication in 1919 of Reginal Heber Smith's book *Justice and the Poor.*[17] Smith's book prompted the American Bar Association to create a Special Committee on Legal Aid Work and to urge state and local bar associations to follow suit. This in turn led to a range of programs, some through charity organizations, some through law schools, and some through the volunteerism of lawyers. In the late 1930s the forerunner of modern legal needs studies was conducted by Charles Clark and Emma Corstvet; the results, published in the *Yale Law Journal,* showed widespread unmet needs for legal assistance.[18]

The patchwork system of legal aid continued through the early 1960s, at which time things began to change. Foundations began funding a range of legal services programs, and President Lyndon Baines Johnson's war on poverty brought federal funding of large numbers of state and local programs along with several national programs to provide information and training as well as some specialized programs targeting particular populations or problems. In the 1970s the Legal Services Corporation (LSC) came into being, serving as the vehicle for funding programs around the country. At about this same time, the first comprehensive study of legal needs was published by the American Bar Foundation (ABF), again showing the depth of the unmet legal needs.[19] A range of studies conducted subsequent to the ABF study have continued to show the extent of these needs.

Legal aid was not the only program employed in an effort to improve access to justice. A second approach was the creation of specialized small claims courts. Although there were antecedents to small claims courts (e.g., justices of the peace courts), what we today call small claims courts in the United States were largely a product of the progressive movement during the first quarter of the twentieth century. The idea was to create a forum for use by individuals that was professional (staffed by lawyers rather than lay justices of the peace), inexpensive (by not requiring legal representation), less formal, and quick.[20] Unfortunately, small claims courts failed to live up to these expectations, with the earliest research on small claims courts showing that they were dominated by businesses seeking to collect debts[21] and in this way did not differ greatly from the justice of the peace and mayor's courts that preceded them.[22]

Although scholars had long expressed concerns about the ability of citizens to obtain redress, it was the Florence Access to Justice Project, led by Mauro Cappelletti, that marked the beginning of contemporary scholarship on the issue and set forth a much wider-ranging set of ideas about improving access to justice.[23] Some of the new ideas focused on expanding on such recourse as class action suits, alternative dispute resolution through both government and private mechanisms, incentivizing private interests to pursue redress for groups, creating procedural alternatives for certain types of cases, and eliminating or modifying legal barriers such as statutes of limitations that served to block access under certain circumstances. Either implicitly or explicitly, most of the new or expanded approaches dealt with the problem of cost.

The Cost Problem in Access to Justice

The issue most associated with limited access to justice in contemporary society is the costs associated with invoking formal legal processes. The cost question has two dimensions. First, many grievances, although real, are so small that it is not rational to spend the time and money required to obtain redress. Many trivial experiences fall into this category; perhaps most common is the soft drink machine that fails to dispense a can or bottle after the machine has swallowed your money. Although many of these events are trivial on an individual basis, they can add up for the entity on the other side to be quite profitable. Few individuals in these kinds of cases would find it worth pursuing redress. However, if the group of those harmed is sufficiently large, some type of aggregate process—what in the United States is called a class action—can be worth pursuing. Aggregate procedures have substantial potential for claims involving consumer issues.[24] In the United States, a series of decisions by the US Supreme Court has largely cut off this avenue of redress for consumers.[25] Specifically, the Court has ruled that consumers who enter into contracts with businesses, even long standard-form contracts that no one ever reads, are bound by arbitration clauses in those contracts waiving the consumer's rights both to turn to the courts and to join with others in an aggregate arbitration claim.[26]

The cost question is not limited to grievances involving very small individual amounts. Even quite substantial claims involve potential costs that greatly exceed the amount of the claim. One area in which this is very evident involves medical negligence claims. Except for the most obvious errors, such as operating on the wrong body part or administering the wrong drug with devastating consequence, the costs of pursuing a disputed claim will typically be in the tens of thousands of dollars even without taking lawyers' fees into consideration. This problem is evident in reports of medical malpractice claims published annually by the Texas Department of Insurance (TDI). Through 2007, TDI separately reported the number of claims with payments of $10,000 or less and the number with payments exceeding $10,000. Of the medical negligence claims paid in 2007, only 14.0 percent involved payments of $10,000 or less; in contrast, for the other categories of commercial insurance covered in the report (general liability, commercial auto, and commercial multiperil), 72.2 percent of the paid claims involved payments of $10,000 or less.[27] Even in some kinds of cases with very substantial damages (e.g., product liability cases[28] and toxic tort cases[29]), the costs of pursuing a single claim can exceed the likely damages, and that does not take into account the possibility that the claim or claims will ultimately fail.[30]

The second cost challenge that applies in cases both modest and large is attorneys' fees. Although in many areas, such as routine auto accidents and problems with everyday consumer purchases, grievances are quickly and readily resolved, pursuing formal legal action typically requires the assistance of a legal professional, the cost of which is likely to be high. There are several ways the attorney fee barrier can be overcome. The first is through some sort of no-win, no-pay fee arrangement that allows the attorney to be paid out of the claimant's recovery; such arrangements are customarily described as contingency fees. A contingency fee can be structured in a variety of ways. In the United States, the most common arrangement is as a percentage of the amount recovered; this is effectively a kind of commission fee.[31] Starting in 1995, England adopted a system labeled as a *conditional fee*, in which the lawyer received a fee based on effort and/or tasks, with an "uplift" of up to 100 percent to compensate the lawyer for assuming the risk of receiving no fee. As originally conceived, the base fee was to be paid by the defendant, and the uplift was to be paid out of the recovery but with a limit of 25 percent of that recovery.[32] Starting in 2001, the uplift was also recoverable from the defendant, although that practice ended in 2013.[33] A third approach is a system whereby the lawyer simply waives any fee if the claim is unsuccessful. This practice has existed for some time in Scotland, in what was referred to as a "speculative fee,"[34] and there is evidence that such a practice existed informally in England prior to institution of the conditional fee.[35] Regardless of how the fee is structured, an attorney handling a case on a contingency-fee basis must be willing to assume the risk of there being no recovery, in which case the attorney's time will not be compensated; moreover, often the attorney has to bear the cost of any expenditures on experts, court fees, and investigators when a claim fails.

The second approach to dealing with the cost of attorneys is through some form of legal aid, either privately funded or publicly funded.[36] Legal aid is almost always means-tested, which limits its availability to a small segment of society. Often legal aid for noncriminal matters is available for only certain types of claims. Into the 1990s, England had an extensive system of legal aid that covered a large proportion of the population;[37] in 1990, for example, 51 percent of the population was eligible for legal aid in personal injury cases, a sharp drop from only eleven years earlier, when 81 percent of the population was eligible. However, legal aid was not available for hearings involving personal injury claims if those hearings were before tribunals rather than courts.[38] In the United States, a significant share of legal aid is provided through the LSC, an agency created in the 1960s as part of the war on poverty. However, legal aid in the United States has never been as broad as it once was in England. The key challenge of legal aid is funding. Convincing legislators to devote tax dollars to civil legal aid has never been easy, and governments seek alternatives that do not involve using tax dollars. In fact, a major motivation for adopting the conditional fee in England was to allow the government to reduce expenditures on civil legal aid.[39]

A third approach to overcoming the cost problem in access to justice is fee shifting, particularly one-way fee shifting. Fee shifting refers to the practice of requiring the loser to pay some, or all, of the winner's legal expenses.[40] In its traditional form, fee shifting is two way, meaning that if the plaintiff wins, the defendant pays the plaintiff's legal expense, and vice versa if the defendant wins. In its two-way form, fee shifting serves as a powerful disincentive to bringing cases because plaintiffs are often risk averse; consequently, two-way fee shifting tends to impede access to justice for most individuals.[41] However, although common around the world,[42] in the United States a general two-way fee shifting system exists only in Alaska.[43] In contrast, one-way fee shifting, whereby only the defendant faces the risk of having to pay the other side's fee, is more common in the United States and is typically seen as a mechanism to increase access to justice.[44] In fact, reforms implemented in 2013 in England formally changed from two-way to one-way fee shifting for certain types of cases as a means of maintaining access to justice in the face of certain other reforms.[45] Two issues arise in one-way fee shifting regimes. First, an attorney who takes on a case under a one-way regime with the understanding that any fee would come from the other side must be prepared to receive no compensation if the claim fails. Second, the calculation of the fee must produce a reasonable return for the attorney's time investment, and often the hourly rate is set low and fails to account for the risk the attorney assumed.[46]

In significant part, the cost issue differentiates the LPL hemispheres in the United States. The LPL-related problems experienced by corporate actors are likely to be of substantial size, and the corporate actor will typically have the resources to pursue redress if it chooses to do so and can bear the cost of losing if a claim fails. In contrast, in the personal services hemisphere, there are questions both of magnitude of the loss relative to the cost of obtaining redress and how to finance those costs if redress is sought. The primary solution to that problem is the contingency fee, usually a percentage fee on the order of one-third or more of the recovery. However, the costs of pursuing an LPL claim, both in an attorney's time and in expenses such as expert witness fees, means that knowledgeable attorneys will consider cases only with losses sufficient to produce what the lawyer views as an adequate fee. Although for the claimant the loss may be substantial, it might not be substantial from an attorney's perspective. This problem might be mitigated in one state, New Jersey, where the state supreme court has effectively imposed one-way fee shifting in LPL cases,[47] with the amount of the fee based on the amount of time expended multiplied by a reasonable hourly rate, what is often called a *lodestar fee*.[48] As will be discussed in Chapter 7, the cost issue is a major barrier to redress for LPL claims coming from the personal services sector.

The Recognition and Attribution Problem

A second issue regarding access to justice is whether those who have been harmed in some way recognize that they have been harmed and then attribute that harm to a party they deem to have caused it.[49] In situations such as motor vehicle accidents, the occurrence of harm is usually clear, even if the person or people responsible for the harm might not be. In some contexts, the actual occurrence of harm might be obscured. Pay discrimination is one such situation if, for example, there is no way to find out if there are differences in pay based on categories that would constitute discrimination.[50] It is likely that in cases of professional negligence, many of the victims never discover that they have been harmed. For example, a hospital patient might experience more pain because of a medication error but never realize that had happened. There is some evidence that most people who suffer harm as a result of errors or negligence during medical care never realize they have been harmed.[51] In the legal services arena, an accident victim might be undercompensated because a lawyer failed to retain an expert assessment that adequately determined the long-term consequences of an injury. A divorce client might receive an inadequate divorce settlement because her lawyer failed to obtain an accurate appraisal of a business that constituted marital property. Although in the medical arena studies have assessed the frequency of errors by systematically examining hospital records, there is nothing comparable in the legal services area.[52] We suspect, but have no way to prove, that many harmful errors committed during legal representation are never discovered by those harmed.

Attribution is a different kind of problem. First, even when people realize that some harm has occurred, they might not attribute responsibility for that harm to another party. They might blame themselves, or they might simply attribute it to bad luck. On the other side, some people might attribute harm to someone even when the other person did nothing to cause the harm.[53] Critics of medical malpractice litigation tend to see this as the major problem in the system and decry the resulting "frivolous litigation."[54] As will be shown in Chapter 5, a large percentage of LPL claims does not result in compensation being paid, and this might indicate a tendency of people to blame their lawyers for less than satisfactory outcomes even if the lawyer was not negligent. This might be particularly common in divorce cases, which frequently result in people upset by the results of the divorce process. Another area of practice with a high potential for similar problems is criminal defense, although as will be discussed in Chapter 3, LPL claims arising from criminal defense have unique problems that limit the potential for success.

PRIOR EMPIRICAL RESEARCH ON LEGAL MALPRACTICE

As noted above, although extensive empirical research on medical malpractice exists, scant attention has been devoted to legal malpractice. As this book was written, there was a renewed scholarly interest in LPL, both in the United States and elsewhere.[55] In the United States the interest has centered largely on insurance-related issues. Levin has examined the frequency and reasons that lawyers choose to go without LPL insurance;[56] her study will be discussed in Chapter 3. She has also examined the limited regulatory role vis-à-vis solo and small-firm lawyers played by LPL insurers.[57] Baker and Swedloff have also been examining insurance arrangements.[58] In one article Baker and Swedloff summarized information gathered from several insurance company sources. Because Chapters 4 and 5 draw in part on the information they assembled, along with additional information from some of the same sources, we defer further discussion until then. Other aspects of Baker and Swedloff's work are discussed in Chapter 3. Here we focus on the earlier research on LPL.

In a 1980 article, Werner Pfennigstorf reviewed available research.[59] He found data from four insurance sources and summarized the information regarding claim rates during the 1970s extending back for one source to the late 1960s. He reported that the rate varied from 1 claim per 100 insured lawyers to about 6 claims per 100 insured lawyers; the average amount of the claims ranged from about $5,000 to as high as $20,000, or roughly $15,000 to $60,000 if converted to the equivalent amount as this is written. Drawing on data reported by the American Home Assurance Company describing claims for the period 1969–1978, Pfennigstorf reported that the two most common alleged types of negligence were missing a deadline set by a statute of limitations (14.8 percent) and improper handling of a title or real estate matter (13.5 percent); an additional 8.7 percent of claims alleged a failure to properly or timely file a document or appeal.

Pfennigstorf also briefly referenced an empirical study conducted by Duke Nordlinger Stern.[60] Stern surveyed lawyers in eleven southern states, asking respondents about claims experience over the period 1972–1977. Only fragmentary reports of that study are available, and there are serious issues regarding response rates. Nevertheless, the survey did show an increasing incidence of claims over the six-year period. The study also showed that missing deadlines was a prominent allegation. Because of the categories Stern used, there is no way to determine how often the claim arose from the handling of a real estate matter. The study also found that only about a third (36.4 percent) of claims resulted in payments and that about two-thirds (64.0 percent) of the payments were $5,000 or less.[61]

The central argument Pfennigstorf advanced was a need for systematic collection of data on legal malpractice claims, and to this end he proposed establishing what became known as the National Legal Malpractice Data Center, which operated under the auspices of the ABA Committee on Professional Liability. In 1985 the chairman of that center, William Gates, published a brief report summarizing some of the findings based on four years of case-level data provided by several LPL insurers.[62] Key points were:

- Almost 80 percent of the reported claims were brought against solo practitioners or lawyers in firms of two to five lawyers.
- Almost half of the claims involved just two areas of practice: plaintiffs' personal injury and real estate.
- About two-thirds of claims were brought against lawyers in practice more than 10 years.
- About two-thirds were closed with no payment, and only about 4 percent of paid claims were a result of a judgment.
- The frequency of payment and the size of payments varied by the area of practice, and amounts paid tended to be relatively modest.

In 1989, what was by then called the ABA Standing Committee on Lawyers' Professional Liability (SCLPL) published a report showing extensive, detailed statistical tabulations[63] and a year later published a more analytical report based on those same data.[64] Subsequently, the SCLPL produced a series of reports, *Profile of Legal Malpractice Claims*, covering four-year periods: 1992–1995, 1996–1999, 2000–2003, 2004–2007, 2008–2011, and 2012–2015, all of which were based on summary statistics provided by insurers rather than on individual case reports. The insurers providing information to the ABA tended to be more oriented to insuring solo practitioners and small-firm lawyers than to lawyers in medium to large firms. The most recent report includes comparative figures for all the studies. Those figures will be discussed in some detail in Chapters 4 and 5.

The only other published empirical study of legal malpractice was reported in a pair of articles by Tulane University law professor Manuel Ramos that appeared in the mid-1990s. In those articles, Ramos drew on a variety of data sources, including his own 20-year experience defending legal malpractice claims.[65] The thrust of Ramos's conclusion was that legal malpractice was a much larger problem than suggested by then-extant research, particularly as indicated by the SCLPL reports.

In the first of the two articles, Ramos discussed his analysis of 42 cases he had defended between February 1991 and December 1992, all but one of which were in suit,[66] plus the SCLPL reports, data on claims reported to the Florida Insurance Commission, and statistics from reports published by two large legal malpractice insurers. Comparing the SCLPL statistics with those from his own experience, Ramos argued that insurers responding to the SCLPL data request must have been underreporting their claims experience. However, Ramos appears to have placed too much confidence in the data he compiled for the 42 cases he handled while in practice. There is no way of knowing how the insurer decided to refer cases to Ramos's firm or which of those cases he handled himself. It is interesting to note that Ramos, who had defended LPL suits, reported that most of his cases resulted in payments to the plaintiff. This might reflect the nature of the cases Ramos handled, heavily weighted toward claims arising from plaintiffs' personal injury matters that had somewhat higher values than the typical paid case in the SCLPL reports or in the reports of the Oregon State Bar's Professional Liability Fund (OSBPLF; PLF for short).[67] Ramos appeared to believe that his personal experience was more typical than that reflected in the various other sets of data, which he saw as biased in a way that understated the significance of legal malpractice as a problem for lawyers and their clients; however, he did seem generally positive toward the information provided by PLF, even though it was not consistent with his own experience.

One interesting aspect of the information provided by Ramos involved figures he abstracted from periodic reports published by the Attorneys' Liability Assurance Society (ALAS), a mutual insurer that provides LPL coverage to corporate-sector law firms with at least 35 lawyers. Although he did note the high value of cases for which ALAS was the insurer, he did not take into account the very different profile of cases in terms of distribution of areas of practice producing those cases. Although for the other insurers he considered, the dominant areas of practice producing claims were plaintiffs' personal injury and real estate, for ALAS the two dominant areas were corporate/banking and litigation. Given the clients of ALAS's insureds, it seems safe to assume that litigation handled by those insureds was seldom, if ever, plaintiffs' personal injury cases.

In his second article, Ramos tried to use case-level data he obtained from the Florida Insurance Commission to assess which factors might be associated with a lawyer facing a professional liability claim. The data included the name of the lawyer whose action generated the claim. This allowed Ramos to merge these data with information from the Martindale-Hubbell legal directory (size of firm, location of practice, areas of practice, Martindale-Hubbell ratings for the firm and the lawyer, birth date, law school attended, date of admittance to the bar, years of practice) and with information from the regulatory authority on any disciplinary complaints faced by the lawyer (any complaints, any actual discipline, and nature of any disciplinary dispositions). Ramos's analysis is difficult to interpret because it consists largely of tables showing various distributions, often comparing malpractice rates to the overall distribution of lawyers without undertaking any statistical tests to see if the distributions differed. Ramos did find some patterns consistent with the SCLPL reports. For example, lawyers facing a legal malpractice claim were more likely to practice solo or in small firms, although solo practitioners were if anything underrepresented compared with the population of lawyers. As discussed in Chapter 3, this might mean solo practitioners were underrepresented among lawyers carrying malpractice insurance. Lawyers facing legal malpractice claims tended to be older rather than younger. He found no particular relationship with quality of law school attended, having been disciplined, practicing in an urban versus a rural setting, or Martindale-Hubbell rating. He zeroed in on lawyers who were the subject of two or more malpractice claims during the period covered by the Florida data and found that they did not differ in major ways from Florida lawyers in general. His overall conclusions were that "nobody is safe" and that "everyone and anyone commits [*sic*] malpractice."

A later, unpublished study by Vidmar and Holman reported a very limited analysis of data also obtained from the Florida Office of Insurance Regulation.[68] However, those authors were limited by a change in the law requiring reporting of claims in the years after Ramos's articles. Specifically, at the time Ramos conducted his analysis, Florida law required reporting of all insurance claims alleging professional liability against a lawyer; in the late 1990s the law was changed to require reporting of only those claims in which some payment was made to the claimant or the loss adjustment expense exceeded $5,000.[69] Vidmar and Holman provided a brief summary of statistics based on the Florida data. The most striking part of the analysis was not surprising: the number of reported claims dropped sharply after the reporting law changed. However, one anomaly was that the number of lawsuits reported also dropped, which seems strange given that it is unlikely that many, if any, lawsuits involving an LPL claim could be defended for less than $5,000. The authors raised questions about the completeness of the Florida data because they located a number of large verdicts in Florida LPL cases that could not be matched to reports in the Florida insurance data.

ERRORS DO NOT EQUAL HARM

The chapters that follow this introduction map how issues of LPL play out through the insurance and court systems. One important point to keep in mind is that errors are quite common in any kind of professional practice, a point well documented by an observational study of medical practice in a hospital setting.[70] Some errors cause great harm, some cause a minimal amount of harm, and some cause no harm at all. In the practice of law many, probably most, errors are detected and corrected before any harm occurs. This detection can be by the lawyer who made the error, by a colleague of the lawyer, or by the client. For example, Kritzer has detected errors in work products of lawyers he has employed for routine tasks: a failure to note a mortgage in a title opinion, an error in an estate tax return, and an error in a draft of a will. Any of these errors could have caused harm if they had not been corrected.

As will be discussed in Chapter 3, the occurrence of harm is one of the required elements of a negligence claim. The simple fact of an error is not enough. There must be harm. In the context of LPL this is a major issue, particularly in claims arising from litigation. Specifically, would the LPL claimant have prevailed, or possibly done much better, if the lawyer had not made the error? The parallel question in medical liability arises when a physician has failed to diagnose a potentially fatal condition, and the patient dies; would the patient have survived if the condition had been diagnosed in a timely fashion? In both the medical and legal contexts, the problem is one of uncertainty: in the absence of the error would the outcome have been different, or in the absence of the error would there have been a higher probability that the outcome would have been substantially different? Many states have adopted mechanisms for dealing with the uncertainty in these kinds of cases when the claim arises in the medical arena; however, no state has done something similar in the legal arena. This issue is one of the challenges discussed in the concluding chapter of this book.

CHAPTER 2

Illustrative Cases of Lawyers' Professional Liability

Chapter 1 opened with two case examples involving claims of legal malpractice, one involving a very large verdict and one that was, in comparison, more modest with regard to how much money was at stake. This chapter presents a sample of additional cases to broaden readers' perspective on the range and variation in lawyers' professional liability (LPL) litigation. The cases are intended to illustrate various legal issues.

Among those issues are the legal bases for LPL claims. Those include (1) breach of contract, (2) negligence, (3) breach of fiduciary obligations, and (4) intentional torts such as fraud and misrepresentation. As will be discussed in detail in Chapter 3, the first three are claims normally brought by a client or someone standing in the place of a client, such as an heir named in a will or some other third-party beneficiary, whereas intentional torts can also be brought by a nonclient.

The cases described in the following pages do not constitute a random sample of all of the cases that can be found on the Internet or elsewhere.[1] Rather, they are cases selected to illustrate various types of claims and some of the legal issues that arise in LPL claims. Getting detailed information on a random sample would be extremely difficult, if not impossible. Even if LPL cases could readily be found in the court records, few would provide information on case outcomes unless the defendant won a motion that ended the case or the case resulted in a trial verdict because court records seldom record details of settlements. Contacting the participants in lawsuits that settle would often be futile because settlements are frequently confidential.[2] Moreover, a large proportion of claims against lawyers are resolved without a lawsuit being filed. The information about such claims, even their very existence, is typically confidential.[3]

We present a total of 10 cases in the following pages. The cases are divided into two groups of five. The first group contains cases involving areas of practice serving individuals, such as personal injury, divorce, sale of a home, and criminal defense. The second group of cases all involved business matters, although none involved large corporations; the cases all deal with problems that arose from business transactions or litigation that arose in connection with such transactions. Across the various cases, readers will see a range of alleged malpractice: missing deadlines, failure to raise issues that should have been raised, failure to sue the correct party, drafting errors, errors in providing advice, lack of due diligence, failure to adequately communicate with the client, and breach of fiduciary duty.

Chapter 1 referenced the mega-verdict against the Andrews Kurth law firm. The case stands out in terms of the magnitude of the jury award, but the basic issues in that case were not atypical. Other malpractice cases have yielded large awards, but many were eventually settled for lesser amounts than the original jury award or were overturned on appeal. One case described below was still pending in the trial court as this was written; interested readers might want to check the internet for updates on that case.

PERSONAL SERVICES SECTOR

Missing a Deadline in a Personal Injury Claim: Kranendonk v. Swapp & Associates *(Utah, 2015)*[4]

In June 2006 Jodi Kranendonk, a Utah resident, was stopped in traffic on a freeway in Portland, Oregon, when she was rear-ended by a tractor-trailer. The impact pushed her vehicle into another lane of traffic, where she was sideswiped by a second tractor-trailer. Kranendonk suffered serious injuries to her knees resulting in multiple surgeries; she eventually needed total replacement of both knees. She subsequently retained a Utah law firm, Gregg & Swapp,[5] to sue the trucking company for its driver's negligence. Gregg & Swapp had an office in Spokane, Washington, and assigned the case to an attorney in that office who had a license to practice in Oregon. That attorney, who was then handling over 100 cases and had no experience with trucking cases, eventually filed suit in Oregon, where the statute of limitations on personal injury cases is only two years.[6]

The suit was dismissed because notice of a lawsuit was not served on the defendant within 60 days of filing as required by Oregon law. A year later Gregg & Swapp refiled the lawsuit, but once again it was dismissed after notice had not been served on the defendant within the required period. It was then too late under Oregon's statute of limitations to try to file for a third time, so Gregg & Swapp filed suit in the state of Washington, where the trucking company also did business and where the statute of limitations was three years rather than two.[7] However, the Washington court dismissed the case on *res judicata* grounds (i.e., that the dismissal in Oregon constituted a final decision). Gregg & Swapp then explained to Kranendonk that because they had failed to file the lawsuit within the statute of limitations, it was now time-barred.

Kranendonk fired Gregg & Swapp and retained a new law firm that filed yet another suit in Oregon. In an effort to circumvent the expired statute of limitations, the new lawyers tried to invoke the Oregon savings statute, which provides for exceptions to the statute of limitations under certain circumstances.[8] As part of this proceeding, the trucking company acknowledged its liability although asserting that the savings statute did not apply making the claim time-barred. When the case went to trial, the jury accepted the statute of limitation defense and ruled for the defendant, ending any possibility of obtaining compensation from the trucking company despite its acknowledgment of fault for the accident.

Kranendonk then filed a malpractice lawsuit against her former lawyers. Gregg & Swapp admitted the firm had been negligent in its failures that led to the lawsuits in Oregon being dismissed. It argued in its defense that Kranendonk had failed to provide evidence that she would have prevailed in the suit in Oregon (i.e., that the trucking company was liable). The defendant also claimed that she had failed to provide evidence of what damages a jury would have awarded if it found full liability against the trucking company. The court disagreed on the damages issue but did grant summary judgment on the viable claim issue, ruling that the admission by the trucking company in the Oregon proceedings constituted hearsay. Kranendonk appealed, as did the defendant law firm, which had lost its argument regarding damages. The appellate court reversed the trial court on the question of liability and upheld it on the damages issue. In 2015, the malpractice case proceeded to trial in Utah. The jury found the defendant firm, by then known as Craig Swapp and Associates, liable for professional negligence and awarded Kranendonk $3.5 million in damages.

Negligence and Breach of Fiduciary Duty by Concealing the Failure to Name the Proper Defendant in a Personal Injury Case: Reece and Long v. Clifford Law Offices *(Illinois; appeal in 2015)*[9]

In July 2005 two workmen, Gregory Reece and Ardis Long, were seriously injured when an elevator in which they were riding fell several floors to the ground. Subsequently the two men retained the Clifford Law Offices (CLO) to prosecute their personal injury claims. Reportedly, the lawyers at CLO reviewed a treatise concerning causes of actions in which persons had been injured or killed in elevator accidents, and that treatise noted that (1) the premises owner would be a potential defendant, (2) the premises owner might be liable as a "common carrier" because an elevator might be deemed to be a public conveyance, and (3) plaintiffs might be able to employ the legal doctrine *res ipsa loquitur* (RIL), "the thing speaks for itself," as a basis for the claim.[10]

The month after the accident, CLO filed suit on behalf of Reece and Long, naming as defendants the building manager and the company with a contract to maintain the elevator. CLO, however, did not name the owner of the building, apparently not having even sought to identify the owner, nor did the complaint invoke *res ipsa loquitur.* About four years later, CLO demanded the limits of their insurance policies from the two defendants, a total of $4 million, but that demand was rejected. Several months later CLO filed an amended complaint on behalf of Reece and Long that included claims based on the management company acting as a common carrier. The defendant, noting that it was not the building owner, unsuccessfully moved to dismiss that part of the claim.

In September 2009, more than four years after the accident, Reece e-mailed the lawyers at CLO asking whether the building owner should bear some liability. He received a reply from Robert Clifford stating, "not just for being a property owner. All of the proper and necessary defendants have been named in your case." However, allegedly this statement was incorrect, and if the case had gone to trial, both the building manager and the elevator company would have had the defense that they bore no liability because the legally responsible party was the owner of the building. Importantly, by this time Illinois's two-year statute of limitations for personal injury claims[11] had expired, which meant that it was too late to add the building owner as a defendant in the lawsuit.

Before the trial began, the defendants offered to settle for $2.25 million. Presumably they made this offer despite their strong defenses because they were uncertain whether their defenses would succeed at a jury trial and were concerned about a possible verdict in excess of their insurance. According to Reece and Long, Clifford "adamantly instructed" them to accept the offer, which they did in March of 2010.

Almost three years later, in February 2013,[12] Reece and Long filed a suit against CLO alleging legal malpractice, breach of fiduciary duty, and fraudulent concealment. The suit alleged Clifford had pressured them to accept the proposed settlement, which the complaint asserted was substantially below the value of their claims. The claim alleged CLO feared that if the case went to trial, the two defendants would defend on the grounds that the owner of the premises bore sole liability, which would have made it clear that CLO had erred in not naming the owner as a defendant.[13] A year later the trial court dismissed the lawsuit. In the dismissal, the court found that the breach of fiduciary duty claim was duplicative of the malpractice claim (i.e., it turned on the same claimed facts). Regarding the negligence and concealment claim, the court ruled that the complaint failed to allege necessary facts to sustain those claims. Specifically, there was no asserted factual basis to potentially conclude that Reece and Long would have turned down a $2.25 million settlement offer even if the owner had been a defendant, and thus there was no evidence that Reece and Long suffered any damages as required for these types of claims (see Chapter 3).[14]

Reece and Long appealed the dismissal. Approximately a year later the appellate court upheld the dismissal for the negligence and fraudulent concealment claims because the appellate brief filed on behalf of Reece and Long failed to provide the type of argument and citations required under Illinois appellate rules.[15] However, the appellate court found that the trial court had erred in dismissing the breach of fiduciary duty claim because it was not duplicative of the legal malpractice claim, and the plaintiffs had alleged sufficient facts in their complaint. Consequently, the breach of fiduciary duty claim was sent back to the trial court for further consideration, which might eventually result in a trial. As this goes to press, the remanded case is still pending in the trial court.[16]

Improper Execution of a Prenuptial Agreement: Frederick v. Wallerich *(Minnesota, 2016)*[17]

In September 2006, Mankato, Minnesota, attorney Kay Wallerich prepared an "antenuptial agreement" (more commonly known as a prenuptial agreement) for wealthy restaurant owner Joseph Frederick and his fiancée, Cynthia Gatliff. On September 28 Frederick and Gatliff came into the office and signed the agreement; Wallerich notarized the document, but the signature spaces designated for two witnesses were left blank. The next day Frederick and Gatliff married. Approximately one year later, Frederick met again with Wallerich to revise his will; at that time, according to the complaint filed in the subsequent legal malpractice case, Wallerich "represented that the September 28, 2006, Antenuptial Agreement was valid and enforceable." Unfortunately for Frederick, the agreement was not valid because it lacked the signatures of the two witnesses, required by Minnesota law.[18] It would not matter that on at least one future occasion Cynthia Frederick, as she was known after her marriage, signed documents acknowledging the validity and enforceability of the antenuptial agreement.

In the fall of 2012, the Fredericks began discussions leading to a divorce petition being filed on January 2, 2013. Joseph Frederick's divorce attorney met with Wallerich, who informed him that the antenuptial agreement was enforceable because it had been notarized by her. The response to the divorce petition asserted that the antenuptial agreement was enforceable and controlled the distribution of assets. Cynthia Frederick's attorney then asserted that the agreement was unenforceable because it lacked the statutorily required signatures of two witnesses. Without the antenuptial agreement, Cynthia was entitled to in excess of $1.5 million more than would be the case under the terms of that agreement.

On September 10, 2013, almost seven years after the execution of the antenuptial agreement, Joseph Frederick brought suit against Wallerich and her law firm, alleging legal malpractice/negligence, breach of fiduciary duty, negligent misrepresentation, and fraudulent concealment. The attorney retained by Wallerich's professional liability insurer moved for judgment on the pleadings on the grounds that the six-year statute of limitations had expired.[19] Joseph Frederick's attorney argued that the continuing representation and later specific reassurance by Wallerich of the validity of the agreement meant that the statute of limitations did not start running until a later date, less than six years from the filing of the malpractice action. However, the trial court rejected Frederick's argument and granted the motion;[20] the court of appeals affirmed the trial court's decision.

Under Minnesota law, the statute of limitations in all types of professional malpractice starts to run when any damages have accrued, what is referred to in the legal malpractice context as the "some damages rule."[21] Although arguably there were no damages until the divorce, Minnesota courts have taken the position that some damage occurred on the date of the marriage, at which time the property interests of each partner to the marriage changed. Moreover, it does not matter under Minnesota law that there was no way for Joseph

Frederick to have known that he had suffered any damage because he had no reason to know that the antenuptial agreement was invalid. In principle, he could have had the agreement checked by another attorney, and if the error had been detected, it could have been corrected through a postnuptial agreement. However, one assumes that an attorney who claims to possess the requisite knowledge and skill to handle a matter does in fact have that knowledge and skill. Even if one might seek a second opinion on the terms written into such an agreement, it would be rare to have such an agreement checked by another attorney to ensure it had been properly executed.

After the trial court's decision was upheld by the Minnesota Court of Appeals, the plaintiff's lawyer successfully petitioned for review by the Minnesota Supreme Court.[22] The issue presented to the state supreme court was not whether the accrual rule should be replaced by a "discovery rule," under which the statute of limitations would only start to run when a client discovered, or should have discovered, the error. Rather the issue the supreme court was asked to decide was whether the subsequent reassurance by Wallerich constituted a separate act of negligence for which a new statute of limitations period began.[23]

Errors during Representation of a Home Seller: Vincent v. DeVries *(Vermont, 2013)*[24]

In May 2003 Leland Vincent, then aged 82, and his older sister signed a contract to sell their home for $52,000. However, shortly before the closing, Leland Vincent's sister died, and he then refused to go through with the sale. In July 2003, the buyers sued Vincent, demanding that he abide by the contract of sale and transfer the property to them; the buyers also sought an order of attachment to prevent Vincent from otherwise disposing of the property. Douglas DeVries, Vincent's lawyer, filed a motion for summary judgment on his client's behalf asserting that the contract lacked specific terms bearing on the sale.

The day before the court hearing on the motion for an order of attachment, the lawyers for both parties filed a stipulation that the court could resolve both the attachment issues and the merits of the summary judgment motion based on both parties' summary judgment pleadings. This action prompted the buyers to file a cross-motion for promissory estoppel, essentially asserting that even if there were some issues with the formal contract, it was sufficiently clear that it should be enforced because the buyers would be harmed if it were not enforced. DeVries did not file a reply to the cross-motion by the deadline, resulting in the court granting summary judgment to the buyers in October 2003.

DeVries tried unsuccessfully to have the summary judgment decision reversed. The court then entered an order for specific performance requiring Vincent to convey the house to the buyers. Subsequent appeals upheld the trial court's decision. Importantly, relatively early in this process, the buyers offered to cancel the purchase contract in exchange for a payment of $15,000, but DeVries had advised his client to reject that offer.

Five years passed by the time these proceedings reached the point that a deed of transfer was about to be executed. In the interim a guardianship had been established for Leland Vincent because of his advancing age and declining mental competence. In June 2008, a new lawyer hired to represent Vincent worked out an agreement with the buyers that allowed him to retain his house in return for a payment of $103,000, about one-third of which was reimbursement of the attorney fees the buyers had incurred over the previous five years. Because of the guardianship, the agreement was subject to approval by the probate court, and that approval was granted.

A month before the agreement allowing Vincent to remain in his house was reached, he (or his guardian on his behalf) brought a legal malpractice action against DeVries alleging that, among a number of other issues, DeVries had failed to timely file an answer to the buyers' motion for promissory estoppel, had advised his client to sign a stipulation that precluded raising defenses to the buyers' suit without explaining the implications of the stipulation, had failed to submit affirmative defenses, had failed to keep the client informed as to the course of the litigation, and had erred in advising his client to decline the offer to cancel the contract in return for a payment of $15,000. The essence of the complaint, paraphrasing the Vermont Supreme Court, was that DeVries had had notice of his 80-year-old client's cognitive limitations "but failed to recognize and timely plead meritorious defenses to buyers' specific performance action." The malpractice suit sought both economic damages and damages for the emotional distress Vincent had experienced during the lengthy dispute with the buyers. DeVries admitted to many of the alleged facts, including his breach of duty, but argued that his actions did not cause any damages to Vincent, or at least much more limited damages than the $103,000 paid to the erstwhile buyers. The case proceeded to trial, and a jury awarded Vincent $103,000 for economic losses, plus $80,000 in emotional distress damages.

DeVries appealed to the Vermont Supreme Court.[25] He argued that the trial court erred in allowing the jury to award damages for emotional distress and that there was insufficient evidence to find that the $103,000 in economic damages had been a reasonable amount for Vincent to have paid to retain his home. The court agreed that damages for emotional distress should not have been awarded. However, the court did affirm the award of economic damages, ruling that there were sufficient grounds for the amount of economic damages awarded, at least in part because the amount paid to the buyers had been approved by the probate court because of the guardianship in place for Vincent.

Negligence in Criminal Defense: Blinn v. Beale *and* Blinn v. Kammen *(Indiana, 2015)*[26]

In the wake of his conviction on federal charges of money laundering, Edwin Blinn Jr., a resident of Indiana, brought malpractice suits against two lawyers who had represented him at different times during various legal processes.

In 2003 Blinn was under investigation by the Federal Bureau of Investigation (FBI) for possible drug offenses and money laundering. Blinn retained lawyer Shane Beal, who advised Blinn that he should enter into an agreement with the FBI to plead guilty to a lesser misdemeanor charge, with a stipulation that Blinn's statements could not be used as evidence in the event that the federal government later decided to file more serious charges. Subsequently, over a period of six months, federal agents attempted to contact lawyer Beal to arrange a follow-up conversation with Blinn. However, after receiving no response, FBI agents confronted Beal at a courthouse in Marion, Indiana. Beal told the agents that Blinn was no longer interested in cooperating with the government. Beal failed to inform Blinn of the conversation at the courthouse. Blinn was subsequently indicted on a federal money laundering charge.

After being indicted, Blinn dismissed Beal and retained attorney Rick Kammen to serve as his new counsel. Because Blinn's earlier offer agreeing to plead guilty to a misdemeanor in return for not using his earlier self-incriminating statements as evidence had expired, the US attorney sought to introduce those earlier statements at the subsequent proceeding. Kammen objected to the use of Blinn's statements but then failed to call attorney Beal as a witness during an initial hearing on the admissibility of the earlier proffer agreement. The federal district court ruled that Blinn's statements were admissible. Kammen successfully sought to have that ruling reconsidered, and at another hearing regarding the proffer, he did call Beal as a witness, who testified at length about his representation of Blinn. However, that court declined to change its previous ruling.

In the wake of this last ruling Blinn dismissed Kammen and hired yet another lawyer, Robert W. Hammerle. Hammerle then negotiated a plea agreement in which Blinn pleaded guilty to a felony of conspiring to launder drug money, with the prosecutor recommending a sentence of between 12 and 20 months in prison. The court accepted the plea agreement, and Blinn was sentenced to 16 months in prison followed by three years of supervised release, including 12 months of home confinement.

In 2007 Blinn filed a legal malpractice claim against Kammen and his law firm. The lawsuit asserted professional negligence in representing Blinn during the prosecution process. Kammen moved for summary judgment, and it was granted by the trial court. The court found that Blinn's only allegation of malpractice was that Kammen did not call Beal to testify at the initial hearing involving whether the government could introduce Blinn's proffer statements, but that failing had been cured by obtaining a hearing to reconsider the admissibility decision at which Beal did testify. The trial court's summary judgment decision was upheld on appeal.[27]

That same year Blinn also filed a malpractice suit against his first attorney, Beal and his firm.[28] Blinn claimed that Beal had been negligent in his failure to communicate with the federal agents and in failing to put Blinn in contact with those agents. The result, Blinn asserted, was that he was convicted of a felony with a longer period of incarceration and other more serious consequences than if the proposed agreement for a misdemeanor plea had gone forward. After extensive proceedings, both sides moved for summary judgment on a variety of grounds. The most important issue was Beal's assertion that in a malpractice case arising from a criminal conviction, the plaintiff must prove actual innocence on the principal that a criminal should not benefit from his or her criminal conduct.[29] After a hearing, the trial court denied all the motions. In a 2014 decision[30] the Indiana Court of Appeals upheld the trial court, noting that if Blinn had met with federal authorities after making the offer to plead guilty to the misdemeanor, the meeting might have resulted in a lesser sentence. The court also rejected Beal's argument that public policy prevents a convicted person from imposing liability on others through a civil action related to that person's own criminal conduct. The Indiana Supreme Court declined a petition to review the decision of the court of appeals. After that ruling, the malpractice case was settled for an undisclosed amount.

BUSINESS CASE EXAMPLES

Bad Legal Advice in a Real Estate Development Matter:
Fairfield Investment Company v. Wilkes Artis Chartered et al.
(Maryland, 2015)[31]

In 2015 Fairfield Investment Company, headquartered in San Diego, California, filed a federal lawsuit against the Wilkes Artis law firm claiming that it had provided bad legal advice regarding a $200 million mixed-use project called Studio Plaza, located in Silver Spring, Maryland.[32] In April 2012, Fairfield joined the development team for Studio Plaza. Fairfield decided to participate in the project after being advised by Wilkes Artis that the project was eligible for up to $13 million in tax credits. However, in August 2013, after the project was well under way, Fairfield learned that the tax credits had been eliminated in 2006.

In 2015 Fairfield filed a legal malpractice suit against Wilkes Artis. Fairfield asserted that the absence of those tax credits drastically affected the economics of the project and that Fairfield would not have gone forward with the project if it had been properly advised about the availability of the tax credit. In reply, Wilkes Artis conceded that it had advised the plaintiff about Studio Plaza prior in 2012. However, Wilkes Artis asserted that Fairfield neither asked about the firm's fee structure nor scheduled any follow-up meetings in connection with the project; hence, Wilkes Artis argued, Fairfield had not actually retained the firm for services related to the project.

Importantly, Wilkes Artis did not dispute its failure to advise Fairfield about the expiration of the tax credit, presumably because there was clear evidence that a lawyer at the firm had told Fairfield in March 2012 that the tax credit program had been amended, when in fact it had been discontinued. The firm's defense that Fairfield was not actually a client meant that the firm was claiming it had no obligations to Fairfield. As will be discussed in Chapter 3, this issue was formally framed in terms of whether Wilkes Artis owed a duty to Fairfield. The question was never formally resolved because after almost a year of trial preparations and pretrial negotiations, the two sides met in a settlement conference conducted by a magistrate judge and settled for an undisclosed amount, with each party paying its own court fees and attorney costs.

Improper Advice, Lack of Due Diligence, and Breach of Fiduciary Duty (Conflict of Interest) in a Business Transaction: Scottie Pippen v. Pedersen & Houpt *(Illinois, 2010)*[33]

In April 2002, former Chicago Bulls basketball star Scottie Pippen and a corporation he formed, Air Pip, purchased a half interest in a 25-year-old Gulfstream II jet airplane for a total of $7 million, $1 million in cash from Pippen, another $1 million from his coinvestor, pilot Craig Frost, and the balance from a $5 million loan cosigned by Pippen and Frost. In order to generate revenue, Pippen and Frost intended to offer the jet for charter through Frost's charter company when Pippen was not using it. After completing the purchase, the two owners found that the jet had to be grounded because the aircraft's engines needed a $1 million overhaul. The $5 million loan went into default, and Pippen and his corporation were sued by the lender because Frost was unable to pay his share of the debt. Pippen ended up incurring multiple millions of dollars in principal, interest, penalties, and litigation expense.

The investment in the aircraft was handled by Pippen's financial adviser, Robert Lunn and Lunn Partners, and the law firm of Pedersen & Houpt. In the wake of the suit to collect the $5 million loan, Pippen brought a suit against the law firm alleging negligence and breach of fiduciary duty. Specifically, Pippen alleged that the law firm had failed to advise them that the deal included the loan obligation, had failed its due diligence obligation by not ensuring the aircraft was inspected prior to the deal closing, and had failed to investigate Frost's financial assets. The suit also alleged conflict of interest because attorney Peer Pedersen had failed to reveal that he was also a member of Lunn Partners and had a past business relationship with Lunn Partners. Pippen also filed suit against Lunn. Pedersen & Houpt denied that it had failed to do anything it was obligated to do and alleged that Pippen was just trying to find a scapegoat for his bad business decision.

In the course of the litigation, testimony showed that Pippen had signed the purchase contract without reading it and, moreover, had received a communication prior to the deal's closing to the effect that the airplane's engines were due for an expensive overhaul. Pippen settled with Lunn, but the claim against the attorneys went to a jury trial after Pippen declined a $1 million settlement offer. During the trial, the judge dismissed the breach of fiduciary duty claim as duplicative, leaving only the negligence claims (improper advice and lack of due diligence). The jury returned a verdict in favor of Pippen, putting the total damages at $8.24 million, but found that Pippen was also 75 percent negligent, which reduced the award to $2.06 million. This amount was further reduced because of the prior settlement with Lunn. Despite the $2.06 million jury award, Pippen appealed the dismissal of the claim for breach of fiduciary duty because, he argued, comparative negligence would not have applied to that claim.[34] However, the Appellate Court of Illinois upheld the dismissal of this latter claim, finding that it was duplicative of the tort claim because it was based on the same set of facts as the negligence claim.[35]

Failure to Advise Insurance Client of Filing Requirements and the Client's Obligations after It Became Insolvent:
Insurance Commissioner of Indiana v. Fillenwarth et al.
(Indiana, 2006)[36]

The Indiana Construction Industry Trust (ICIT) provided health coverage to nonunion construction workers. The trust became insolvent and was liquidated in 2002, leaving $8 million in unpaid medical claims, $7 million of which was then paid by the Indiana Department of Insurance (IDOI). As the effective successor to ICIT, IDOI brought a legal malpractice lawsuit against Fillenwarth, Dennerline, Grothe & Towe, the firm at which ICIT's outside counsel, Frederick Dennerline, was a partner.

Dennerline had begun providing legal counsel to ICIT in 1995 and became its outside counsel in 1998. Dennerline lacked expertise on the core Indiana statute and associated regulations governing the operation of insurance trusts such as ICIT; further, he had failed either to research those requirements or to consult with anyone familiar with them. One of the requirements was that ICIT obtain a certificate of operation. After learning of the requirement and determining that ICIT had failed to obtain the required certificate, Dennerline determined that ICIT could continue to operate without obtaining a certificate because there were no regulations concerning how the certificate was to be obtained. Dennerline drafted a trust agreement for ICIT that included a provision that the trust "shall cease and terminate . . . in the event the Trust Fund or Funds shall be inadequate to carry out the intent and purposes of

[the] Trust, or to meet the payments due or to become due under this Trust."[37] However, after learning in September 2001 that ICIT's liabilities exceeded its assets by almost $700,000, Dennerline failed to notify the trustees of the termination provision. As it turned out, some of the supposed assets, a set of precious stones, were not actually owned by ICIT, and thus the actual deficit was $2.7 million.[38] By the end of 2001, because of the deficit, claims were not being paid. However, even after obtaining this information, Dennerline failed to inform the trustees of the termination provision or of their duty to inform IDOI of the impending insolvency of the trust.

IDOI's lawsuit against Fillenwarth, Dennerline, Grothe & Towe involved several claims, two of which dealt with the specific issues described above:

- Fillenwarth Dennerline failed to advise ICIT and its trustees of the legal ramifications of operating without a certificate of registration from the Indiana Department of Insurance.
- Fillenwarth Dennerline failed to advise ICIT and its trustees of the legal implications of its insolvent status, particularly its obligation to cease operating altogether, after Dennerline learned that leased "precious stones" were listed as an asset on ICIT's financial statement, which meant that ICIT was insolvent.

IDOI offered to settle the case for $1 million, the limits of Fillenwarth Dennerline's LPL insurance policy, but Fillenwarth Dennerline's insurer, ProAssurance, refused to do so. The case proceeded to trial in October 2006, and a jury returned a verdict against Fillenwarth Dennerline in the amount of $18 million. The verdict was upheld by the Indiana Court of Appeals and appealed, unsuccessfully, to the Indiana Supreme Court.

This did not end the case, however. Even before the verdict in the malpractice trial, Fillenwarth Dennerline filed a federal suit against ProAssurance and its parent company, ProNational Insurance Company alleging bad faith for failing to settle the case.[39] In June 2008, after losing in the Indiana Court of Appeals, Fillenwarth Dennerline entered into an agreement with IDOI to pay a fine of $50,000 to the department and to transfer its claim against ProAssurance to IDOI. In return, IDOI released Fillenwarth Dennerline from an obligation to pay the $18 million judgment.[40] IDOI refiled the bad faith suit in June 2008. Approximately four months later, IDOI settled that suit for $16.5 million.[41]

Improper Drafting and Bad Advice in a Business Transaction: Karadsheh v. Kempski *(Michigan, 2015)*[42]

In 2009 Akram Karadsheh entered into a purchase agreement with Daniel Chudik to buy his restaurant for his son, Rakann. However, in order to use the existing liquor license while Rakann was seeking his own license, the Michigan Liquor Control Commission (MLCC) required that Rakann have lease and management agreements with the seller. Attorney John Kempski provided legal assistance with these agreements. After entering into the agreement, Rakann discovered that there was a substantial tax lien outstanding, and because of this, the liquor license had been suspended. The lien had to be satisfied before the liquor license would be reinstated. A revised purchase agreement was reached in which the Karadshehs paid the back taxes in return for a reduced purchase price.

Over the next year, the relationship between the Karadshehs and Chudik became increasing acrimonious, leading to Chudik terminating the lease and management agreements with Karadsheh. In the wake of this development, Chudik asked the MLCC to cancel the liquor license, which it did. As this conflict was going on, attorney Kempski withdrew from representing Karadsheh because of the acrimony involved in the dispute. Karadsheh continued to operate the restaurant without the liquor license and retained new lawyers, who filed a suit against Chudik seeking specific performance that would serve to have the liquor license reinstated. However, after obtaining a default judgment, Karadsheh abandoned his efforts to obtain the transfer of Chudik's liquor license and temporarily closed the restaurant. Eventually, Karadsheh did obtain his own liquor license and reopened the restaurant.

Subsequently, Karadsheh filed a legal malpractice claim against Kempski alleging several failings. These charges included failing to ascertain the presence of the tax lien, failure to advise the client about the possibility of such liens, and errors in drafting the lease and management agreements. Kempski did not dispute these breaches of his duty to his client but asserted that none of the errors caused actual injury to Karadsheh. Both sides asked the trial judge to grant summary judgment, Karadsheh on the allegations of breach of duty and Kempski on the issue of causation. The judge granted summary judgment in favor of Karadsheh on most of the alleged breaches and denied summary judgment to Kempski, ruling that there was sufficient evidence for the issue of causation to be decided by a jury. The case was tried in late 2014. The jury found that Kempski's negligence had caused harm to Karadsheh and awarded damages of $1,559,000.

Inadequate Representation in a Business Dispute:
Takahashi v. Snell and Wilmer *(California, 2011)*[43]

This case has its origins in a business relationship that turned sour. In 1993 William Takahashi and Harold Yamanuha entered into an agreement to invest in a 55-unit apartment building in California. The property was sold the following year, thereby generating a substantial profit. Takahashi and Yamanuha then invested the profit in a much larger property they held for five years and subsequently sold with an overall profit of about $7 million. After that sale, a dispute arose between Takahashi and Yamanuha over whether Yamanuha was a partner in the second purchase—thus entitled to a share of profits equal to his share of what was originally invested (about $4.7 million)—or simply a lender entitled to repayment under the terms of the agreement (double his original investment, or a total of about $600,000).

The dispute between Takahashi and Yamanuha resulted in two trials. At the first trial, the jury found for Yamanuha, and the court entered a judgment for $4.5 million against Takahashi. At that point Takahashi retained Snell and Wilmer to represent him on appeal. The appeal was successful, with the trial court judgment overturned because of an error in jury instructions. While the appeal was pending, Takahashi found copies of documents he maintained demonstrated Yamanuha's status was as a lender and not a full partner. The documents also included notations indicating that some of the "loans" had been paid. Takahashi's assistant faxed the documents to his appellate lawyer at Snell and Wilmer. The Snell and Wilmer lawyer added the documents to his file of correspondence for the case but informed Takahashi's assistant that the documents could not be used in the appeal because they had not been introduced at trial.

Takahashi subsequently retained a different lawyer at Snell and Wilmer to handle the retrial. That attorney obtained documents from Takahashi's prior trial attorney. Those documents included the same items faxed to the appellate attorney three years earlier. Neither the appellate attorney nor Takahashi's assistant recalled the documents, nor did the new trial team at Snell and Wilmer find them in files received from the prior attorney. A new trial took place in

February 2005, with testimony focusing on the issue of partnership versus lender. Six days into the trial, after Yamanuha had completed his testimony, Takahashi remembered the documents, and they were then retrieved by his assistant. The Snell and Wilmer attorney sought to introduce the documents, arguing that they corroborated his client's position. However, the judge refused to admit the documents because they had not been produced during discovery prior to either trial. Despite Takahashi's testimony and other documents ostensibly supportive of that testimony, the jury again found for Yamanuha, this time awarding $3.1 million. Takahashi later settled with Yamanuha for approximately $3.5 million.

By the time of the settlement, Takahashi owed Snell and Wilmer more than $600,000 in legal fees and expenses. Despite repeated promises to pay those outstanding fees, Takahashi did not do so. In April 2006, Takahashi filed a legal malpractice suit against Snell and Wilmer claiming the firm was negligent in failing to locate and produce the documents that ostensibly supported Takahashi's contention that Yamanuha was simply a lender. As noted above, Takahashi's original trial lawyer had provided those documents to both the trial and appellate lawyers at Snell and Wilmer. Takahashi also claimed that it was negligence on the part of Snell and Wilmer not to have sought a mistrial when the judge refused to allow those documents into evidence. Snell and Wilmer counterclaimed for the $605,000 it was owed in outstanding legal fees.

At the subsequent malpractice trial, Takahashi did not testify, supposedly because in the previous litigation with Yamanuha he had had serious problems when testifying. Those problems included giving inconsistent and contradictory answers, taking long pauses during his testimony, being combative and prone to outbursts, and repeatedly impeaching himself. In fact, because of his outburst during the second trial with Yamanuha, Takahashi had almost been thrown out of the courtroom.[44] In lieu of live testimony, Snell and Wilmer in its defense introduced portions of Takahashi's videotaped deposition. In closing arguments, Snell and Wilmer, over the objections of Takahashi's counsel, was permitted to make several references to Takahashi's failure to testify.[45]

The trial court in the malpractice trial submitted two verdict forms to the jury. On the malpractice claim, the jury found (10 to 2) that Snell and Wilmer had been negligent but that the negligence was not a significant factor causing harm to Takahashi. The jury then awarded Snell and Wilmer $604,794 in its cross-complaint for unpaid legal fees. With interest, the judgment in Snell and

Wilmer's claim was $838,837.35. Takahashi appealed the decision to the California Court of Appeals based on the trial court's allowing references to his failure to testify. However, the court affirmed the judgment of the lower court.

CONCLUSION

We reemphasize that the cases above, and in Chapter 1, are illustrative rather than representative of all cases. The cases illustrate some of the issues that arise in a professional liability claim brought against a lawyer. Two prominent types of cases not included among the examples are those arising out of wills, estates, and trusts and those arising out of intellectual property matters. Also missing are any of the types of cases in which a law firm is sued not by its (former) client but by parties harmed by actions of a client of the firm; these may involve claims that the firm aided the client in behavior that caused harm. As we will discuss in later chapters, this latter type of case involves what some LPL insurers refer to as the *bad client problem*. These are the kinds of cases that tend to result in the greatest liability because they typically involve significant malfeasance by large corporations.

CHAPTER 3

Preliminary Issues: Insurance, Bases of Claims, Important Legal Issues, and Differences between Medical Professional Liability and Lawyers' Professional Liability

This chapter sets the context for the discussion of lawyers' professional liability (LPL) claims and their outcomes by discussing several important issues that arise regarding those claims. The first issue is insurance. As will be discussed in later chapters, knowledgeable practitioners who prosecute LPL claims want to be sure that there is a source of payment of damages; that source will typically be the lawyer-defendant's professional liability insurance. Rarely will a lawyer experienced in LPL claims take on a case if the defendant is uninsured. Furthermore, as will be explained, there are significant differences in insurance arrangements depending on whether a lawyer or law firm is working in the corporate or personal services sector.

The second issue concerns the bases for LPL claims. Often LPL claims are labeled "legal malpractice," which sounds similar to "medical malpractice." Medical malpractice involves matters of negligence on the part of one or more physicians or a hospital and in some contexts is referred to as medical or clinical negligence.[1] Although many LPL claims reflect negligence on the part of the lawyer-defendant, there are bases for LPL claims that do not involve negligence as it is formally defined in the law. The discussion of the legal bases for LPL claims below spells out the types of claims that occur and the factors that define or distinguish those claims.

The third issue concerns three specific legal problems that can arise in LPL claims: proving causation, statutes of limitations, and the requirement to prove "actual innocence" in claims arising from representation of criminal defendants. Although the first two of these issues can arise in other types of claims, some special challenges can arise in an LPL claim.

The fourth issue is the relationship between civil liability of lawyers and the rules of professional practice administered by regulatory bodies. Although one might expect there to be a close relationship between these two ways of regulating lawyers, that turns out not to always be the case.

The final section briefly describes major differences between the liability setting of medical professionals compared with that of legal professionals. We include this discussion because of the prominence of litigation regarding medical negligence.

INSURANCE

Requirements for Insurance

In most other major common-law countries, lawyers who serve private clients are required to carry professional liability insurance.[2] Similar requirements exist for legal professionals in most European countries that draw on the civil law tradition.[3] The issue of whether lawyers in the United States who provide legal services to private clients should be required to carry LPL insurance has come up with some regularity. However, as of 2016 only one state, Oregon, requires all private practitioners to carry professional liability insurance, and that insurance is through the Oregon State Bar's Professional Liability Fund (PLF).

In 2016 the required liability coverage provided by Oregon's PLF was $300,000. The PLF provides an additional $50,000 for claims defense, with any costs exceeding $50,000 depleting the liability coverage. In 2016 the $3,500 cost of this coverage was not affected by past claims experience and was uniform for all practitioners.[4] Oregon practitioners may choose to carry insurance in addition to the basic required insurance provided by PLF. That "excess coverage" can be obtained through PLF or on the open insurance market.[5] Unlike most other LPL insurers, PLF does not have a deductible as part of its standard policy.[6] PLF's policies are on a "claims made" basis, the norm for LPL insurance. A "claims made" policy is one that covers any claim made during the term of the policy regardless of when the alleged error or behavior occurred or the damages were incurred.

A survey of the states by the ABA's Center for Professional Responsibility (CPR) published in 2014 showed that 18 states had rejected proposals for mandatory LPL insurance, 2 were studying the issue, and 14 had never considered mandatory insurance; the remaining states either did not respond to the survey or did not provide information regarding LPL insurance.[7] A variety of arguments has been advanced in opposition to requiring lawyers to carry liability insurance:

- There is lack of evidence of large numbers of uncompensated victims of lawyers' malpractice.
- Mandatory insurance would boost insurance rates because low-risk lawyers would be subsidizing high-risk lawyers.
- The increased costs would force many lawyers to increase their fees, making their services less affordable.
- These increased costs would drive substantial numbers of solo practitioners and part-time lawyers out of practice, thus increasing problems of access to legal services.
- There are problems in determining the appropriate level of coverage for different categories of lawyers, leading to problems setting premiums and deductibles.
- Mandatory insurance could encourage frivolous malpractice claims.
- Mandatory insurance would lead to insurance industry regulation of the profession because underwriting decisions would force some lawyers out of practice or force some lawyers to limit their areas of practice.[8]

Although mandatory insurance exists only in Oregon, some other states require lawyers who organize in some form of limited liability entity to carry insurance for that entity.[9] There are various forms for these limited liability structures including a limited liability company (LLC), a professional limited liability company (PLLC), a limited liability partnership (LLP), and a service corporation (SC). One example is in Wisconsin, where the Rules of Professional Conduct (SCR 20:5.7) require attorneys organized as an LLC, an LLP, or an SC to carry professional liability for their firms. The required coverage amount varies depending on the size of firm, starting at $100,000 per claim/$300,000 in aggregate for firms of 1 to 3 lawyers, and increasing to $10 million/$10 million for firms of 51 or more lawyers. We identified nine states with such a requirement, seven imposed by practice rules and two by statute.[10]

Some states require that practitioners disclose in some way whether they are covered by LPL insurance.[11] The first state to create such a requirement was California in 1988.[12] The CPR report for 2011–2013 listed 19 states that have some requirement of this type and noted that 6 states have rejected proposals for such a requirement.[13] The mechanism of these disclosures varies from state to state. South Dakota has probably the most stringent requirement: a lawyer who does not have professional liability insurance with limits of at least $100,000 must include a statement on the lawyer's letterhead that the lawyer or firm "is not covered by professional liability insurance," and that notice must "be included in every written communication with a client."[14] Other states require that a client be informed of the lack of insurance at the time the lawyer is retained, sometimes as a statement in the retainer agreement. Some states require clients to be notified of any changes in the lawyer's insurance status, whereas others have no such requirement. Still other states require that lawyers report whether they have insurance each year when they renew their licenses to practice; 10 states make this information available on a searchable website, whereas others (e.g., Rhode Island) do not make the information as easily available.[15] According to one report, only 4 percent of practitioners in South Dakota were uninsured,[16] suggesting that the kind of stringent disclosure requirement that exists in South Dakota pushes lawyers to obtain LPL insurance.

Going Bare

The absence of a requirement for LPL insurance in most states raises two questions. First, how frequently do lawyers serving private clients forgo insurance? Second, what reasons do lawyers who do choose to "go bare" give for their decisions not to purchase insurance?

Percentage of Lawyers Who Work without LPL Insurance. Whereas, as noted just above, according to one report only 4 percent of South Dakota practitioners chose to "go bare," nationally a significant number of legal practitioners working solo or in small firms do not purchase LPL insurance. Although there are no national figures for the proportion of private practitioners who choose to work without liability insurance, there is information for several individual states. A survey of Texas lawyers in 2005 found that 36 percent of private practitioners and 63 percent of solo practitioners did not carry such insurance.[17] In California, a demographic survey of the state bar conducted in 2001 found that 18 percent of private practitioners had no LPL insurance.[18] In her study of decisions to forgo LPL insurance, Leslie Levin obtained information from several of the states that require lawyers to report their insurance status. She found that the percentage of private practitioners without insurance in those states ranged from 6 percent in South Dakota to almost 21 percent in Michigan.[19] A

Table 3.1: Percentage of Private Practitioners without LPL Insurance

	Percentage Private Practitioners Uninsured (1)	*Percentage of All Private Practitioners Solo or in Firms of 5 or Fewer*[a] (2)	*Estimated Percentage Small Firm or Solo Uninsured* (3)	*Actual Percentage Solo Uninsured* (4)
South Dakota	6.0	71.1	8.4	
Pennsylvania	6.9	52.2	13.2	
Virginia	10.2	61.3	16.6	
West Virginia	13.5	79.0	17.1	
Washington	14.3	63.4	22.6	
New Mexico	15.3	73.8	20.7	
Illinois	15.7	56.5[b]	25.6[b]	41.1
Colorado	17.0	63.5	26.8	
Minnesota	18.0	53.5	33.6	
California	18.0	61.7	29.2	
Arizona	24.8	61.1	40.6	
Texas	36.0	64.8	55.6	63.0

[a]Clara N. Carson with Jeeyoon Park, *The Lawyer Statistical Report 2005* (Chicago, IL: American Bar Foundation, 2012).

[b]10 or fewer lawyers; James Grogan to Herbert Kritzer, e-mail, August 16, 2016. Carson reports 51.5 percent of Illinois private practitioners in firms of 10 or fewer lawyers in 2005. The percentage shown as uninsured is the actual percentage rather than an estimate.

2012 examination of registration data in Minnesota found that 18 percent of lawyers representing private clients did not report having insurance.[20] Information for 2016 provided by the Attorney Registration & Disciplinary Commission in Illinois showed that among all private practitioners, 15.7 percent were uninsured, but for solo practitioners this figure rose to 41.1 percent.[21] Table 3.1 summarizes all of the information we could find on the percentage of private practitioners forgoing LPL insurance.

With the exceptions of the percentage of solo practitioners in Texas and Illinois, the figures reflect the percentage of all private practitioners without LPL insurance. It seems very unlikely that many firms over some size would go without insurance. If one assumes that all firms with more than five lawyers carry insurance, which is probably close to reality,[22] that would mean virtually all uninsured private practitioners are solo or in firms of five or fewer lawyers.

With this assumption, it is possible to estimate the percentage of lawyers in solo practice or firms of five or fewer lawyers who are uninsured. Column 2 in Table 3.1 reports the percentage of all private practitioners in solo practice or in firms of five or fewer lawyers as of 2005 (the latest figures available). Column 3 combines Columns 1 and 2 to estimate the percentage of small-firm lawyers/solo practitioners who are uninsured. These figures suggest that clients using small-firm lawyers or solo practitioners have a substantial chance of dealing with a lawyer who lacks insurance. The numbers for Texas are particularly striking.

Why Do Lawyers Choose to Forgo LPL Insurance? There are a variety of reasons a lawyer might lack LPL coverage. In one of our interviews, a lawyer who prosecutes legal malpractice cases said he that did not carry LPL insurance because he did not want to have to worry about suing a lawyer covered by the carrier that had his policy. Other lawyers might lack LPL insurance because their record of past claims makes them such a risk that LPL carriers either decline to insure them or demand a premium that is not economical for them.

Levin summarized several small surveys that included lawyers who did not currently have LPL insurance.[23] The surveys provide some insights into decisions to forgo insurance.[24] One group of uninsured lawyers was composed of semiretired practitioners who often performed work only on behalf of family members. Another group comprised lawyers doing exclusively pro bono work. Something less than a quarter of the uninsured lawyers was working fewer than 15 hours per week, although a majority was working at least 30 hours per week. In all the jurisdictions where the surveys were conducted, the cost of a minimum level of coverage ($100,000 per claim up to $300,000 per year) was around $3,000. When asked why they did not have insurance, about 60 percent cited cost: they felt that they could not afford it. However, it was unclear what proportion knew what the cost would be. For some lawyers the issue was not financial but rather more of a philosophical objection to such a requirement. Almost 60 percent of the lawyers responding to one of the surveys reported that if they were required to purchase insurance, they would stop practicing. About the same percentage said they would be able to afford to retain counsel should they be sued by a former client. Many of the respondents, 43 percent, reported that their areas of practice did not expose them to any risk of liability. Very few lawyers reported that they could not obtain insurance because of their past claims experience.[25]

Regardless of why a lawyer might choose to forgo LPL insurance, that decision does have consequences not only for the lawyer but also for the lawyer's clients. As we will show in Chapter 7, a client harmed by the actions of his or her uninsured lawyer will encounter great difficulty in securing experienced representation to pursue a claim against that lawyer. We know of no way to estimate how much harm is caused by uninsured lawyers that goes uncompensated, but statistics on the amounts paid out in claims against solo practitioners who are insured suggest that this harm is in the tens, if not hundreds, of millions of dollars every year.

Structure of LPL Insurance

The markets for lawyers' professional liability insurance differ for large corporate firms and for the smaller firms that serve individuals and small businesses. In both sectors, there is a mix of commercial insurers and mutual insurers, although the nature of the mutual insurers differs greatly between the two sectors, as does the structure of the insurance arrangements.

Insurance for the Personal Services Sector and Other Small Firms. The providers of insurance for solo practitioners and small firms, with the latter defined as firms with no more than 30 lawyers, include 13 mutual insurers affiliated with state bar associations.[26] All of these insurers are members of the National Association of Bar Related Insurance Companies (NABRICO). Although originally started by specific state bars, NABRICO-affiliated companies currently write LPL insurance in 38 of the 50 states.[27] In some states a NABRICO-affiliated insurer writes the bulk of LPL insurance. For example, in 2014 the Missouri Bar Plan Mutual had 71 percent of the market (in terms of number of insureds) for LPL insurance in Missouri.[28] Some of the NABRICO mutuals limit the size of the firm they will insure. Others specifically decline to insure firms practicing in areas in which there is a risk of very substantial damage claims; one such area mentioned in interviews was intellectual property claims.

In addition to the bar-related mutual insurers, several commercial insurers write policies in the solo and small-firm sector. Some of the better-known companies include Travelers, Hartford, CNA, Swiss Re, and Zurich American.[29] A portion of commercial insurance is sold directly to solo practitioners and small law firms with the rest sold through insurance brokers. Insurers come and go in the commercial sector. For example, OneBeacon wrote LPL insurance in several states but sold off that part of its business in 2014,[30] very soon after being hit with a $34 million judgment for failing to pay a claim in Texas.[31] Some of the commercial companies have different programs or offerings for large and small firms.[32]

LPL policies in this sector start with limits of $100,000 per claim/$300,000 per year and can go up to several million dollars. For example, California Lawyers Mutual offers limits up to $5 million per claim,[33] as does The Hartford's program for small firms (20 or fewer lawyers).[34] Wisconsin Lawyers Mutual writes policies with coverage up to $10 million,[35] as does Minnesota Lawyers Mutual.[36] Some insurers offer special programs with reduced rates for lawyers with less than a certain number of years of practice, part-time practitioners, or those whose practice is limited to a specific area in which risk is low, such as criminal defense.[37] For most policies, the limits include the cost of defense ("defense within limits"), although some insurers include a separate allocation for the cost of defense such that the indemnity limit is not reduced unless the allocation for defense costs is exceeded. Most LPL policies in this sector include a deductible that can range from as low as $1,000 to $50,000 or more, although, as noted previously, the required insurance sold through Oregon's PLF has no deductible. Although the deductible can apply to both indemnity and cost of defense, or only to indemnity ("loss only"), the former is most common.

Premiums for this insurance vary based on a number of factors. We found references to premiums as low as $750 per year.[38] The required insurance offered by PLF has a uniform premium of $3,500 per year with a limit of $300,000 per claim.[39] Premiums generally are tied to the policy limit, the size of the deductible, areas of practice, and claims experience. With the exception of PLF, both mutual and commercial insurers can, and do, decline to cover lawyers based on past claims experience and/or the lawyers' area of practice.

Insurance for this sector is sold much like auto or homeowners insurance. Insurers have a set of standard programs they offer on essentially a take-it-or-leave-it basis. The underwriting process is minimal, meaning that it is based on a small set of factors such as areas of practice, prior claims experience, use of engagement letters, and the like. Levin likens the offerings to what one would find if looking to buy a men's suit "off the rack" in a store. This contrasts sharply with how LPL insurance is written in the large-firm sector, which Levin likens to buying a bespoke suit.[40]

Insurance for Lawyers in the Large-Firm Corporate Sector.[41] As in the small-firm/personal service sector, there is a mix of mutual and commercial insurers offering policies. Attorneys Liability Assurance Society (ALAS) is by far the most prominent insurer. ALAS will only insure firms with at least 35 lawyers.[42] According to its 2014 annual report, ALAS covered almost 58,000 lawyers in 219 law firms around the country.[43] The average ALAS firm has 270 lawyers, and the median firm has in excess of 100 lawyers. For historical reasons, ALAS does not cover the very large firms based in New York or California. There are several much smaller large-firm mutuals: Bar Assurance and Reinsurance Ltd. (BAR), MPC Insurance Ltd., and Attorneys Insurance Mutual Risk Retention Group (AIM). The first of these serves some of the large firms based in New York City, and the other two are heavily oriented toward firms in California.[44] Whereas ALAS underwrites all of its own policies, the other large-firm mutuals are somewhere between policy writers and buying groups that purchase insurance on the commercial market through brokers.

ALAS offers its members policies with per-claim limits starting at $10 million and going as high as $75 million. Premiums are not experience based. Rather, all members of ALAS pay the same rate per lawyer for a policy with a specific limit and a specific "self-insured retention" (SIR). An SIR operates similarly to a deductible with one key difference. The insured must expend that SIR before the insurer steps in and starts to pay; in a contract with a deductible, the norm in the solo/small-firm market, the insurer usually will recoup the deductible from the insured after paying the claim and the defense costs. The per-claim SIR with ALAS ranges from a minimum of $175,000 up to a maximum of $5 million. In 2015, a policy with the lowest claim limit had a premium of $5,075 per lawyer if the SIR was $175,000; the premium declined to $3,128 with a $1 million SIR and to $1,450 with a $5 million SIR. The comparable figures for a policy with a claim limit of $50 million were $9,398, $6,444, and $4,128, respectively; for a policy with the maximum claim limit of $75 million, the figures were $10,664, $7,594, and $5,225, respectively.

Commercial LPL insurance for large firms is typically secured through a broker with expertise in this type of insurance. The most prominent broker is Aon, and a second large broker in the area is Marsh.[45] Because of the potential size of LPL claims that can occur in the corporate sector, most insurers limit the amount of coverage they will provide to typically no more than $10 million per firm in a given year. Because large firms might seek several hundred million dollars of coverage,[46] brokers assemble multiple sets of "syndicates" to form a "tower" of insurance.[47] For example, assume a firm wants to buy $100 million of coverage. That insurance might be arranged in a tower with three layers. The first $40 million would be covered by a syndicate comprising four insurers each taking on a quarter of the risk, or a "quota share" of $10 million. If a claim arose that resulted in a $20 million loss, each insurer in the syndicate would pay $5 million. The second layer of $30 million would be composed of another syndicate consisting of three insurers, each with $10 million at risk; however, the insurers in this layer would pay nothing unless the loss exceeded $40 million, and then each insurer would pay a proportion of its $10 million coverage. The third layer of the final $30 million would be handled by another syndicate, again with three insurers each with a $10 million quota share. Only if the total loss exceeded $70 million would the insurers in the third syndicate have to pay out anything, and then they would pay out proportionately based on their quota share.

Note that our discussion of syndicates and towers referred to "loss" rather than to "payments." Loss here refers to "incurred loss," which combines any indemnity payment with expenditures on defense. Policies in the sector are normally "defense within limits," meaning that any amount expended on defense reduces the amount available to cover awards or settlements. Some people interviewed for this chapter referred to defense within limits as "declining limits" or even "wasting limits." Importantly, expenditures on defense also count toward an insured's SIR, and in a large claim it is not uncommon for the entire SIR to be expended on defense even if the claim does not result in any payment to the claimant.

BASES OF CLAIMS

Although the term "legal malpractice" is typically used to refer to claims brought against lawyers arising from their professional activities, that term is most closely associated with only one of the legal bases for professional liability claims. There are in fact several ways in which lawyers can face professional liability claims.[48] In this section we discuss four broad bases used in claims against lawyers. Note that the discussion that follows is by necessity highly simplified; the leading treatise on legal malpractice consists of five volumes totaling about six thousand pages.[49] The goal of this discussion is to set the frame for material discussed in the chapters to follow.

Negligence

The first and most common type of claim is one of negligence, a common type of tort claim. The defendant in a tort claim is referred to as the tortfeasor, or more properly during the claim process, the alleged tortfeasor. A negligence claim requires the claimant to prove four elements: the alleged tortfeasor had a duty to the claimant, the alleged tortfeasor breached that duty, the breach of duty actually caused harm to the claimant, and as a result of that harm the claimant suffered damages. We discuss each of these in turn.

Duty. Duty is not an issue in most claims of professional negligence. A lawyer has a duty to his or her client to meet the standards of the profession. The issue of duty arises in two situations. First, there might be questions as to whether a party is a client of the lawyer. Simply consulting a lawyer does not make the party a client. For example, when a potential client approaches a lawyer with a possible tort case, smart lawyers take care to make clear that they are simply declining a case and not providing legal advice regarding the case. A second situation is when the harmed party was not the lawyer's client. This question most commonly arises when someone retains a lawyer to prepare documents, such as a will or a trust, intended to benefit a third party. States vary regarding whether lawyers owe a duty to a third-party beneficiary even when there is no question that the work was intended for that person's benefit.

Breach. Given the presence of a duty, the claimant must prove that the lawyer breached that duty. The usual definition of breach of duty in negligence is that the tortfeasor failed to exercise "reasonable care." That is, the alleged tortfeasor does not function as the absolute insurer against harm, and the tortfeasor is not even required to take every possible measure to avoid harm to parties to whom a duty is owed. In the context of the negligence of professionals, including lawyers, "reasonable care" becomes the "standard of care" a member of the profession is expected to exercise. That is, "a lawyer is negligent only if the lawyer does what no reasonably prudent lawyer could do, or fails to do what every reasonable lawyer must do."[50] This clearly does not mean that a lawyer is negligent if another lawyer would not have done what the alleged tortfeasor did. Certain types of errors, however, clearly breach this standard of care; for example, missing a filing deadline, failing to identify a lien on a title when preparing a title opinion, or failing to inform a client of the tax consequences of a transaction the lawyer is handling on behalf of the client.

Other errors are more ambiguous, and this ambiguity might turn on what is referred to as the "professional judgment rule." The professional judgment rule states that it is not negligence if the lawyer made a reasonable professional judgment to do or not to do something. For example, it is not a breach of duty for a lawyer to decide not to make a particular legal argument in a case unless the argument is such that no reasonable lawyer would fail to raise it. It is not negligence when a lawyer decides not to pursue a line of investigation if, in his or her reasonable judgment, that investigation has a very low likelihood of yielding useful information. In contrast, if the law governing a case requires a certain line of investigation, such as obtaining a police report or retaining an expert witness, and the lawyer fails to do so, the omission would constitute a breach of the standard of care. This is not to say that all errors of judgment are immune from constituting a breach; the error of judgment must be reasonable.

Except when the error is something clear-cut that cannot be readily contested, such as missing a filing deadline or failing to follow explicit directions from the client, proving breach can be challenging. How does one show what the standard or custom of behavior is in a specific situation? The normal way is to employ an expert who will testify as to what the standard or custom is and opine that the lawyer-defendant failed to meet that standard.[51] This requires finding another lawyer with expertise in the practice area involved who will provide the necessary testimony. Without an expert who will testify to the standard of care and the occurrence of a breach of that standard, a legal malpractice case is likely to be dismissed prior to trial. The need for this kind of expert testimony is one of the significant costs involved in bringing a legal malpractice claim.

Causation. Not all breaches cause harm. If some harm was going to happen regardless of whether the lawyer did or did not breach the profession's standard of care, then the breach did not cause harm. For example, if a client was going to lose her medical malpractice claim if it had gone to trial, then the failure of the lawyer to file the lawsuit by the deadline did not cause any harm to the client. The challenge for the claimant in this situation is how to prove that the lawsuit would have been successful. Similarly, in a case in which a lawyer negligently fails to raise a particular issue on appeal, and the appeal is unsuccessful on the grounds raised, there is no causation if the appeal would have been unsuccessful even if that issue had been raised. A different kind of example can occur regarding a transactional matter when the transaction turns out to produce less of a benefit or payoff than anticipated. It might be that after the disappointment arose, the client discovered that the lawyer had failed to identify an issue that might have led to the loss; the question then becomes whether the loss was sufficiently connected to the issue the lawyer failed to identify. The language of tort law refers to this as "but-for" causation; that is, but-for the lawyer's breach of duty, the injury would not have occurred. Essentially, proving but-for causation requires the plaintiff to prove that an alternate set or sequence of events would have occurred in the absence of the lawyer's breach, and that alternate sequence would have resulted in a different outcome.[52]

In a negligence claim arising from a lawsuit, the specific challenge is determining whether the outcome of the underlying lawsuit, the "case-within-the-case," would have been different. For such claims, this necessitates what amounts to a trial of the case-within-the-case as part of the larger trial; the larger trial can also involve the issue of whether the lawyer breached the standard of care. In some situations, such as when the breach was missing the filing deadline for a lawsuit, the only issue might be what would have happened in the case-within-the-case; a trial in such a situation would focus solely on the but-for issue.

The causation element in tort law can include a second aspect involving what is commonly called "proximate cause." A succinct definition of proximate cause has eluded legal scholars. One way to think of proximate cause is that it turns on the issue of whether the breach of the alleged tortfeasor is close enough to the alleged harm that the tortfeasor should be required to compensate the victim. The analysis of proximate cause turns somewhat on foreseeability; that is, whether the alleged tortfeasor should have foreseen that the breach would lead to harm. It also turns on whether there were any significant intervening causes. A simple example from the personal injury context illustrates both of these issues.

At 6:05 p.m. on August 1, 2007, the Interstate 35W bridge over the Mississippi River in Minneapolis collapsed, resulting in the deaths of 13 people and injuring another 143. Suppose that Jane Doe was driving home from work crossing the bridge and was severely injured in the collapse. Normally, she would have crossed the bridge 20 minutes earlier, but she had been delayed by a traffic accident several miles before the bridge caused by a negligent truck driver changing lanes. "But-for" the negligence of the truck driver, Jane would not have been on the I-35W bridge when it collapsed. The truck driver's negligence constitutes a "but-for" cause but not the proximate cause because

(1) there was no way the negligent truck driver could have foreseen an event like the bridge collapse, and (2) the collapse itself constituted an intervening cause.

Generally, in most legal malpractice cases, the cause-in-fact also constitutes a proximate cause, and hence there are seldom separate issues of proximate cause. Proximate cause issues might arise in an LPL case when there was a sequence of attorneys involved in a case. For example, proximate cause might be lacking if a second attorney either made another error or failed to identify the error of the earlier attorney when it was remediable, and the standard of care required the second attorney to examine the prior work in such a way that the original error would have been detected.

Damages. The final element in a negligence claim, actual damages, requires a distinction to be drawn between harm and damages. Assume that a lawyer makes an error in drafting a contract. That error is discovered only after something goes wrong. The result is that the client must delay some planned activity and/or experiences some emotional upset. Either the delay or the emotional upset can reasonably be characterized as harm. However, there is no financial loss, and hence no economic damages to be recovered. With certain exceptions, largely in personal injury tort cases or certain types of intentional torts, a breach producing only emotional harm is not compensable.[53] In a divorce-related matter, for example, a lawyer's failure to correctly advise a client on issues related to child visitation or child custody that results in emotional distress on the part of the client is not compensable. One possible exception arises in some states when a lawyer's negligence results in the imprisonment of a client. However, there are other special issues (discussed below) that arise in malpractice claims related to criminal defense work.[54] A second exception might arise in situations where the lawyer's failure was particularly egregious, bordering on being willfully or grossly negligent.[55]

Breach of Fiduciary Duty

Two of the cases discussed in Chapter 2, *Reece and Long v. Clifford Law Offices* and *Scottie Pippen v. Pedersen & Houpt,* involved allegations of breach of fiduciary duty. In some respects, this type of claim resembles negligence. It involves breaching a duty in a way that causes harm to the party to whom that duty is owed. The central difference turns on the nature of the duty owed.

Under negligence the standard is "reasonable care," which translates into the "standard of care" a member of the profession is expected to exercise. Fiduciary duty is a more stringent standard involving "the utmost good faith, complete fair dealing, and full disclosure."[56]

One aspect of fiduciary duty is that it explicitly puts the client's interest ahead of the lawyer's interest. Claims of a breach of fiduciary duty often assert that the lawyer acted in his or her own interest rather than the client's interest. An attorney breaches his fiduciary duty when he benefits improperly from the attorney-client relationship by, among other things, subordinating his client's interest to his own, retaining the client's funds, engaging in self-dealing, improperly using client confidences, failing to disclose conflicts of interest, or making misrepresentations to achieve these ends.[57]

Thus, fiduciary duty involves avoiding conflicts of interest that have the potential of harming the client. Assume, for example, that the attorney's spouse is a stockbroker, and the attorney refers the client to the spouse to handle the proceeds of a large settlement without revealing that the spouse will charge above-market fees. Such behavior would be a breach of the attorney's fiduciary duty because the referral is in the attorney's interest and clearly harmful to the client's interests.

A second, and often related, aspect of fiduciary duty concerns the lawyer's disclosure obligations to the client. In some instances, this has been described as a duty of "absolute and perfect" candor to clients.[58] A simple example is the lawyer's duty to disclose to his or her client offers of settlement made or received unless the client has authorized the lawyer to proceed in a way that does not require such disclosure (e.g., authorizing the lawyer to settle within some range). In short, although absolute candor may be required as part of fiduciary duty, that does not mean everything must be disclosed; a lawyer is not required to disclose things that the lawyer in good faith deems immaterial or unreliable.

Breach of Contract

A claim against an attorney can also be brought based on a breach of contract. Terms of a contract can be explicit (express contract) or implied. Contract claims against attorneys are typically based on the implied terms of a representation agreement; specifically, the agreement implies that the attorney will exercise ordinary skill and knowledge in rendering professional services to the client.[59] In this sense, there is little difference between a contract claim and a negligence claim. The contract/agreement creates the duty, and the implied terms are essentially the same standard as for determining breach under negligence theory.

It is also possible to have express terms in a representation agreement that go beyond the implied terms of exercising ordinary skill and knowledge. The agreement might call for the attorney to complete certain tasks in accord with an explicit schedule or to handle a matter to a certain conclusion. Failing to do so would constitute a breach of the express contract, and if that failure causes loss to the client, the client has a claim in contract.

One potential feature of an express contract is that it might specify the damages payable in the case of breach, what is termed "liquidated damages." However, a liquidated damages clause is probably very rare in a representation agreement because such a clause might run afoul of ethical rules. Absent such a clause, the same causation issues arise regarding needing to prove damages as in a negligence claim.

There are some potentially significant differences between a negligence claim and a contract claim. The statute of limitations under contract may differ from that for a negligence claim, and if longer, that can work to the benefit of a claimant in some circumstances.[60] However, a contract-basis claim can also work to the disadvantage of a claimant who was not an explicit party to either the implied or express contract, such as a beneficiary to a will or trust. In the language of contract law, there is an absence of "privity" between one party to a contract and someone who was not a party to the contract. Thus, it might be harder for a third-party beneficiary to bring a claim under contract than under negligence.

Fraud and Misrepresentation

The final major basis for a professional liability claim against an attorney is fraud and/or misrepresentation.[61] Misrepresentation is conveying false information, and that constitutes fraud if the misrepresentation is intentional or results from a reckless disregard for the truth constituting gross negligence; there also must be an intent for the recipient to act upon the false information. In the absence of intent or reckless disregard, misrepresentation can be a form of negligence ("negligent misrepresentation") if the lawyer failed to exercise reasonable care in ascertaining whether the information was true. For either fraud or negligent misrepresentation to create liability, the claimant must have acted based on the false information (i.e., the claimant did rely on that information) and consequently suffered harm. Given the intentional nature of fraud, it opens up the defendant to the potential of punitive as well as compensatory damages.

An example of fraud would be telling the client that the opposing party had only $20,000 of insurance with the goal of inducing the client to agree to a settlement when the attorney knew that $100,000 of insurance was available. It would also be fraud for a lawyer to tell an opposing party that the lawyer's client had only $20,000 of insurance when the attorney knew that $100,000 of insurance was available.[62] It can also be fraud if an attorney fails to reveal information the attorney has when specifically asked for it either by the client or by the adverse party unless the information is privileged; in the former instance silence can constitute fraud.

Negligent misrepresentation generally lacks the intent elements of fraud.[63] Although a negligent misrepresentation claim does require that the claimant relied upon the information that turned out to be false, there is no requirement that the intent of the lawyer was to induce some action on the part of the claimant. In assessing a negligent misrepresentation claim, normal standards of negligence apply: an attorney must take reasonable care to ascertain the truth or falsity of information prior to conveying it to either the client or the adverse party. Moreover, as is the case with negligence more generally, the recipient of the information must have exercised reasonable care in assessing the truth of the information received in accordance with the standard of comparative or contributory negligence existing in the state where the claim arises.

A claim of either fraud or misrepresentation can be brought by both clients and nonclients. In fact, fraud and/or misrepresentation are typically the basis of claims brought against law firms in connection with securities-related claims and/or major business failures, such as the Enron debacle, in which share prices plummeted from around $90 per share in 2000 to less than $1 by the end of November 2001 after extensive accounting irregularities by the company came to light.[64] The plaintiffs' argument in such cases is that the lawyers working on behalf of the corporation aided and abetted their client in perpetrating a fraud on stock purchasers, bond purchasers, or lenders. Often the allegation is that the firm either intentionally or negligently assisted its client in preparing disclosures containing false information that either the law firm knew to be false (fraud) or should have known to be false if the lawyers had acted with due diligence (negligent misrepresentation).

LEGAL ISSUES

Aside from the choice of the basis to bring a professional liability claim against a lawyer, the claimant's attorney must deal with several key issues of law and/or evidence. The issues described here reflect the kinds of problems that came up during our interviews with lawyers who regularly handle LPL claims.

Causation (of Damages/Injury)

As illustrated by *Karadsheh v. Kempski,* discussed in Chapter 2, a significant issue in LPL cases is often whether the claimant has in fact suffered any damages because of the lawyer-defendant's negligence. In the medical malpractice setting, an error constituting malpractice is likely to produce at least some physical impact, usually in the form of pain or other unpleasant consequences accompanied by emotional distress,[65] all of which are compensable under tort law. In claims brought against lawyers, damages are almost always limited to provable financial loss; in only very limited circumstances is there a claim for emotional distress.[66] In the medical context, even if the error can be treated so that there are no lasting consequences, it is still possible to claim damages for any lost wages incurred and for pain and suffering. However, in the legal context, errors can often be "fixed," and even when a legal error gets as far as a professional liability claim, it is not uncommon for the insurer to assist the lawyer-defendant in what is referred to as "claim repair," which will be discussed in Chapters 6 and 8.

Even when the claimant can prove that the lawyer-defendant had failed to meet the standard of care or due diligence, or had engaged in either intentional or negligent misrepresentation, the claimant must prove that some loss was caused by that failing or behavior. In many states, the plaintiff must provide expert testimony to the effect that there was an actual loss on the part of the plaintiff, and a failure to produce the required testimony by a qualified expert will lead to a (summary) judgment in favor of the defendant that ends the case. This can be particularly problematic in an LPL claim arising from a litigation matter. In many jurisdictions, the expert in a litigation-related case might be required to testify that the party bringing the claim would have won had the underlying case gone to trial.[67] It is not sufficient for the expert to say that it was likely the claimant would have won, or that it was "more likely than not"—the usual standard of proof in a civil case—that the claimant would have won. Generally, lawyers are reluctant to state with certainty what would have happened in a trial because of the unpredictability of how witnesses will be perceived or the general unpredictability of how a jury will assess the evidence it hears. If expert testimony is required at the summary judgment stage to the effect that the plaintiff would have won the underlying case at trial, a failure to produce such testimony will result in a summary judgment decision in favor of the defendant. We will return to this issue in our concluding chapter.

Statutes of Limitations

A second issue that arises in LPL cases concerns statutes of limitations (SoL). As illustrated by *Frederick v. Wallerich*, discussed in Chapter 2, the primary question of concern is not the length of time specified by the SoL but rather exactly when the clock starts running. There are two basic rules governing the start of the clock: the occurrence rule and the damages rule. The former refers to when the error was made, and the latter refers to when the damages occurred. For example, assume a lawyer makes an error in investigating a claim and fails to identify some information that would have produced a different outcome at trial. Under the occurrence rule, the clock starts when the error was made; under the damages rule, the clock does not start until the trial is final (i.e., after any appeals are completed), at which time the damages would have been payable. A crucial question is whether the SoL clock starts when the relevant event occurs or when the relevant event is discovered or should have been discovered. Additional considerations are how to factor in continuous representation and whether the lawyer sought to conceal the error, thereby preventing discovery by the client until after the SoL has expired.[68]

The occurrence rule in LPL litigation can be particularly problematic for potential claimants, either because of delay in the proceedings or because of the nature of the representation. The latter is easy to understand. Assume a lawyer drafts a stock distribution plan and makes an error that increases the tax liability that would accrue when the shares are sold. Further assume that the statute of limitations is six years, but it is not until eight years after the distribution plan was put into place that anyone seeks to sell shares. Under the occurrence rule, a liability claim would be time-barred unless there was also a discovery rule. This type of problem is particularly likely to arise in cases in which the lawyer made an error drafting a will or a trust agreement, but the error was not discovered until some years after the drafting was completed, the situation in *Wallerich v. Frederick*.

Jurisdictions vary substantially as to both the actual length of the SoL and what controls when the clock starts. The SoL might be as short as one year and as long as six years, or even more in certain circumstances. A majority of states set the SoL as three or fewer years. In some states, it depends on whether the claim is based on contract or tort, and if the former, whether the contract was oral or written. By our count, roughly one-third of jurisdictions employ the occurrence rule and two-thirds the damages rule.[69] The majority of states operates with a discovery rule; however, a number of states start the SoL from when either the error occurred or the damages accrued, regardless of when the problem is discovered.

Actual Innocence Rule

A final legal issue is specific to LPL claims arising out of a criminal defense matter. Many jurisdictions have a requirement that a criminal defendant bringing a claim against a defense lawyer must prove actual innocence, although there might be some exceptions as illustrated by the two *Blinn* cases discussed in Chapter 2. It is not sufficient for the claimant to prove that the lawyer was negligent in a way that led to the claimant being convicted. For example, it might be that if the defense lawyer had challenged the introduction of certain evidence, the case would have been dismissed before trial because the prosecution would have been unable to meet its burden of proof beyond a reasonable doubt. The "actual innocence" requirement means that the claimant bears the burden of proving that he or she was factually innocent of the criminal charges.[70] Moreover, in some states it is not sufficient to prove innocence on the charge that resulted in the conviction; the claimant must also prove innocence to any lesser included charges. That is, it would not be sufficient to show that the claimant was innocent of the charge of aggravated assault; the claimant would also have to prove that he or she was innocent of simple assault.[71] Some jurisdictions with a requirement that the plaintiff prove actual innocence make an exception for errors related to sentencing; that is, given that sentencing is often based on specific factors, a defense lawyer can be held negligent for a failure to bring forth evidence that would have resulted in a lesser sentence even if the claimant is either factually guilty of the offense or cannot prove actual innocence.[72] As we will discuss in Chapter 4, there are relatively few LPL claims arising from criminal defense, and this is at least in part because of the actual innocence requirement.

THE LAWYER DISCIPLINE SYSTEM AND CIVIL LIABILITY

In his influential article "Who Should Regulate Lawyers," David Wilkins identified four methods of lawyer regulation, one of which is civil liability. The other three methods are disciplinary controls administered by the courts and/or the profession itself, regulation by the venues before which lawyers appear, and regulation by a legislatively established administrative agency.[73] Most prominent of the three in addition to civil liability is disciplinary controls through rules of professional conduct (RPC). Those rules are generally promulgated by the state supreme court and administered in a system that involves members of the profession acting as investigators and possibly as prosecutors who may recommend sanctions, with the sanctions themselves usually imposed through orders of the supreme court. One might expect that there is a close relationship between the disciplinary system and civil liability, but that is not the case.

Although states do vary in the specific rules they adopt, those rules are generally based on the Model Rules of Professional Conduct (MRPC) promulgated by the American Bar Association. Included in MRPC's Preamble is the following statement:

> Violation of a Rule should not itself give rise to a cause of action against a lawyer nor should it create any presumption in such a case that a legal duty has been breached. In addition, violation of a Rule does not necessarily warrant any other nondisciplinary remedy, such as disqualification of a lawyer in pending litigation. The Rules are designed to provide guidance to lawyers and to provide a structure for regulating conduct through disciplinary agencies. They are not designed to be a basis for civil liability.[74]

That is, the fact that a lawyer was found to have violated an ethics rule does not in itself establish civil liability, nor does a violation indicate per se that a lawyer has breached his or her professional or fiduciary duty to a client.[75]

This does not necessarily mean that rules of professional conduct are irrelevant in an LPL claim. Moreover, some states do not strictly follow the approach of the MRPC. The relevance of the RPC might depend in part on whether the claim is one of negligence or breach of fiduciary duty, with the RPC being relevant in the latter but not the former.[76] Regarding negligence claims, states differ in how they treat the RPC as evidence of the standard of care governing lawyers' work. There are four approaches:

1. "Professional ethical standards conclusively establish the duty of care and any violation constitutes negligence per se."
2. "A professional ethical violation establishes a rebuttable presumption of legal malpractice."
3. "Professional ethical standards [can be admitted] as evidence of the common law duty of care."
4. "Professional ethical standards [are] inadmissible as evidence of an attorney's duty of care."

The third approach is the most common.[77]

All four of the alternatives speak to the issue of whether evidence based on the RPC, such as what constitutes the standard of care or an alleged violation of the RPC, can be admitted into evidence. A second and distinct issue is whether an actual finding of a violation of the RPC by an ethics tribunal can by itself establish civil liability. This relates to the legal concept of "collateral estoppel" or "issue preclusion," which prevents a party from relitigating a legal or factual issue previously decided in another legal proceeding involving that party. This would appear to mean that if a disciplinary proceeding found a lawyer to have had a conflict of interest or a breach of fiduciary duty involving a client, that client would not need to prove that conflict or breach in a subsequent LPL suit. Alternatively, if in a civil suit a lawyer was found to have had a conflict or a breach of fiduciary duty, the lawyer could not contest that in a subsequent disciplinary proceeding. Although only the latter situation has received significant attention in court decisions, it turns out that issue preclusion generally does not apply in either situation but for different reasons.

A finding by a court in an LPL cases that a lawyer acted in a way that would constitute an ethics violation does not generally preclude a lawyer from contesting that before an ethics panel. The reason is that in most states an ethics panel requires "clear and convincing evidence" to find a violation, whereas in most civil court proceedings the standard of proof is the less stringent "preponderance of the evidence."[78] An exception is a criminal conviction, which requires proof "beyond a reasonable doubt"; lawyers cannot contest criminal convictions in disciplinary proceedings,[79] and ethics panels will impose discipline based on criminal convictions without requiring further proof of the attorneys' criminal behavior.

For different reasons, collateral estoppel based on findings of a disciplinary panel does not apply in a subsequent LPL civil proceeding. The primary reason for this is that the defendant in an LPL lawsuit enjoys the right to a jury trial.[80] A second issue is that in some states, for collateral estoppel to apply, both parties (including those in privity with parties) in the previous forum must be bound by that forum's decision; generally, the plaintiff in an LPL matter is in no sense bound by the findings of a previous disciplinary proceeding even if the plaintiff initiated the complaint that led to the discipline.[81] Finally, even if collateral estoppel based on a disciplinary finding was granted in an LPL lawsuit, the plaintiff would still have to prove having suffered some damage.

Even if collateral estoppel did not apply, there is the question of whether the findings of a disciplinary tribunal are admissible as part of the evidence in a civil proceeding. The central problem with the use of such findings in a civil proceeding is that they technically are "hearsay," which is not admissible.[82] We could find only one case in which such findings were admitted.[83] In that case, there was substantial additional evidence of the lawyer-defendant's malfeasance, and the objection raised to the admission of the disciplinary tribunal's finding was not that it was hearsay but that it was "unfairly prejudicial" to the defendant.[84] The Tennessee Court of Appeals found that the trial judge had not abused his discretion in finding that the "probative value" of the evidence was not "*substantially outweighed* by the danger of unfair prejudice."[85]

Regardless of the admissibility of an ethics tribunal's finding of a violation of the RPC, it is unlikely that such findings are a common part of the evidence introduced by a plaintiff in an LPL case. As we will discuss in Chapter 7, we specifically asked many of the plaintiffs' lawyers we spoke with whether there had been an ethics proceeding running alongside the most recent LPL claim the lawyer had completed. The lawyers told us that they discouraged their clients from pursuing an ethics complaint while the LPL claim was pending. Their rationale was that the ethics complaint would put the defendant's license to practice at risk, and that would stiffen the defendant's resistance to the LPL claim. The lawyers said they advised their clients to wait until after the LPL claim was resolved before filing an ethics complaint.[86]

Although the civil liability system for LPL and the system regulating lawyers under the RPC are distinct, there is one important commonality. As we will discuss in Chapter 4, lawyers in the kinds of solo and small-firm practices that serve the personal services sector are overrepresented among the lawyers facing LPL claims. The same is true of lawyers facing disciplinary proceedings.[87] This does not mean that ethical issues do not arise in corporate-sector firms,[88] but they differ in frequency and type from the issues arising in the personal services sector as we will show in Chapter 4 is true for LPL claims.

DIFFERENCES IN THE LIABILITY WORLDS EXPERIENCED BY LAWYERS AND PHYSICIANS

As noted in Chapter 1, there is very little empirical research on LPL. In contrast, there is an extensive literature on the liability of medical professionals. It might be tempting to assume that the liability of these two professions raise similar issues and that one can draw from the research on medical professional liability (MPL) to understand LPL. Although it is certainly the case that there are common elements, the differences between MPL and LPL are so vast that relatively little about the empirical world of LPL can be assumed to be the same as that for MPL. In this section, we highlight those differences.

Insurance Differences

Several insurance-related differences are relevant for understanding claims and claim handling.[89] As we discussed previously in this chapter, only one state requires private practice lawyers to carry malpractice insurance. The result of this is that large numbers of lawyers serving private clients practice without insurance. In contrast. seven states explicitly require physicians to have liability insurance, and another seven require insurance for a physician to benefit from limits on physician liability passed by state legislatures.[90] Probably more important is that most medical doctors want to have admitting privileges at a hospital, and hospitals typically require that those with admitting privileges carry liability insurance. The result is that few physicians practice without insurance in contrast to the substantial number of lawyers lacking insurance. This is important because of the unwillingness of knowledgeable lawyers to prosecute LPL claims if the defendant is uninsured, most of whom are lower-end practitioners from whom it would be difficult to collect a judgment.

Problems collecting judgments are less likely to be the case with an uninsured physician, who is likely to have seizable assets.

A second difference regarding insurance is in the structure of the insurance policies. First, although deductibles and/or SIRs are the general norm for LPL insurance policies, few medical liability policies have deductibles requiring physicians to bear some part of the loss when a payment is made. In a study of 15,065 paid medical malpractice claims of $10,000 or more in Texas over the period 1985–2005, only 350 (2.3 percent) involved the insured having to pay a deductible.[91] A related difference concerns how the insurance handles the cost of defense. In MPL policies, the cost of defense is generally in addition to the indemnity coverage (the amount available to pay in compensation) and is not limited, whereas LPL policies seldom provide for unlimited defense costs. As noted previously, some LPL policies do provide a specific amount in addition to the indemnity coverage for defense, but if that amount is expended, additional defense expenditures reduce the amount available for paying a successful claimant. More common in LPL policies is a single limit on the amount available to pay both defense costs and indemnity, which means all defense expenditures reduce the amount available to pay the claimant. Importantly, the presence of a deductible or SIR often means that a lawyer-defendant is paying the first dollars of the cost of defense up to the amount of the lawyer's deductible or SIR.

A final insurance difference concerns premiums. In the MPL market, premiums are largely determined by the nature of a physician's area of practice. There is little in the way of "experience rating" in MPL insurance; that is, a physician's premium is not generally affected by the physician's claims experience. With some exceptions, experience rating is common in the LPL market. The major exceptions were described earlier: the Oregon State Bar PLF, which charges the same premium regardless of either area of practice or claims experience (with discounts for lawyers in practice less than three years), and the Attorneys' Liability Assurance Society (ALAS), which sets premiums based solely on the combination of the selected policy limit and the SIR.

Features of Claims

Most legal malpractice claims are singular; that is, they involve a single lawyer or a single law firm. In some types of situations typically involving large corporate matters, there might be multiple defendant firms, but this represents a very small percentage of LPL claims. The presence of multiple defendants in MPL claims is more common. This arises because there are often several independent actors involved in an alleged medical injury: a surgeon, an anesthesiologist, nurses, a hospital, and so forth, each of which might have his, her, or its own MPL policy. How often an incident leads to multiple MPL claims is not known on a national basis, but using a dataset on medical malpractice claims in Missouri, we found that 36.9 percent of incidents leading to claims involved multiple claims.[92] Other studies report 60 percent or more of incidents involving multiple claims[93] or multiple actors involved in the incident.[94]

Another difference concerns what in the LPL setting is referred to as "claim repair." This refers to the idea that an error made by a lawyer might be correctable in such a way that the client is left uninjured, other than perhaps some delay in resolving or completing a matter. In fact, as we discuss in Chapter 5, "claim repair" is accomplished in approximately 10 percent of incidents that come to LPL insurers. In the medical arena, even if it is possible to correct, repair, or mitigate an injury arising from some error, it is seldom possible to undo the injury completely because the victim will have suffered at least some compensable harm even if that is only pain or discomfort.

In the MPL arena, a significant group of lawyers specializes in representing persons claiming injury by medical providers. For example, a study of medical malpractice claims in Illinois identified a set of 112 law firms for which the average number of claims handled was 61.5; for the top 22 firms, the average was 158.4 claims.[95] As we will detail in Chapter 7, although there are lawyers who specialize in prosecuting LPL claims, they are few and not always easy to locate. We would estimate that in Illinois there might be a dozen lawyers who have handled 20 or more LPL claims on behalf of claimants, and we would not be surprised if the actual number was considerably less than a dozen. Only a small fraction of LPL claims is brought by lawyers with substantial expertise in this area.

Both small and large claims can arise in either the MPL or LPL context. However, for various reasons, small claims are much less common in the medical context. As discussed in the previous paragraph, a substantial proportion of MPL claims is handled by specialist lawyers, and they limit the claims they will handle to those involving substantial damages. Even most nonspecialists apply screening criteria requiring substantial damages in order to take on representation for medical malpractice claims.[96] Although lawyers with significant expertise in bringing LPL claims also tend to limit their work to substantial claims, the much larger group of nonexperts who bring such claims does not appear to be particularly selective vis-à-vis claim size. Nonetheless, as the Andrews Kurth case referenced in Chapter 1 makes clear, there is potential for monster LPL claims well beyond the magnitude of what one sees in the MPL setting. This explains why law firms that handle large commercial matters frequently have LPL insurance that could cover claims of $100 million or more.

Claim Resolution

One reason lawyers expert in prosecuting MPL claims are selective in the cases that they pursue is that MPL insurers have a reputation for fighting every claim up to the courthouse door. This perception is clearly an overstatement because there is evidence that insurers do settle some claims even before a lawsuit is filed.[97] LPL insurers generally do not have a reputation for pursuing scorched-earth defenses when their insured was clearly negligent, such as in claims involving an insured who missed a deadline in a case in which liability of the original defendant was undisputed. Although we did hear comments about one LPL insurer that was very resistant to paying claims, that seemed to be the exception rather than the rule, unlike the situation in MPL cases.

One possible reason why MPL insurers are so willing to fight claims is that the physicians they insure do not want to admit liability. This might be partly because of professional pride on the part of the physicians, but it also might reflect an important practicality. Specifically, any indemnity payment made on behalf of a physician must be reported to the National Practitioner Data Bank (NPDB),[98] and this information is available to qualified health-care organizations. Also important is that in most LPL claims, the insured will incur expenditures to cover the cost of defense, and the cost of defense eats into the indemnity coverage. This can create an incentive to settle rather than fight, particularly with small claims. The nature of MPL insurance does not create a similar set of incentives.

Only a small fraction of either LPL or MPL claims ever proceeds to trial. However, there are significant differences in what happens when trials do occur.[99] As we will discuss in more detail in Chapter 6, almost all MPL trials are before juries, whereas about one-half of LPL cases are tried without a jury. Defense verdicts are more likely in MPL cases than in LPL cases. We suspect that this higher percentage of defense verdicts might be because juries are more willing to give the benefit of a doubt to physician-defendants than to lawyer-defendants. One experiment using simulated juries in a hypothetical case specifically designed to involve negligence on the part of a physician reported that only 47 percent of the subjects found the physician-defendant negligent,[100] although this might also have been at least in part because of the nature of the evidence presented to the subjects.

As noted in the previous section, a substantial portion of MPL cases involves multiple claims and hence multiple defendants. In such cases, it is common for only some claims to be resolved with payment. Drawing on the same Missouri data on medical malpractice claims, we found that about half (50.6 percent) of multiclaim incidents resulted in some payment.[101] However, in 80.1 percent of the incidents producing some payment, one or more of the individual claims resulted in no payment. This leads to the possibility that the higher likelihood of defense verdicts in MPL cases might arise because the clearly liable defendants settle and only the shakier claims get to trial.[102] We tested this hypothesis using the data on Missouri MPL claims. The specific hypothesis was that the likelihood of a defense verdict would be higher in a multiple-claim case in which only some claims went to trial compared with either a single-claim case or a multiclaim case in which none of the defendants had settled by making a payment. What we found was the opposite of the hypothesis: the plaintiff verdict rate was 31 percent in multiclaim cases, with some of the defendants having settled, compared with 23 percent for the other two scenarios.[103]

CONCLUSION

This chapter has laid out a range of issues central to understanding how LPL claims are handled, from the decision by a lawyer to take on representation of a claimant through what a claimant might have to prove at trial. As the following chapters will show, the broad effect of many of these factors is to create barriers to redress for persons harmed by the actions of their lawyers. In the concluding chapter, we will address how at least some of these barriers might be mitigated.

CHAPTER 4

Claims: Rates, Sources, and Issues

The ideal place to start developing a statistical profile of lawyers' professional liability (LPL) would be with some estimate of the frequency of negligence by lawyers, including breaches of the standard of care, breaches of fiduciary duty, and breaches of contract. In the medical malpractice arena, researchers have sought to identify the frequency of medical negligence in the hospital setting by reviewing medical records.[1] Nothing even roughly equivalent to hospital records is available for lawyers, and we have not been able to identify any other way to establish a baseline of the frequency of incidents as a basis for bringing an LPL claim. Consequently, rather than starting with some measure of incidents of legal malpractice, we must start with a measure of LPL insurance claims.

Thus, in this chapter we consider several aspects of LPL claims brought to insurance companies. We start with claim rates measured as the number of claims recorded by LPL insurers per 1,000 lawyers insured. As we will discuss below, one problem with these measures is that insurers differ as to what they count as a "claim." We then look at the areas of practice that generate claims. Ideally, we would have information that would allow us to benchmark the areas of practice that generate claims against some measure of how many lawyers work in each area of practice and how much time in aggregate lawyers devote to each area. However, we do not have such information. We also look at the size of law firms producing claims, and on this we do have information to assess whether practices of certain sizes are over- or underrepresented in the claims brought. We have a small amount of information that allows us to look at the relationship between claims frequency and the length of time lawyers have been practicing. The final piece we look at in this chapter involves the kinds of errors alleged in LPL claims. Before turning to our analysis, however, we describe in some detail the sources of data upon which we rely in this chapter and in Chapter 5, on claim resolution.

DATA SOURCES

We draw on four broad types of data sources, each of which differs in coverage and content. Because the years covered by the multiple sources varied and sometimes extended over a period of as long as 20 or more years, we have, whenever possible, adjusted any dollar amounts to 2010 dollars using standard cost-of-living tables provided by the US Bureau of Labor Statistics.[2]

Reports of the American Bar Association's Standing Committee on Lawyers' Professional Liability

In our discussion of previous research, we described the study conducted in the 1980s on behalf of the ABA's Standing Committee on Lawyers' Professional Liability (SCLPL). Since that initial study, the SCLPL has published reports about every four years. Whereas the initial study was based on case-level reports provided by the participating insurers, subsequent reports rely upon a compilation of summary information provided by the insurers to the SCLPL. Participants in the SCLPL's data collection effort include a combination of bar-related mutual insurers and commercial insurers,[3] but missing from the contributors are some of the insurers that focus on large firms (100 or more lawyers).[4] The SCLPL has now published seven reports: the initial report published in 1986 plus reports covering claims closed in 1990–1995, 1996–1999, 2000–2003, 2004–2007, 2008–2011, and 2012–2015.[5] The 2008–2011 and 2012–2015 reports provide a substantial amount of information comparing patterns across the various reports, and we look to these reports as major sources for discussion.[6] We also draw on and expand from summaries of the first six SCLPL reports compiled by Professors Tom Baker and Rick Swedloff.[7]

Information from Individual Insurers

One type of insurer in the legal malpractice marketplace is bar-related companies, all of which are affiliated with the National Association of Bar Related Insurance Companies (NABRICO). Our second source of data comes from reports published by six of these insurers:[8] Minnesota Lawyers Mutual Insurance Company (MLMINS),[9] Wisconsin Lawyers Mutual Insurance Company (WILMIC),[10] Lawyers Mutual Insurance Company of North Carolina (LMICNC),[11] Lawyers Mutual Insurance Company of Kentucky (LMICK),[12]

Bar Plan Mutual Insurance Company (of Missouri) (BPMIC),[13] and Oregon State Bar Professional Liability Fund (OSBPLF; PLF for short); this last source is the provider of the mandatory malpractice insurance for all lawyers serving private clients in Oregon.[14] Given the relatively small amount of change over time, we generally focus on the reports published for 2013, the most recent year for which reports were available from the companies as this book was written. Some reports cover just the most recent year, some show the previous five years, and some show claims experience from the inception of the company. In addition to the published reports, PLF provided limited case-level data. Although these data include only a small number of variables, given that Oregon is the only state requiring LPL insurance and all Oregon private practitioners must obtain their basic insurance from PLF, the data provide unique information on what claim patterns would probably look like were LPL insurance required in all states.

Baker and Swedloff compiled information from the reports of the Attorneys' Liability Assurance Society (ALAS). Although the information they were able to distill from the ALAS reports is limited, it does provide a sense of how claims brought against large firms differ from claims brought against the much larger number of lawyers practicing solo or in small firms. We draw on this information plus some of our own examination of materials published by ALAS.

We also use information compiled by Aon, an insurance brokerage for larger, corporate-sector firms. Aon collects data on the claims experience of its clients as part of the underwriting process. In 2015 Aon published a report providing an extensive summary of that claims experience.[15] We draw on this report to provide a second portrait of corporate-sector LPL claims in addition to that provided by the data compiled by Baker and Swedloff from ALAS reports.

Data Reported to State Insurance Regulators

We found two states that require insurers to report claim-level information to insurance regulators regarding some or all legal malpractice claims brought against lawyers and firms in their states, and that allowed access to some claim-level data.

Since approximately 1988, legal malpractice insurance carriers writing policies in Missouri have been required to report all claims to the Missouri Department of Insurance's Division of Financial Institutions & Professional

Regulation (DIFP). The Statistics Section of DIFP publishes a detailed report each year, typically going back 10 years.[16] DIFP generously made the data available for our analysis. One insurer, BPMIC, has been the dominant LPL insurer in Missouri, with a market share exceeding 70 percent in recent years. Typically, only one or two other insurers have had as much as 20 percent of the market.[17] BPMIC has been even more dominant regarding claims reported to DIFP. Over the history of the reporting requirement through March 2015, BPMIC claims constituted 79.4 percent of all claims; on a year-to-year basis, BPMIC's share of claims ranged from a low of 61.2 percent to a high of 93.2 percent.[18]

Since approximately 1981, Florida law has required LPL insurers to report claim-level information to the Florida Office of Insurance Regulation (FLOIR). Through 1997 insurers had to report all claims regardless of whether a payment was made to the claimant; however, starting sometime in 1998, insurers have been required to report only those claims that either involved a payment to the claimant or defense expenses of $5,000 or more. Late in 1994 FLOIR changed the reporting form in a major way, requiring additional information not included on the original form. When we examined the data from the years prior to the form change in 1994, it appeared there might have been some previous changes to the form in the mid-1980s; prior to that time there was little or no published information on the area of practice generating the claim. These various quirks placed limits on the analyses we could conduct using the Florida data.[19]

Limitations of Our Data Sources

It is important to understand the limits of the data sources described above and those that we will describe in later chapters. We have nothing clearly representative of the entire legal profession or the entire universe of LPL claims. However, the general consistency across sources suggests that the portraits we draw of areas are probably broadly accurate regarding the dominant areas of practice producing claims, the types of errors involved in the claims, and the magnitude of the claims. We are confident that our portraits of claims involving solo and small-firm lawyers, and the separate portrait for large (50 or more lawyers) firms, are broadly representative. We are less confident about what the picture looks like for medium-sized firms (11 to 49 lawyers); it probably falls somewhere between what we describe for small firms and for large firms. We

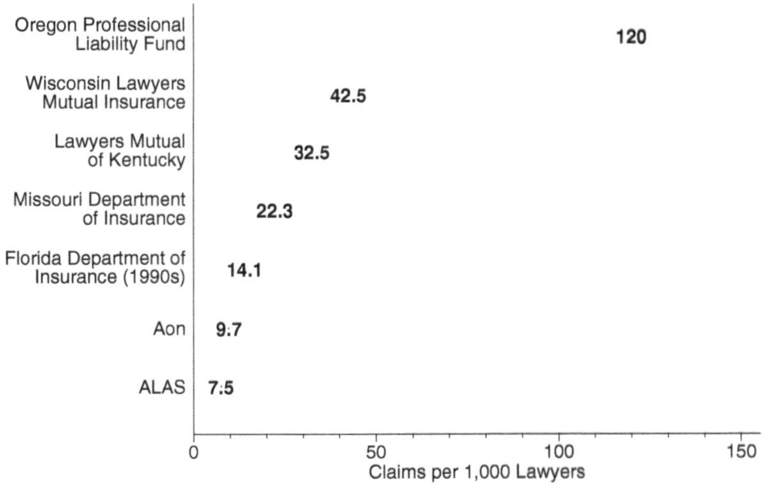

Figure 4.1 Claim Rates

also caution that specific percentages and dollar amounts should be understood as approximations at best.

CLAIM RATES

As discussed above, in an ideal world we would have information on the incidence of legal malpractice to examine the rate at which such incidents matured into claims. As also noted, incidence data have been compiled for hospital-based medical malpractice by reviewing samples of hospital records and identifying the frequency of negligence occurring in that setting.[20] Unfortunately, there is no practical way to review large numbers of files of legal matters because there is no setting that keeps records in a manner similar to hospitals; even if it were possible, those files might not document or otherwise reveal many of the types of errors that would constitute legal malpractice. It is possible, however, to examine the rate of claims filed with insurers on a per capita basis; that is what we do in this section.

Figure 4.1 summarizes the claim rates information we could locate or estimate. The specific sources and the patterns are discussed in what follows. The figure represents all claim rates on a per 1,000 basis.[21] Where rates were available for several years, the figure shows the average of those rates.

An important caveat to this figure is that insurers vary in what they label a claim.

Reports from several of the insurance companies included information on claim rates. Two of the companies, LMICK and WILMIC, reported frequency of claims per 100 lawyers insured, and both provided figures for 2009 through 2013. WILMIC showed rates ranging from about 3.75 to 4.75 per 100 lawyers, whereas for LMICK the corresponding rates ranged from 2.71 to 3.79 claims per 100 lawyers.[22] The LMICK reports further divided their data into "incidents," "claims," and "total" (i.e., the sum of incidents and claims). Presumably, incidents were situations reported to LMICK or inquiries received by LMICK that did not mature into actual claims. A representative at WILMIC indicated that the same reporting practice was used by that company.[23] Incidents that did not mature into claims at these companies were not included in the calculation of claim rates.

The claim rates experienced by Oregon's PLF were much higher than those of the above companies were. Their reports showed the number of claims, and the director of PLF provided the number of insureds for 2011, 2012, and 2013.[24] Based on those figures, PLF's claim rate was about 120 per 1,000 insureds, three to four times higher than that reported by either LMICK or WILMIC. PLF counted as a claim any case in which either a demand was made or an investigation or other action (e.g., claim repair) was undertaken by PLF even if there was never a demand from a claimant. However, it did not count situations in which it had simply been notified by an insured that there could be a problem, situations it tracked as "suspense files."[25] PLF also counted a small number of instances in which it covered the costs of representation when a lawyer was being deposed in an action in which the lawyer was not the defendant. Even with these differences, the Oregon claim rate was much higher than that reported by other insurers, and we can only speculate as to why this was the case. The fact that all private practice lawyers had to be insured might have encouraged disgruntled clients to bring claims because the clients might have known that insurance was available. In fact, in 2014 roughly half of the claims in Oregon were brought directly by claimants, on a *pro se* or *pro per* basis.[26] One might speculate that lawyers in the other states who were most likely to face malpractice claims did not seek coverage because of a concern about the cost of that insurance or might even have been denied coverage. This speculation is supported by some comparisons to information from three Canadian provinces that also require LPL insurance[27] and provide that insurance in a similar fashion to Oregon—without any underwriting—meaning that a single premium is charged for the required amount of insurance regardless of area of practice or prior claims experience.[28] The claim rates per 1,000 lawyers reported by the insurers for Ontario, British Columbia, and Alberta for 2014 are respectively 103,[29] 123,[30] and 118,[31] all in the same range as Oregon.

We also used information on claims reported to the insurance regulators as a means of estimating claim rates per 1,000 private practice lawyers for certain years: 1995, 2000, and 2005 for Missouri and 1985, 1991, and 1995 for Florida. The period for which we have information for Florida is limited by the change in the reporting requirement there in the late 1990s, which subsequently did not require reporting of claims unless the claim resulted in a payment to the claimant or an expenditure of at least $5,000 by the insurer in investigating or defending the claim. For each of the six years listed above, we averaged the number of claims reported for two years prior, the exact year, and two years following. We then used the number of private practitioners as reported in the periodic versions of the Lawyer Statistical Report published by the American Bar Foundation to compute number of claims per 1,000 private practitioners. The rates for Florida were 20.5, 11.2, and 10.5 for the three years, respectively, and 22.8, 23.4, and 20.8 for Missouri, respectively.

Information from ALAS and Aon provided a measure of the frequency of claims experienced by larger corporate-sector firms. ALAS measured claim rates in terms of claims per 1,000 insured lawyers and characterized what it counted as "real claims," by which it means "all claims other than those initially classified as without merit."[32] The rates reported by ALAS were much lower than those discussed above. The claim rate for ALAS insureds peaked at about 10.5 claims per 1,000 lawyers in the early 1990s and varied between about 6.5 and 8.5 per 1,000 lawyers in the years since about 2000.[33]

The information from Aon referred not to claims but to "notices." Notices included contacts from potential claimants plus situations in which the insurer had been notified by its insured that there might be a problem, even if no contact or claim was subsequently received from a potential claimant. The approximately 275 firms insured through Aon had a total of 68,000 lawyers.[34] Between 2004 and 2013, Aon's clients reported an average of 662 notices each year. Combining the estimate of the number of insured lawyers with the average number of notices produced an estimated annual rate of 9.7 notices per 1,000 lawyers, a figure slightly larger than the numbers reported by ALAS, although the difference probably reflects the fact that Aon included all notices, whereas, in contrast, ALAS restricted its count to "real claims."

The lower figures for ALAS and Aon might be misleading. Although each lawyer in a firm is covered by the firm's liability policy, claims against large firms frequently arise from work by a team of lawyers rather than a single lawyer, as is the case with solo practitioners. This is likely to be the case in most claims against firms with five or fewer lawyers because lawyers in such settings seldom collaborate on individual matters. If one could count all lawyers involved in a matter resulting in a claim, the claim rates for ALAS and Aon might be less different from the claim rates experienced by the insurers of solo practitioners and small firms. If it were possible to obtain a measure of claim rates based on the number of matters handled rather than number of lawyers, it might well be the case that large firms experience as many or more claims per 100 matters handled than do small firms and solo practitioners. Obtaining such a measure would raise a range of issues, most prominently defining what exactly counts as a "matter" when there is ongoing representation involving general counseling and advice.

SOURCES OF CLAIMS

In this section, we consider the areas of practice, the law practice setting, and the characteristics of individual lawyers against whom claims are brought.

Areas of Practice Producing Claims, Including Possible Change over Time

The SCLPL reports have employed consistent categorization of areas of practice that tend to produce claims. Figure 4.2 displays the areas producing at least 8 percent of the claims in one or more of the seven reporting periods.[35] It shows that, except for one report, the top two areas of practice producing claims were real estate and plaintiffs' personal injury (the one exception was the 1990–1995 report, for which our combined category of commercial transactions plus corporate/business organizations surpassed real estate). Although there was variation from one report to another, the overall pattern was generally consistent. Table 4.1 shows average percentages across the seven reports;

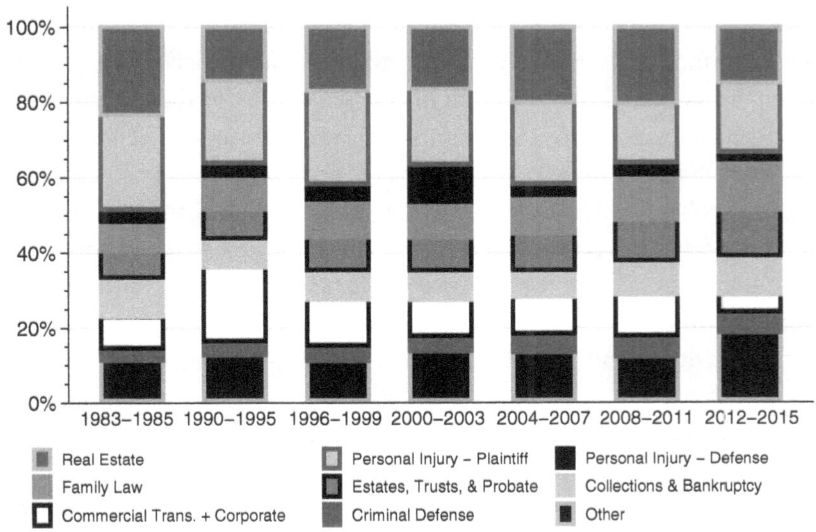

Figure 4.2 Areas of Practice Producing Claims, SCLPL Reports

Table 4.1: Average Percentage of Claims by Area of Practice, SCLPL Reports

Area of Practice	*Average Percentage*
Plaintiff's personal injury	21.0
Real estate	18.0
Commercial transactions or corporate/business organization	11.4
Family law	10.4
Estates, trusts, and probate	9.2
Collections and bankruptcy	8.8
Criminal defense	4.5
Personal injury defense	4.1
All other areas of practice	12.6

on average, almost 40 percent of the claims involve either plaintiffs' personal injury or real estate.

In the reports produced by four of the five NABRICO insurers, the top areas of practice producing claims appear the same as reported in the SCLPL's composite studies: real estate, personal injury litigation (LMICNC lumps all litigation other than criminal and family law together), family law, trusts and estates (T&E), and bankruptcy and collections. For three of the four reports, real estate and personal injury were the top two areas; for PLF real estate dropped to fourth place, with personal injury and family law tied as the most frequent areas. A higher proportion of claims reported to the Oregon insurer involved business transactions/commercial law or criminal defense than was the case for the other three insurers. The higher proportion of business-related claims is probably a result of the requirement that all firms in Oregon insure through PLF, whereas the other three mainly insure solo and small firms, meaning that a smaller proportion of their insureds handle business transactions or commercial work. The higher proportion of cases involving criminal defense in Oregon probably reflects the fact that many criminal defense lawyers in other states do not carry malpractice insurance, which undoubtedly discourages plaintiffs' malpractice lawyers from agreeing to bring claims against criminal defense lawyers.

Using the data from Missouri's DIFP, Figure 4.3 shows that the areas of practice producing the largest share of claims varied over time. For clarity and stability, the figure shows the data collapsed into two-year periods. Similar to the SCLPL data, in this figure the category we label "Business, Commercial, and Corporate" combines DIFP's categories "Corporate and Business Organizations" with the category "Business Transactions/Commercial Law." The other categories shown in the figure are real estate, T&E, family law, collections and bankruptcy, and an "Other" category that combines a wide range of areas, none of which represented more than 4 percent of the cases in the dataset. There are some trends worth noting. First, plaintiffs' personal injury declined slightly as a proportion of claims in recent years, with collections and bankruptcy increasing. The latter is not surprising given the economic crisis of 2008–2009. Similarly, the increase in the percentage of real estate cases is not surprising given the economic crisis; further, it is interesting that the more recent level for real estate claims is similar to that from the late 1980s, when the savings and loan (S&L) crisis occurred. There was also a decline in T&E cases, perhaps in part because of the more limited inheritance tax now in operation, although reduced inheritance taxes could also increase the assets over which heirs fight.

The BPMIC reports open claims rather than claims received or claims closed. Its figures showed a slightly different distribution of areas of practice involved in currently open claims as compared with the claims patterns of the other companies. The highest percentage of cases (19 percent) involved collections and bankruptcy, followed by real estate and plaintiffs' personal injury, both at 15 percent. The next three areas were corporate and business

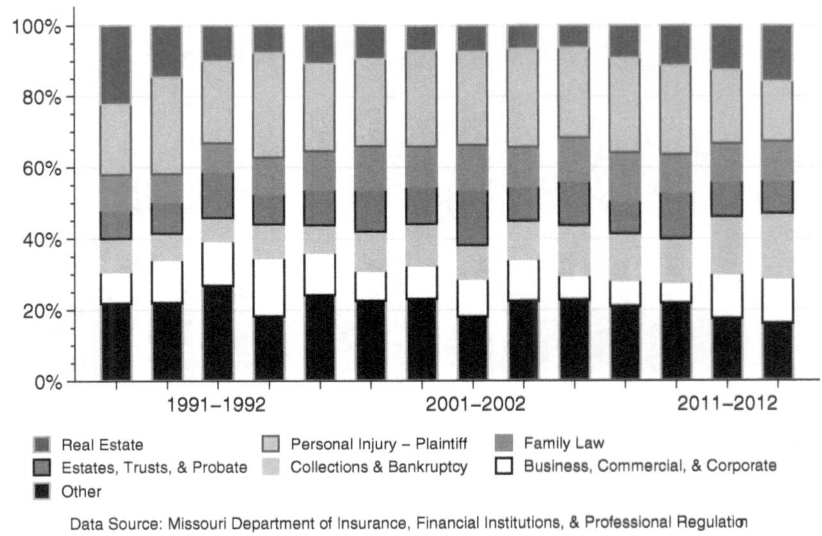

Figure 4.3 Areas of Practice Producing Claims, 1987–2014, Missouri Data

organizations (13 percent), T&E (12 percent), and family (11 percent). It is possible that this distribution reflects that BPMIC might have a larger proportion of lawyers in firms of the size that handle commercial matters—the 2013 report noted that "67% of Missouri lawyers choose The Bar Plan for Lawyers' Professional Liability Insurance."[36]

Figure 4.4 shows the breakdown by area of practice over time using the data we obtained from PLF. PLF combines plaintiff- and defense-related claims arising from personal injury work; however, staff at PLF report that approximately 95 percent of personal-injury-related claims arise from the plaintiff side. Whereas the Missouri data include all LPL claims in Missouri, the Oregon data go one step further because they cover all claims involving all private practitioners in Oregon as a result of LPL insurance being mandatory in that state. The areas that show an increasing proportion over time are family law, T&E,[37] and collection and bankruptcy. Over time there has been a continuing decline in the proportion of cases arising from the practice areas labeled "Business, Commercial, and Corporate" and from the practice areas of real estate and workers' compensation.[38]

Given the difference in the types of firms ALAS and Aon insure, it is not surprising that the areas of practice producing claims for ALAS and Aon were very different than from the insurance claims reported by the NABRICO com-

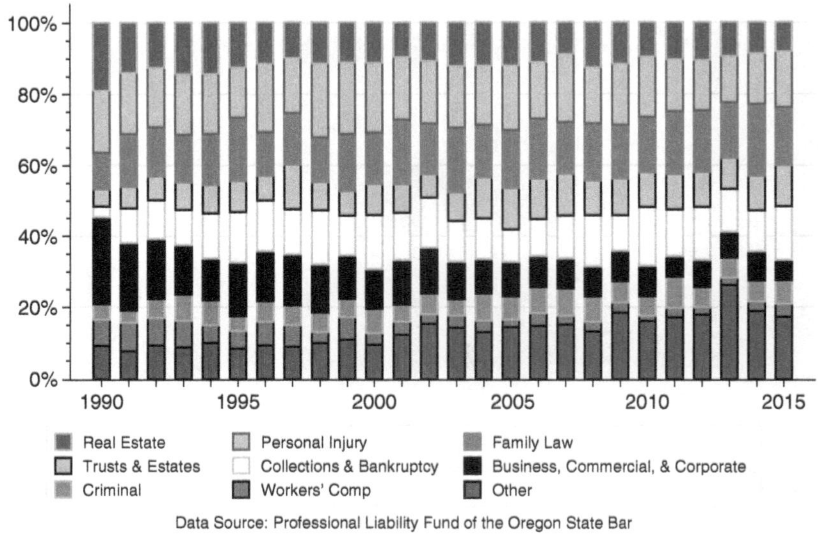

Figure 4.4 Areas of Practice Producing Claims, 1990–2015, Oregon Data

panies, of which the insureds are dominated by solo practitioners and small firms. The simple explanation is that large corporate firms do not generally handle significant numbers of matters that produce a large percentage of claims against solo and small firms. The dominant areas for claims against large firms, as indicated by the ALAS reports and the Aon materials, are claims arising from corporate/transactional matters and claims-related litigation work, including general corporate litigation, securities and intellectual property litigation, defense of major product liability claims, and major consumer claims.

For ALAS, litigation constituted 39 percent of claims between when ALAS started operating and November 2014, with corporate/transactional claims accounting for 26 percent of the total. Real estate accounted for 7 percent of claims, as did T&E, with lesser percentages—on the order of 3 to 4 percent each—for other areas of practice, including intellectual property, bankruptcy, tax/ERISA, and securities.[39] Although litigation constituted 39 percent of claims, it accounted for only 17 percent of ALAS's accumulated loss payments.[40] In contrast, corporate/transactional matters, accounting for 26 percent of claims, produced 41 percent of accumulated losses.[41] The contribution of securities-related claims to accumulated losses was 11 percent, whereas it constituted only 4 percent of claims. Each of the remaining categories accounted for 6 percent or less of the accumulated loss.

For the firms insuring through Aon, between 2004 and 2013 litigation made up 31.7 percent of notices, whereas corporate/transactional accounted for 21.4 percent. Similar to ALAS's experience, the reverse was the case when measured in terms of loss. For Aon's clients, corporate/transactional matters accounted for 39.6 percent of the total loss, including amounts paid as part of self-insured retentions, whereas litigation accounted for 17.7 percent of losses. Real estate–related claims constituted 8.6 percent of notices and 8.6 of accumulated losses; securities issues were only 2.4 percent of notices but accounted for 6.1 percent of losses. It is important to note that the categories used by ALAS and Aon are not identical, and some of the differences between the two sources might reflect similar sounding categories that are slightly different in actual content.

The differences in the claims/notices reported by ALAS and Aon compared with the other sources reflect the two-hemispheres issue. Although some of the other sources included claims against the kinds of firms handled by ALAS and Aon, the bulk of the insureds reporting claims to PLF (Oregon), FLOIR (Florida), and DIFP (Missouri) are geared more toward the personal and small-business sectors rather than to the corporate sector. Hence, it is not surprising that the claims reported by ALAS and Aon were predominantly corporate in nature, with relatively few dealing with family law or T&E and virtually none involving either plaintiffs' personal injury matters or criminal matters.

Size of Firms/Practices Producing Claims

The SCLPL reports included information on the practice size from which claims arose. The previous five reports used a common set of categories, except that the 1992–1995 report collapsed solo practitioners with firms of 2 to 5 lawyers. Figure 4.5 shows the distribution of practice sizes producing claims for all but the 1983–1985 report, which used a different set of categories.[42] The figure shows clearly that solo practitioners and firms of fewer than 5 lawyers accounted for between 61 percent and 73 percent, with firms of 6 to 10 accounting for another 10 percent of the claims. Roughly equal numbers of claims came from solo practitioners and firms of 2 to 5 lawyers. Firms of 100 or more accounted for 8 to 11 percent of claims, except in the 1999 study, when they generated less than 3 percent. The 2012–2015 report provided more specific information for firms of 100 or more lawyers: 2.0 percent of claims came from firms of 100–199 lawyers, 2.4 percent from firms of 200–499 lawyers, and

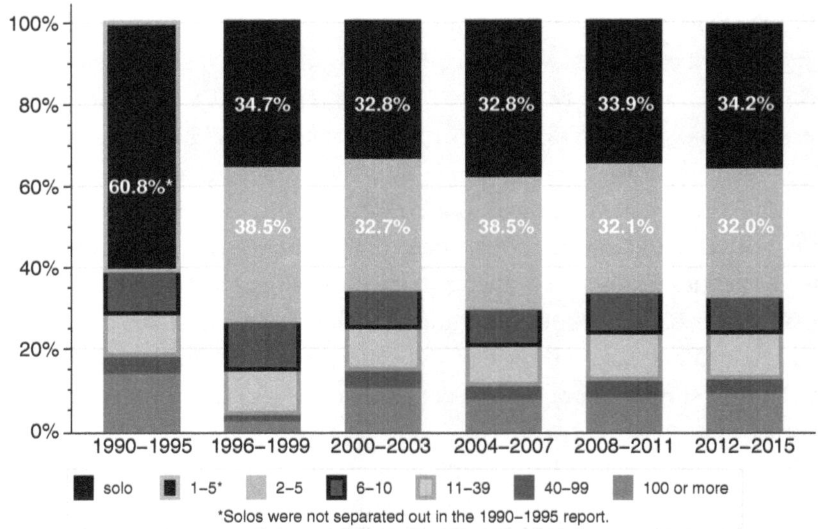

Figure 4.5 Practice Size Producing Claims, SCLPL Reports

5.1 percent from firms with 500 or more lawyers. The variations from report to report do not suggest any trend and most likely reflect differences in which insurers provided data for a given report.

Clearly the bulk of the claims come from solo and small firms. However, it is important to keep in perspective the distribution of practice settings for private practitioners. Based on information provided by the American Bar Foundation's *Lawyer Statistical Reports*, which covered the profession in 1991, 1995, 2000, and 2005,[43] most lawyers in private practice work in solo and small firms. Those reports showed solo practitioners constituting between 45 and 49 percent of lawyers in private practice, lawyers in firms of 2 to 5 comprise 14 to 15 percent of private practitioners, and lawyers in firms of 2 to 10 comprise 20 to 23 percent. Lawyers working in firms of more than 100 lawyers made up 12 to 15 percent of private practitioners. Comparing the claim sources to the distribution of practice settings, claims from large firms were only slightly underrepresented. The group most underrepresented was solo practitioners, whereas the most overrepresented group was small firms with 2 to 10 lawyers, particularly the firms with 2 to 5 lawyers.

Also important is the fact that the SCLPL figures were derived from insurers that voluntarily participated in the data collection, many of which insure mostly solo practitioners and small-firm lawyers. This means that larger firms might be underrepresented in the SCLPL figures. Because the Missouri DIFP requires all insurers writing legal malpractice policies in Missouri to report claims, its data avoid the problem of some insurers not being included.[44]

The DIFP's report form uses four categories of practice size: solo, 2–5, 6–30, and more than 30 lawyers. Almost exactly two-thirds (66.4 percent) of the claims involved practices with 5 or fewer lawyers, a figure consistent with the SCLPL figures. In contrast, substantially fewer claims were in the largest firm category: just under 5 percent came from firms of more than 30 lawyers. According to the 1995, 2000, and 2005 *Lawyer Statistical Reports*, the proportion of Missouri private practitioners in practices of 5 or fewer lawyers was somewhere between 51.5 and 56.9 percent. The DIFP data show that the largest share of claims, 40 percent, came from small firms with between 2 and 5 lawyers; lawyers working in these settings constituted 16 to 18 percent of private practitioners. The large-firm categories in the lawyer statistical reports do not match the categories used by DIFP; however, it is noteworthy that although those reports showed between 15.3 and 21.5 percent of Missouri private practitioners in firms of more than 50 lawyers, only 4.9 percent of the legal malpractice claims came from firms of more than 30 lawyers. The other underrepresented group was again solo practitioners, who accounted for between 32.7 and 40.9 percent of private practitioners in Missouri but generated only 26.5 percent of the claims reported to DIFP.

The SCLPL data and the DIFP data show that solo practitioners were quite underrepresented as a source of legal malpractice claims. Exactly why this is the case is not clear. At least part of the underrepresentation might reflect the fact that a disproportionate share of solo practitioners does not obtain LPL insurance and hence would not appear in any reports provided by insurers. This might also reflect that many lawyers in solo practice had small caseloads, perhaps only practicing on a part-time basis. As noted in Chapter 3, a survey in Texas found that almost two-thirds of solo practitioners in that state were uninsured,[45] and data provided by the Illinois Attorney Registration & Disciplinary Commission showed that 41.1 percent of solo practitioners in Illinois were uninsured.

There were differences not only in the claim rates depending on the size of practice, but also in the areas of practice producing claims depending on practice size. Table 4.2 shows the area of practice producing claims for each size practice identified in the Missouri data. The patterns for solo lawyers and those practicing in firms of 2–5 lawyers were similar, with plaintiffs' personal

Table 4.2: Claims by Area of Practice and Practice Size, Missouri Data, 1987–2014

	Firm Size				
Area of Practice	*Solo (%)*	*2–5 (%)*	*6–30 (%)*	*> 30 (%)*	*All (%)*
Personal injury, plaintiff	28.4	28.3	19.8	7.9	24.9
Real estate	10.8	9.4	10.3	8.9	10.0
Family law	13.6	11.3	9.0	5.9	11.0
Trusts and estates	12.8	11.6	8.0	8.2	10.7
Collections and bankruptcy	8.7	10.8	16.2	5.6	11.5
Business, commercial, and corporate	8.3	8.9	13.7	17.1	10.5
Securities	0.3	0.5	1.1	10.9	1.1
Personal injury, defendant	1.5	2.8	5.4	20.1	4.0
Criminal defense	5.7	4.2	3.1	2.0	4.2
Other	10.0	12.3	13.2	13.2	12.0
N	1,706	2,578	1,850	303	6,437

injury producing the largest proportion of claims and family law the second largest (leaving aside the "Other" category). In the 6–30 lawyer setting, plaintiffs' personal injury still produced the largest proportion of claims, but the second and third largest categories involved collections/bankruptcy and business/commercial/corporations matters. For firms with more than 30 lawyers the differences were even greater: personal injury defense was the largest source of claims, followed by business/commercial/corporations; securities-related matters were also a noticeable contributor to claims for the larger firms.[46]

The "Bad Client" Problem

The ALAS reports do not provide information on the nature of the problem leading to the claim, but they speak of problems of "client quality." Essentially what the reports appear to be asserting is that one cause of liability claims brought against lawyers relates to the behavior of clients. Lawyers could face liability if they failed to recognize that a client was engaging in illegal or shady behavior, and the lawyer's work somehow facilitated that behavior. There is some evidence that many of the largest claims brought against major law firms arise from client dishonesty. This is part of what some have labeled the "bad client" problem, which also includes clients who are dishonest with their lawyers. Indeed, some commentators have suggested that bad clients might be the "number one cause of legal malpractice actions."[47]

LPL insurance policies normally cover claims of this type in addition to more traditional types of negligence or contract claims. This means some portion of LPL claims does not reflect traditional types of errors affecting clients (or intended beneficiaries, such as heirs to an estate or beneficiaries to a trust) but rather claims by third parties injured because some failing by the lawyer allowed the lawyer's client to engage in fraudulent activity. This is particularly a problem for large firms that have found themselves facing liability related to corporate scandals, such as Enron, WorldCom, and the banks involved in the S&L crisis of the 1980s. For 2011 ALAS incurred losses totaling $455 million, and 7.3 percent of this amount was attributed solely to problems created by an "unworthy" client, with another 36.5 percent partly attributable to "unworthy" clients.[48]

A short report by Douglas Richmond, a loss prevention specialist with Aon, provides a further illustration. Richmond looked at large, publicly reported verdicts and settlements in claims brought against lawyers or law firms from the mid-1980s through early 2015. He found 67 cases involving payments or verdicts exceeding $20 million, with the largest verdict and largest settlement each slightly over $100 million. He described 41 of the 67 cases as being entirely a result of "dishonest clients," with another 4 cases partially resulting from "dishonest clients."[49] Richmond identified an additional 70 cases involving payments between $3 million and $20 million, 17 of which involved dishonest clients.[50]

Other Factors Influencing the Volume of Claims

Years of Experience. The DIFP data from Missouri provide information on the number of years the insured lawyer had been in practice at the time of the alleged error, but only three response alternatives were provided: under 4 years, 4 to 10 years, and more than 10 years. The claims were heavily skewed toward the "More-Than-10-Years" category, with 87.5 percent of claims in that category, leaving 10.2 percent in the "4-to-10-Years" category and only 2.3 percent in the "Under-4-Years category.

The reports of WILMIC provide a more detailed breakdown of the proportion of claims by years in practice. From 1986 through 2013, that distribution is:

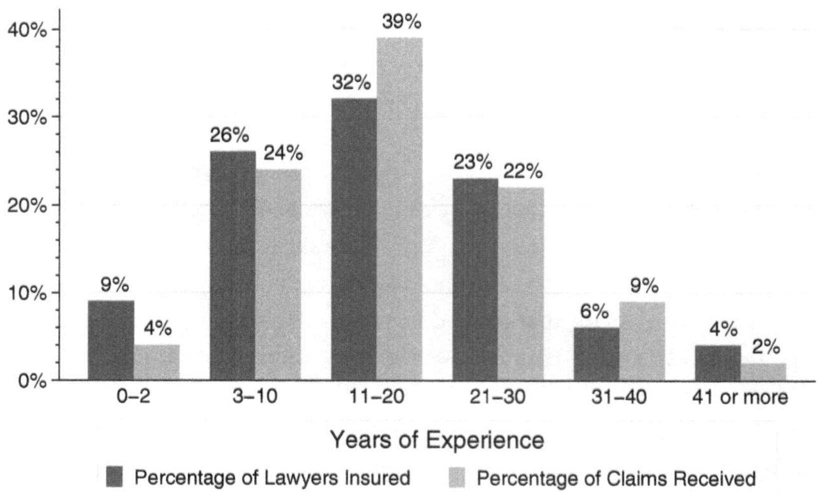

Source: Todd C. Scott, "Who Has the Most Malpractice? Hint: It's Not the New Lawyers," *The View* 29, no. 2 (April 2013).

Figure 4.6 Years of Experience for Insureds and Claim Targets, Minnesota

11 percent	0–5 years
14 percent	6–10 years
14 percent	11–15 years
15 percent	16–20 years
14 percent	21–25 years
12 percent	26–30 years
20 percent	31 or more years[51]

It is difficult to know how to interpret these figures from Missouri or Wisconsin in the absence of information on the distribution of years of experience, either among all private practitioners or among those covered by insurance. Fortunately, MILMIC published some figures showing both the years of experience of all its insureds and of the lawyers against whom claims were filed.[52] Figure 4.6 displays these distributions. The figure clearly shows the inexperienced lawyers did not produce a disproportionate share of the claims; rather it was lawyers practicing 11 to 20 years. The first SCLPL study, covering the early 1980s, did include some information on experience, and reports drawing on that study gave a minimal experience breakdown: 65.5 percent of claims involved lawyers with more than 10 years of experience,

30.2 percent 4 to 10 years, and 4.3 percent 0 to 3 years.[53] As a comparison the 1980 *Lawyer Statistical Report* reported that 56.8 percent of private practitioners had been admitted before 1971,[54] again suggesting that more experienced lawyers were overrepresented among those facing legal malpractice claims. An interesting question is why this is the case. Possible explanations include

- Underrepresentation of new lawyers might be because they have few clients and little revenue, and therefore are less likely to purchase insurance because of its cost.
- New lawyers even in smaller firms might be less likely to deal directly with clients, and if a problem comes up, the more senior lawyer is the subject of the claim.
- It could be that the group of lawyers overrepresented is the most overwhelmed by both the demands of the practice along with outside demands, such as those of family. It might be that at this period in lawyers' careers, they are most likely to be experiencing burnout and hence become sloppy in their work. This is consistent with some research on disciplinary proceedings that indicates that lawyers with some years of experience are disproportionately likely to face disciplinary proceedings.[55]

Nature of Activity Leading to Claim. One last item of information from the SCLPL reports and from the data we obtained from Missouri and Oregon is the nature of activity in which the lawyer was engaged that produced the alleged error. Five types of activities accounted for about three-quarters of the claims.[56] Table 4.3 displays the distribution. The sources differ as to which activity was most likely to lead to a claim: document preparation or transmittal for SCLPL and commencement of action for Missouri and Oregon. The reason for this difference is unclear. There was one interesting variation in the Missouri data based on firm size: advice led to 20 percent of claims for firms of more than 30 lawyers, compared with between 5 and 8 percent of claims for the other sizes of practices; the activity less likely to lead to a claim for the larger firms was commencement of an action, which accounted for about 19 percent of their claims compared with about 28 percent for the other sizes of practices (chi square = 175.08, $p < .001$, df = 42).

Table 4.3: Type of Activity That Gave Rise to Claims, SCLPL, Missouri, and Oregon Data

	SCLPL *All Reports (%)*	*Missouri* *1987–2014 (%)*	*Oregon* *1990–2015 (%)*
Preparation or transmittal of nonpleading documents	25.83	10.9	16.2
Advice	13.8	7.6	11.4
Commencement of action or proceedings	18.7	27.6	23.2
Pretrial or prehearing activities	10.2	10.5	12.9
Settlement or negotiation	7.4	9.7	9.2
All other activities	24.2	22.3	27.0

NATURE OF ALLEGED ERRORS OR BEHAVIOR IN LPL CLAIMS

Several of the data sources provide information on the types of errors or other allegations that underlie claims. The SCLPL reports and the Missouri DIFP data share a set of detailed categories for the nature of the allegation. SCLPL groups the allegations into four broad categories: administrative errors, substantive errors, client relations, and intentional wrongs. We have slightly modified these categories to separate out four specific claims that involve missing deadlines. Oregon's PLF has a more extensive set of 33 types of errors; the PLF staff does this coding by simply ticking off errors from the list of possible problems. They can identify multiple issues without indicating which one might be the primary issue. About one-third of claims listed only alleged error, with the median claim listing 2 errors; the maximum was 13 errors, although about 98 percent of claims listed 6 or fewer alleged errors.

Table 4.4 shows the distribution of the allegations aggregated across all of the SCLPL reports and for Missouri for the period 1987–2014, using both the detailed categories provided by SCLPL and DIFP, and as aggregated into our five summary categories. For the 1990–2015 Oregon data, the table shows only the percentage for the summary categories; that column adds to more than 100 because a claim can involve allegations of multiple types of errors.[57] Substantive errors constituted the plurality for both the SCLPL reports and the Missouri data; within that broad category SCLPL and Missouri differed with "Failure to Know or Properly Apply the Law" as the largest subcategory for

Table 4.4: Types of Allegations in LPL Claims, SCLPL, Missouri, and Oregon Data

Type of Error or Behavior	*SCLPL (%)*	*Missouri (%)*	*Oregon[a] (%)*
Deadline related	24.3	32.3	41.6
Procrastination in performance/ follow-up	6.4	9.1	
Failure to calendar properly	7.0	4.0	
Failure to react to calendar	2.8	3.1	
Failure to know/ascertain deadline	8.1	16.1	
Other administrative errors	9.9	5.4	48.5
Lost file, document evidence	2.5	0.3	
Clerical error	2.9	2.2	
Failure to file document/no deadline	4.5	2.9	
Substantive errors	40.3	36.3	63.2
Failure to know/properly apply law	14.2	8.9	
Inadequate discovery/investigation	8.7	6.7	
Planning error/procedure choice	7.4	12.3	
Conflict of interest	4.5	5.0	
Error in public record search	3.2	1.1	
Failure to understand/anticipate tax issues	1.5	1.5	
Math calculation error	0.7	0.7	
Client relations	15.0	11.4	30.2
Failure to obtain consent/inform client	7.8	4.2	
Failure to follow client's instructions	5.0	5.8	
Improper withdrawal of representation	2.2	1.4	
Intentional wrongs	10.4	14.6	1.6
Fraud	4.0	4.5	
Malicious prosecution/abuse of process	3.9	6.0	
Violation of civil rights	1.4	3.1	
Libel or slander	1.3	1.1	

[a]Percentages for Oregon add up to more than 100 because of multiple errors being coded.

SCLPL and "Error in Planning or Procedural Choice" as the largest category for Missouri. The important subcategory of "Conflict of Interest" represented roughly equal proportions of claims for the two data sources. Administrative errors that were not deadline-related constituted less than 10 percent of the allegations, with the remaining two broad categories, "Client Relations" and "Intentional Wrongs," constituting between 10 and 15 percent of claims.

The patterns in the Oregon data are very different, no doubt reflecting the ability of the PLF staff who code information about a claim to list multiple errors or allegations. There are two ways to understand this difference. First, some errors might logically fall into multiple categories. For example, one of the detailed categories in the Oregon data is "Inadequate Office System," which we grouped under "Other Administrative Errors." A deadline-related error could also be coded as involving an inadequate office system. There is a range of errors that could cross the boundary between the broad categories. Second, a client might raise multiple issues that themselves could fall in two or more of the categories. More broadly, one can interpret the Oregon data as suggesting that the issues underlying LPL claims might be more complex than the single-error coding reported by SCLPL and used by Missouri's DIFP. Even with these caveats, one particularly striking difference is the very low percentage of claims alleging "Intentional Wrongs."

Using the Missouri data, it is possible to explore whether the types of alleged errors varied on key factors such as area of practice and firm size. Figure 4.7 shows the broad category of alleged error for six areas of practice producing the most claims: real estate, T&E, family law, plaintiffs' personal injury, collections and bankruptcy, and corporate/commercial. The factor that leaps out in Figure 4.7 is that more than half of the claims arising from plaintiffs' personal injury involved allegations of a deadline problem, compared with between 6 and 12 percent of claims from the other five areas of practice. It is not particularly surprising that deadlines are less of an issue for other areas because the other areas do not typically involve the same kind of strict deadlines one finds in civil litigation such as personal injury. Although there was some variation among the other areas of practice, that variation pales in comparison with the role of missed deadlines in plaintiffs' personal injury.[58]

Figure 4.8 shows the relative frequency of the five error categories by the size of the practice. The pattern is quite clear: there is a sharp drop in administrative and deadline errors combined for firms of 6 or more lawyers, and a further drop for firms with more than 30 lawyers. This pattern and the pattern in Figure 4.7 are undoubtedly related because solo and small-firm lawyers dominate in the practice area of plaintiffs' personal injury. It is worth noting that the two categories of errors that increase in relative frequency for the firms of 30 or more are "Substantive Errors" and "Client Relations" issues; those firms have the smallest percentage of claims alleging intentional wrongs.

Using the Oregon data, it is possible to look at variation by area of practice but not by size of firm because the latter information is not included in the

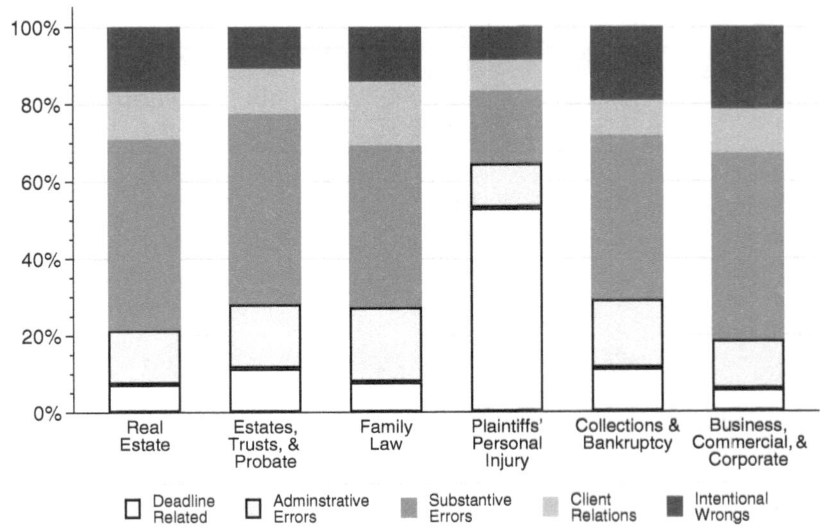

Figure 4.7 Alleged Error by Area of Practice, Missouri Data, 1987–2014

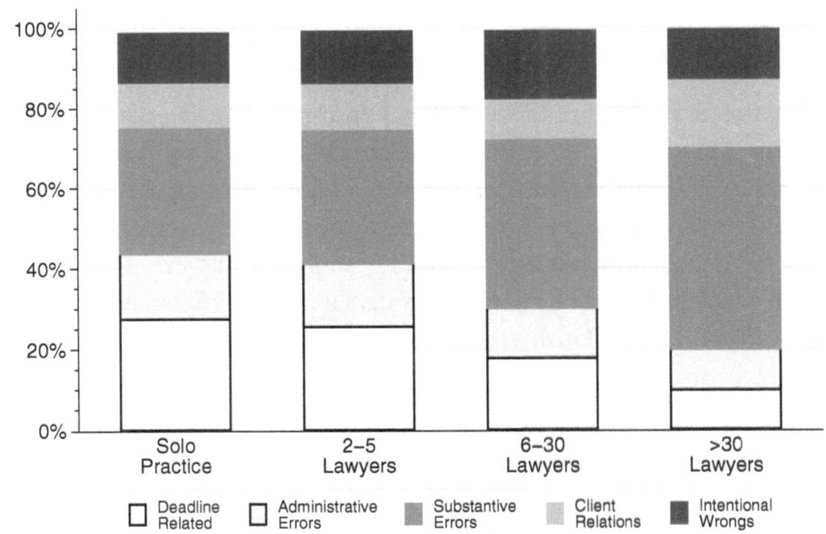

Figure 4.8 Alleged Error by Size of Practice, Missouri Data, 1987–2014

Table 4.5: Alleged Errors by Area of Practice, Oregon Data, 1990–2015

	Deadline Related (%)	*Other Administrative Errors (%)*	*Substantive Errors (%)*	*Client Relations (%)*	*Intentional Wrongs (%)*
Real estate	21.8	26.7	59.0	35.0	1.7
Personal injury	52.1	54.0	53.0	25.8	1.7
Family law	25.2	28.5	50.3	47.8	1.1
Estates, trusts, and probate	17.3	21.5	66.7	27.2	2.9
Bankruptcy and collections	28.9	37.4	54.9	36.5	1.8
Business, commercial, and corporate	18.9	24.6	54.9	37.1	2.8
Criminal	13.3	11.5	39.1	46.5	1.3
Workers' compensation	40.2	51.0	43.7	36.8	0.6
Tax	27.9	27.4	54.7	34.2	3.7
Securities	9.0	9.0	61.6	24.9	9.6
Other	40.5	37.5	51.1	41.6	1.5
All cases	29.9	33.3	53.6	36.6	1.9

information from Oregon. Table 4.5 shows the broad error categories for all of the areas of practice coded by PLF. There are some interesting variations. Personal injury and workers' compensation stand out regarding deadline issues. T&E and probate stand out for substantive issues, as does securities. "Client Relations" issues most commonly arise in family law and criminal matters, areas in which clients can be particularly demanding and frequently have unrealistic expectations.[59] Finally, securities stands out for the proportion of such claims involving allegations of intentional wrongs.

Although the ALAS reports do not include information on the nature of the conduct that led to claims brought against its insureds, the Aon publication did include that information, albeit using a very different set of categories than used by SCLPL or Missouri. Aon categorizes claims as arising from conflicts of interest, dishonest clients, dishonest lawyers, fraud and misrepresentation, malicious prosecution or abuse of process, and "mistakes."[60] As shown in Table 4.6, the broad category of "Mistakes" accounted for 53.0 percent of the notices, 55.6 percent of claims with some loss, and 45.6 percent of total losses. The other category that stands out is "dishonest client," which produces 25.4

Table 4.6: Conduct Causing Claims, Aon Data, 2004–2013

	% of Notices	*% with Loss*	*% of Total Loss Paid*	*Median Loss (thousands of $)*
Conflicts of interest	8.0	10.6	7.6	199.3
Dishonest client	12.9	10.3	25.4	348.5
Dishonest lawyer	1.6	3.3	5.4	396.7
Fraud and misrepresentation	17.3	14.0	11.4	124.6
Malicious prosecution/abuse of process	7.2	6.2	4.5	25.0
Mistakes	53.0	55.6	45.6	195.0
All cases, total or n	(5,941)	(1,170)	$1,848.5m	190.5

Source: Richmond et al., "The Aon Claims Experience," 6.

percent of total losses although constituting only 12.9 percent of notices and 10.3 percent of claims with losses.

Figures 4.9 and 4.10 disaggregate the information in Table 4.5 in two ways. Figure 4.9 shows the information by area of practice. Corporate/transactional stands out for the proportion of total loss attributable to dishonest clients; in terms of total loss, the category "Dishonest Clients" is relatively unimportant for the other areas of practice. The category "Mistakes" stands out in the real estate area and the T&E area for all three measures (percentage of notices, percentage of claims with loss, and percentage of total lost). Most likely these mistakes are some combination of drafting errors or mistakes in understanding the law. Fraud and misrepresentation stand out for intellectual property and securities, although less so regarding total losses for matters arising from intellectual property.

Because the information in the Aon report did not include the percentage of claims with losses attributable to each type of conduct by firm size, Figure 4.10 includes only the number of notices and amounts of loss. This figure suggests some differences, although not ones in a sense linear with firm size. Two subsets of firms stand out, those with between 101 and 500 lawyers and those with more than 1,500 lawyers. For both of those subsets, dishonest clients caused a prominent percentage of the total losses, although the percentage of total notices attributable to dishonest clients is not greatly different for those firms compared with those for the other sets of firms. Exactly what accounts for this pattern is unclear.

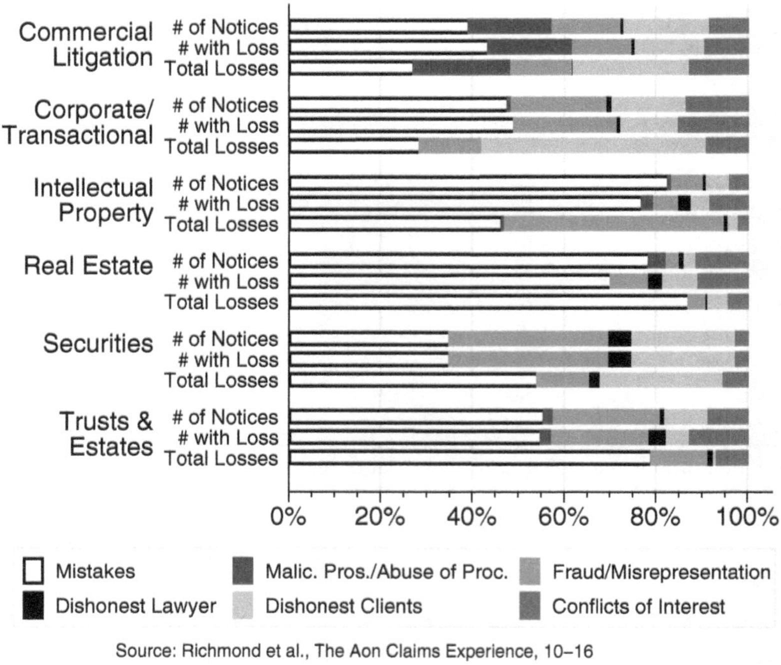

Figure 4.9 Conduct Causing Claims by Practice Area, Aon Data, 2004–2014

The figures discussed above confirm the significance of the "bad client" problem for large firms. As shown in Table 4.5, bad clients account for a quarter of the losses experienced by firms that insure through Aon. Figure 4.9 shows that this is a problem particularly for work in the corporate/transactional area and is not insignificant for securities work and for commercial litigation. However, bad clients do not appear to be a major issue for the other areas of practice regarding actual loss. As shown in Figure 4.10 bad clients appear to be a minor problem for firms of 1,000 to 1,500 lawyers. The reason for this variation based on the size of the firm is not clear.

THE TWO HEMISPHERES OF LAWYERS' PROFESSIONAL LIABILITY CLAIMS

The patterns described in this chapter clearly show major differences in the frequency and types of professional liability claims faced by lawyers in the cor-

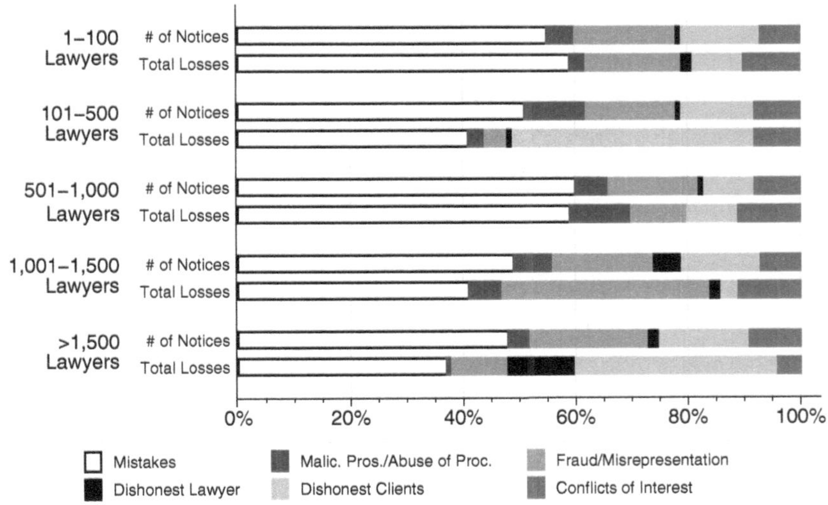

Source: Richmond et al., The Aon Claims Experience, 17

Figure 4.10 Conduct Causing Claims by Firm Size, Aon Data, 2004–2013

porate services sector versus the personal and small-business-services sector of the profession.

Measured on a per capita basis, lawyers in the corporate sector are much less likely to have a liability claim brought against them. One explanation for this finding is that there are more likely to be procedures by which work is reviewed and checked in the corporate sector, which in turn should lead to lawyers taking more care as they work and to having many or even most of the errors that they make caught in the review process. A second explanation derives from corporate lawyers tending to be dependent on a relatively small set of clients. This surely produces strong motivations for those lawyers to keep those clients happy.[61] If a problem is discovered by the client, the law firm will probably try to find some way to satisfy the client and avoid turning the matter over to the firm's LPL insurer. A third explanation for lower claim rates in the corporate sector is that lawyers in that sector might be less concerned about keeping time spent on a matter low, which allows those lawyers to take more time to double-check for possible errors. In contrast, lawyers in the personal services and small business sectors might feel they need to keep their billed time as low as possible in order to keep their fees at a level their clients can afford or because the nature of the fee arrangement, such as fixed fee or contingency fee, creates an incentive to minimize time, particularly in smaller matters.

However, as previously discussed, measuring claims on a per-lawyer basis could be misleading. Corporate-sector lawyers usually work in teams, sometimes quite large teams. Moreover, the number of individual matters handled by a lawyer in the corporate sector is likely to be much smaller than that for lawyers in the personal services sector. If it were possible to measure claims on a per-matter-handled basis, or on a per-client basis, one might find that lawyers in the corporate sector produce a rate of claims not all that different, and possibly even higher, than that for lawyers in the personal services sector.

The second major difference in LPL claims between the corporate and personal services sectors involves the areas of practice generating claims. This is unsurprising given that areas of practice differ between the two sectors, reflecting the needs of the clients served. In the personal services sector the major areas of legal need are personal injury, real estate, family law, T&E, and criminal defense. Except for criminal defense, these same areas dominate LPL claims involving solo and small-firm lawyers. Earlier we discussed the legal problems that arise in bringing LPL claims from criminal defense (i.e., most states require plaintiffs in such cases to prove "actual innocence"), and thus it is likely many criminal defense lawyers forgo LPL insurance and are therefore less likely to be sued when they have been negligent. In contrast the major areas of work in the corporate sector involve corporate/transactional matters (including securities and intellectual property) or business litigation. Some firms do take on personal injury defense, particularly in major toxic tort or product liability areas, and general insurance defense is often undertaken by midsized firms that fall into the corporate sector. Additionally, some real estate work is undertaken in the corporate sector, plus a small amount of work involving T&E. However, litigation and corporate/commercial are the areas producing the bulk of LPL claims involving lawyers in the corporate sector.

The fact that some lawyers forgo LPL insurance complicates the comparison of the two hemispheres. Virtually all, if not all, lawyers practicing in larger firms are covered by LPL insurance purchased by the firm, whereas, as discussed in Chapter 3, some unknown but probably substantial proportion of lawyers working in the personal services sector forgoes insurance. As we will discuss in Chapter 7, lawyers with expertise in prosecuting legal malpractice claims almost never take on a case involving an uninsured defendant. Furthermore, the amounts involved in LPL claims from the personal services sector are often relatively small, another factor limiting the interest of plaintiffs' lawyers in taking on a case. Indeed, even if a potential claimant has the resources to pay a lawyer on something other than a contingency fee basis, the amount at stake will frequently be considerably less than the cost of bringing the claim. This suggests that although the per capita measure of claims in the corporate services sector might understate the likelihood of an LPL claim arising, some other factors substantially reduce the likelihood of bringing even strong claims in the personal services sector.

In Chapter 5, we turn to the patterns of resolution in legal malpractice claims. The major apparent difference between the two sectors concerns the amounts at stake and the resulting amounts of damages paid. Although the number of claims arising in the personal services sector is much greater than in the corporate services sector, the amount of the damages paid in the corporate sector tends to be much greater. In fact, as will be discussed in Chapter 5, as best we can estimate, the total amounts paid out in LPL claims in the corporate sector are roughly the same as those paid out in the personal services sector despite many fewer claims arising in the corporate sector.

CHAPTER 5

Resolving Claims: Lawsuits, Claimant Success, and Payments

We now turn to the resolution of claims received by lawyers' professional liability (LPL) insurers. Although this chapter looks at how often claims became lawsuits, we defer to Chapter 6 a consideration of the outcomes of trials that result from those lawsuits. A second aspect of claim resolution discussed in this chapter is the likelihood that the claimant obtained some compensation; that is, in simple terms, whether the claim was successful from the claimant's perspective. The third question considered is the amount of compensation claimants obtained when a claim was successful.

As the analysis that follows will show, the outcome of claims varied substantially depending on the area of practice involved and the nature of the alleged error. The size of the payments also varied substantially, more by the area of practice than by the nature of the alleged errors. Not surprisingly, the data show that the amounts of damages paid differed radically, by an order of magnitude, for claims arising in the corporate sector of practice compared with the personal services sector.

FREQUENCY OF CLAIMS BECOMING LAWSUITS

Some claims are abandoned after the claimant's lawyer assesses the merits of a claim, perhaps after some investigation by the insurer. Other claims are settled presuit if an insurer determines the insured was culpable and the claimant did incur a loss because of the lawyer's negligence. Other claims get into a suit, where they can be settled, dismissed on the defendant's motion, or resolved at trial. This section briefly considers the likelihood of a claim leading to a lawsuit being filed. As discussed in the previous chapter, an important caveat to keep in mind is that insurers might differ in what they count as a claim, with some insurers equating simply opening a file as a claim, whereas others count as claims only an actual demand or some action requiring expenditures by the insurer.

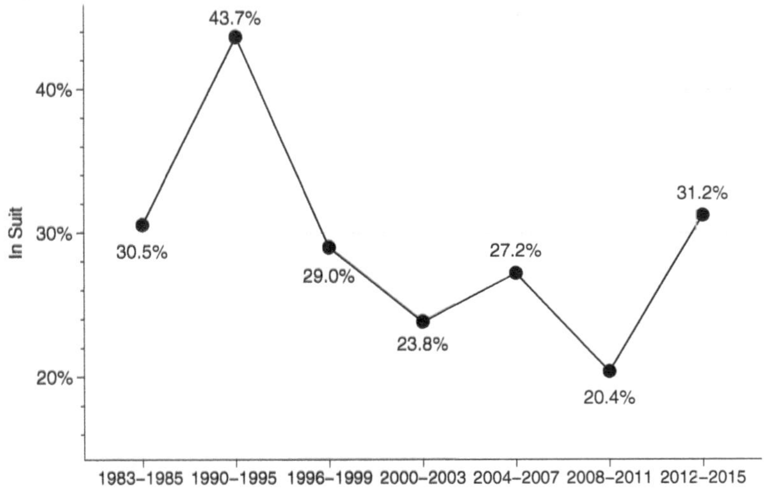

Figure 5.1 Percentage of Claims in Suit, SCLPL Data

Figure 5.1 shows the percentage in suit for each of the seven Standing Committee on Lawyers' Professional Liability (SCLPL) reports. With one exception, between 20 and 31 percent of the claims reported to SCLPL were in suit; the one exception is the 1992–1995 report, which showed 43.7 percent of claims in suit. What might account for the report-to-report variation can only be a matter of speculation, but it is likely that differences in which companies participate is part of the explanation. In contrast to the SCLPL figures, the Oregon State Bar's Professional Liability Fund (PLF) reports typically show that under 10 percent of claims result in "litigation," which presumably means a lawsuit.

It is also possible to derive estimates of the likelihood of a claim maturing into a lawsuit using the data from the Missouri Department of Insurance's Division of Financial Institutions & Professional Regulation (DIFP). One caveat regarding the DIFP data is that the coding used for disposition refers to "before filing suit or demanding hearing." A hearing might occur if the retainer agreement contained an arbitration clause. Unfortunately, there is no way to distinguish between filing suit and seeking arbitration; hence, we will treat them both as constituting "filing suit." A second caveat is that one disposition category is "Claim or Suit Abandoned," which was treated as indicating "before a suit was filed" if the claim adjustment expense was zero (88.2 percent of the abandoned claims or suits) and in suit if there had been claims adjustment expenditures.[1] Over the period 1987–2014, a suit had been filed in 48.8 percent

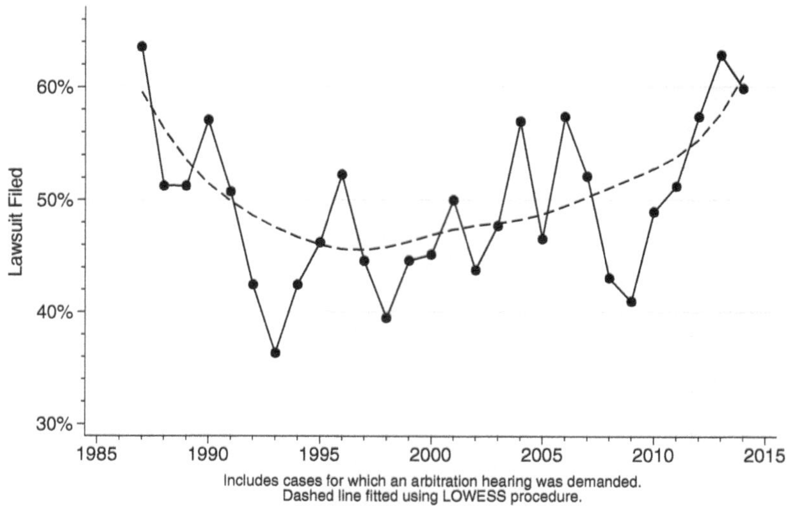

Figure 5.2 Percentage of Claims in Suit, Missouri Data, 1987–2014

of claims reported to DIFP, with some variation from year to year. As shown by the dashed lines in Figure 5.2,[2] there was a pattern of increase starting in the late 1990s. The overall percentage of cases in suit in the Missouri data was considerably higher than equivalent figures in the SCLPL reports. However, in looking at the pattern in the Missouri data, it is important to keep in mind that one company, the Bar Plan Mutual Insurance Company (BPMIC), accounted for about three-quarters of all claims, and shifts of the type shown in Figure 5.2 might have resulted from changes in how BPMIC was handling claims.

Because it stopped requiring the reporting of all claims after 1997, we have limited information from the Florida Office of Insurance Regulation (FLOIR) on the likelihood of a claim leading to a lawsuit. Looking only at the period 1981–1997, the percentage of reported claims in suit was 50.6 percent, very similar to the figure from Missouri. As in Missouri, there was year-to-year variation, with a slight pattern of a rising proportion in suit over the 17-year period.

The variation in the reported proportion of legal malpractice claims becoming lawsuits is striking, ranging from a low of 6 percent of claims made to the PLF to around half of claims reported to the insurance regulators in Florida and Missouri. The aggregated figures in the SCLPL reports fell somewhere between these two extremes. Importantly, 70 percent or more of the claims in Missouri involved an insurer that also participated in the SCLPL data

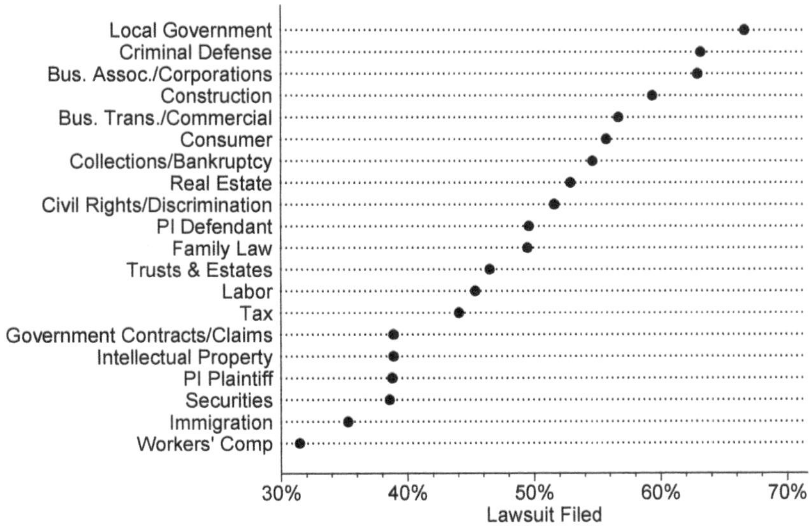

Figure 5.3 Likelihood of Suit by Area of Practice, Missouri Data, 1987–2014

collection. This raises the question of whether some of the differences in the likelihood of claims resulting in lawsuits reflect what was counted as a claim and whether that differs between what was reported to SCLPL and to the state insurance regulators. For example, Oregon's PLF only counted as claims those situations in which an actual claim was made or it had incurred some expense, with the result that it labeled only 7 percent of claims as having resulted in "litigation." The low proportion of suits among Oregon claims might indicate a very different philosophy of responding to claims, perhaps resulting from the mandatory nature of LPL insurance in Oregon, which requires all private practitioners to buy insurance through PLF.

The Missouri data made it possible to look at whether the likelihood of a claim leading to a lawsuit varied depending on several other factors. First, size of practice showed some relationship with claims getting into suit (chi square = 33.95, $p < .001$, df = 3): about 46 percent of claims against practices comprising 5 or fewer lawyers got into suit compared with about 54 percent of claims against lawyers in firms of 6 to 30 lawyers and 52 percent in firms of more than 30 lawyers. Second, as shown in Figure 5.3, whether a claim became a lawsuit varied sharply depending on the area of practice involved (chi square = 177.10, $p < .001$, df = 23). This figure omits areas of practice with fewer than 10 observations, and the only areas with fewer than 50 claims were immigration (17),

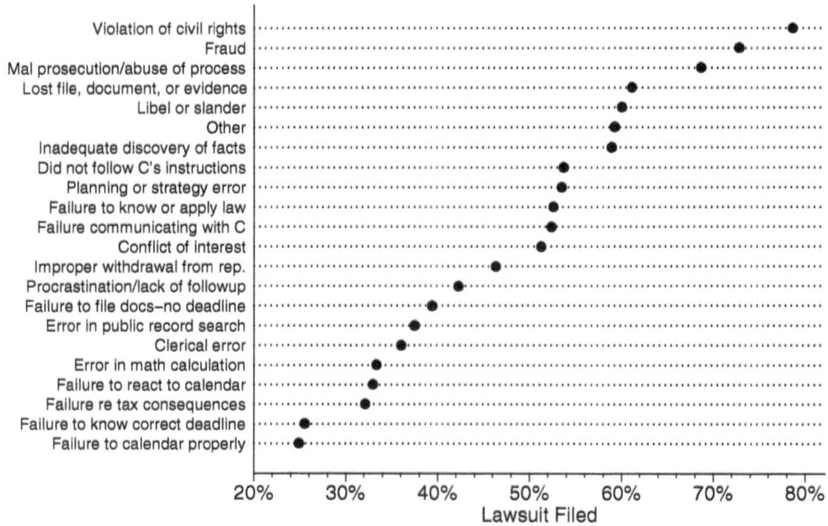

Figure 5.4 Likelihood of Suit by Alleged Error, Missouri Data, 1987–2014

government contracts (18), construction (32), and intellectual property (36). Interestingly, two areas toward the bottom in the likelihood of resulting in a lawsuit were workers' compensation (31.5 percent in suit) and personal injury (PI) plaintiffs (38.8 percent). It might be that this pattern indicates that the errors in these cases were often clear (e.g., missing a deadline). For three areas of practice—business associations/corporations, criminal defense, and local government cases—more than 60 percent of the claims resulted in lawsuits.

A second factor even more strongly linked to cases leading to a lawsuit is the nature of the alleged error or behavior (chi square = 547.06, p <.001, df = 21). Figure 5.4 shows this variation. Errors related to timing, such as missing deadlines, were the least likely to get into suit, with two having less than a 20 percent chance of leading to a lawsuit. Other types of alleged errors having a low likelihood of producing a lawsuit were math or clerical errors. At the top of the continuum, with as high as 80 percent resulting in a lawsuit, were four types of claims related to intentional behavior: violation of civil rights, fraud, malicious prosecution/abuse of process, and libel or slander. Alleged errors associated with interacting with the client—failure to communicate, conflict of interest, failing to follow the client's instruction—fell toward the middle with 50 to 60 percent getting into suit.

OUTCOME OF CLAIMS

In this section, we turn to the outcome of claims and consider three primary issues: the frequency of claim repair, the likelihood of a claim leading to payment, and the magnitude of the payments made. For the latter two questions, we examine how outcomes vary along several key dimensions.

Frequency of Claim Repair

One of the things we learned through the interviews with lawyers who regularly defended legal malpractice cases and representatives of several of the National Association of Bar Related Insurance Companies (NABRICO) insurers discussed in Chapter 7 was the practice of "claim repair," that is, finding a way to fix or mitigate the problem that led to the claim. For example, during Kritzer's study of contingency fee legal practice, one of the firms he observed was working with its LPL insurer to overcome the effect of having missed an ostensible filing deadline by one day.[3] The case involved a claim against a municipality, and under Wisconsin law a claimant cannot file suit until a municipality has been notified of the claim and has had the opportunity to settle it. After the municipality notifies the claimant that it is disallowing the claim, the claimant must file suit no later than six months after the rejection has been served on the claimant. The trial court dismissed the suit as time-barred because the suit had not been filed until six months plus one day after the date the notice of disallowance had been mailed. The firm was successful in arguing on appeal that the six-month deadline should not have applied because the notice was mailed to the law firm, not the claimant, and the relevant statute stated that the notice of denial be "served on the claimant by registered or certified mail."[4] Ultimately the suit was voluntarily dismissed without payment for factual reasons unrelated to the missed deadline.

Although we heard many references to claim repair in our interviews with defense lawyers and insurers, we found virtually no statistics on the frequency of claim repair. In fact, the only information we found that specifically identified claim repair as a mode of case disposition was from PLF. PLF's report covering the decade ending December 31, 2014, showed that 19 percent of disposed claims were closed after successful claim repair.[5] Using the data obtained from PLF, we found that over the period 1990–2015, 16.6 percent of claims were disposed through repair. There was some variation by area of law, with claim repair most frequent in personal injury cases (22.0 percent) and least frequent in securities cases (5.6 percent). Interestingly, workers' compensation matters could be repaired in only 8.8 percent of cases. Claim repair disposed of 16 to 19 percent of cases arising from family law matters, debt-related cases, trusts and estates, and tax. Claim repair was accomplished in 14 to 15 percent of criminal-related matters and business-related matters.

Claim Success: Was Any Payment Made to the Claimant?

Three sets of data contain information on the success of claims, that is, the likelihood of a claimant obtaining some payment. The dots connected by the long-dashed solid line in Figure 5.5 show the success rate as reported in seven SCLPL reports. It is hard to see any kind of clear trend in seven points. There are too few points to apply locally weighted scatterplot smoothing (LOWESS), but if one fits a linear regression line to the points, there is a downward slope. However, that slope is essentially generated by two of the seven points (2008–2011 at 19.6 and 1991–1994 at 43.6); the remaining five points are in a narrow range (29.6 to 33.9). The solid line shows the percentage of claims paid each year between 1988 and 2013 based on the Missouri data; the smoothed, curved line, produced with the LOWESS smoother, suggests a slow increase in success through about 2004, followed by a decline. There was a particularly sharp drop in 2013; exactly why is unclear, and there is no explanation of it in either the DIFP report or the BPMIC report. The success rate rebounded in 2014. Leaving aside 2013, the percentage of claims paid fluctuated between approximately 25 and 30 percent in recent years in contrast to substantially more variation in earlier years. The short-dashed lines represent the frequency of success based on the Oregon data. The level of success in Oregon was considerably higher than in Missouri and would be much higher if claim repair were treated as success from the claimant's perspective. There is, however, a clear pattern of declining success in Oregon, from more than 40 percent in the early 1990s to between 30 and 33 percent in the most recent years. The decline appears to be linear, even though the smoothed line was fitted using LOWESS, which allows for nonlinearity. The interesting question is, why have claims in Oregon have been so much more successful than claims in Missouri, or as reported by SCLPL in its periodic studies? One possibility is that PLF feels an obligation to settle claims that are valid, whereas other insurers choose

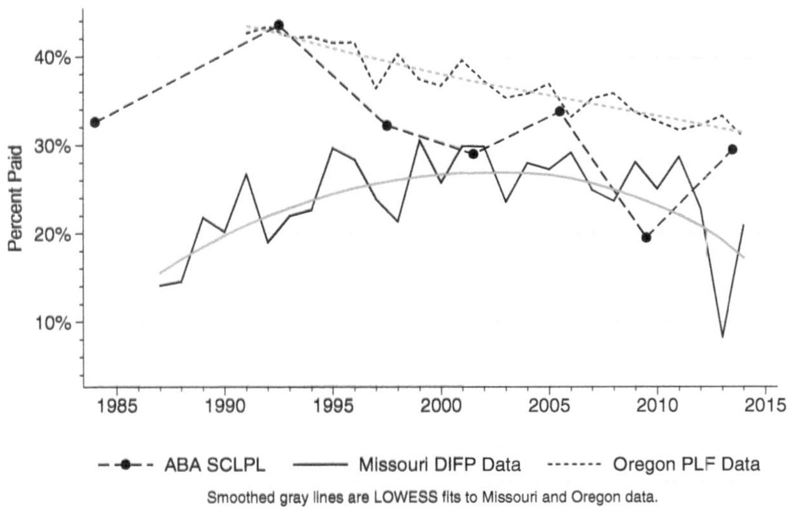

Figure 5.5 Claim Success

to resist paying claims unless they are hopeless from a defense perspective. It might also be that many strong, low-value claims are brought to PLF by unrepresented claimants, and PLF settles those claims, whereas other insurers choose not to deal with unrepresented claimants, and it is difficult to find experienced representation for even a very strong claim if the size of the claim is small.

One caution is in order in interpreting the figures discussed above. Recall that insurers vary in what they define to constitute a "claim." It does not necessarily mean that a demand for payment was ever received. As we will discuss in Chapter 7, when we asked insurers and insurance defense lawyers about the percentage of claims that resulted in payment, the figures we heard tended to be on the order of 50 percent or more, considerably higher than what is shown in the statistical analysis discussed in this chapter. We suspect that the respondents were thinking specifically in terms of claims that involved something resembling an actual demand for payment.

The Missouri data allow an exploration of several factors related to the lawyer against whom the claim was brought that might be correlated with claim success. First, regarding firm size, there was a moderate effect of decreasing success as the size of the firm increased (chi square = 22.48, $p < .001$, df = 3). For solo practitioners and lawyers in firms of 2 to 5 lawyers, 25.9 and 26.4 percent of claims, respectively, resulted in payment to the claimant; for lawyers in firms of 6 to 30, claim success decreased to 21.5 percent, and in firms of more than 30 lawyers only 18.2 percent of claims resulted in payment.

There was little difference in the success of claims brought against lawyers with more than 10 years of experience compared with those with 4 to 10 years of experience: 24.4 percent and 26.6 percent success, respectively. However, for claims against lawyers with less than 4 years' experience, the success of claims fell to 17.4 percent. Contrasting this least experienced group with the two other groups combined produced a statistically significant result (chi square = 4.05, p = .044). Why claims against young lawyers would be less successful is unclear, although it might be that the kinds of matters they handled tended to fall among the areas in which claims tended to be less successful. We consider the relations between practice area and claim outcome below.

The form used to report claims to DIFP asked whether the claim arose in one of the insured's normal areas of practice. A logical hypothesis would be that the likelihood of a claim succeeding would be greater if it involved an area less familiar to the lawyer-defendant. Only about 10 percent of claims involved a lawyer working outside of his or her usual areas of practice. About 27 percent of such claims resulted in payment compared with 25 percent of claims in which the lawyer had been working in a usual area of practice, a difference too small to rule out chance variation (chi square = 1.80, p = .180).

Another item on DIFP's form asks whether the claim arose after the lawyer attempted to collect a fee. This was the case for almost 9 percent of the claims. The claims arising in this context were less successful, producing payments in only 16.4 percent of claims as compared with 25.2 percent of claims in which there was no reported link to the lawyer trying to collect a fee. This is a difference that cannot be attributed to chance variation (chi square = 21.67, p <.001). Oregon's PLF coded whether there was a dispute about the lawyer's fee as one of the allegations; 6.4 percent of cases included such a dispute.[6] Consistent with the general payment of a higher percentage of paid claims in Oregon, where there was a fee dispute along with some alleged error, payments were made in 28.0 percent of claims compared with 37.4 percent of claims in which there was no fee dispute.[7] Hence, the pattern in Missouri and Oregon is similar: substantially fewer claims are paid when they are connected to some issue related to the lawyer's fee.

Figure 5.6 uses both the Missouri and Oregon data to examine how claimant success depended on the area of practice producing the claim and shows that there is significant variation (chi square = 193.04, p <.001, df = 22 for Missouri; chi square = 666.08, p < .001, df = 10 for Oregon).[8] As was true for

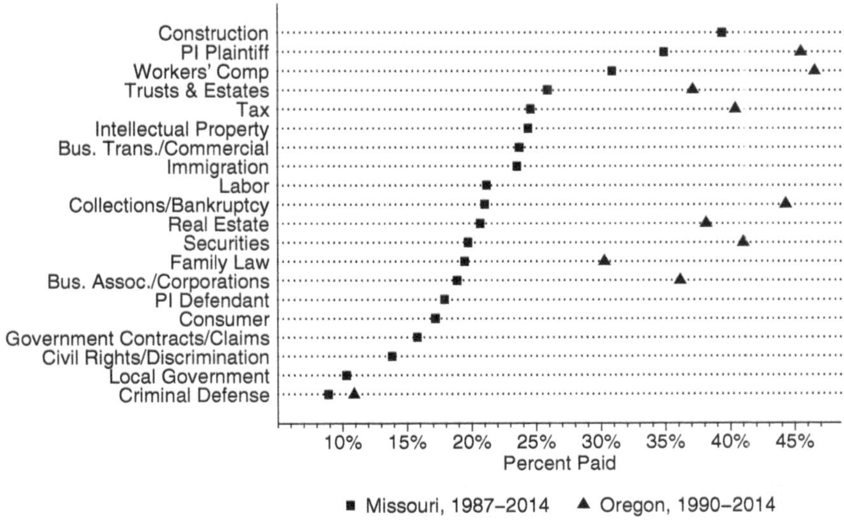

Figure 5.6 Claim Success by Area of Practice Producing the Claim, Missouri and Oregon Data

the overtime variation in success, the likelihood of payment was greater in every area of practice category for the Oregon data. For more than half of the categories in the Missouri data, claimants obtained recovery in 20–25 percent of the cases. The three areas that stand out are construction (contracts) with a success rate of almost 40 percent, plaintiffs' personal injury, and workers' compensation with success rates in the 30 to 35 percent range. In the Oregon data, five of the categories—personal injury, collections/bankruptcy, workers' compensation, tax, and securities—exceeded 40 percent, with three others—real estate, trusts and estates, and business/commercial between 35 and 40 percent. At the bottom of the figure, one finds cases arising from criminal defense for both states with very similar success rates: 11 percent in Oregon and 8 percent in Missouri. Missouri cases arising from issues with local government had a similarly low success rates of just over 10 percent. Other areas with a success rate below 20 percent in Missouri involved government contracts/claims, consumer cases, personal injury defense, and civil rights/discrimination cases. Thinking about the kinds of matters that tend to be concentrated in one or the other of the two hemispheres, personal services or corporate, there was no pattern suggesting higher claimant success in one or the other.

In Chapter 4 we showed that claims were most associated with certain types of activities: the combination of commencement of action, preparation

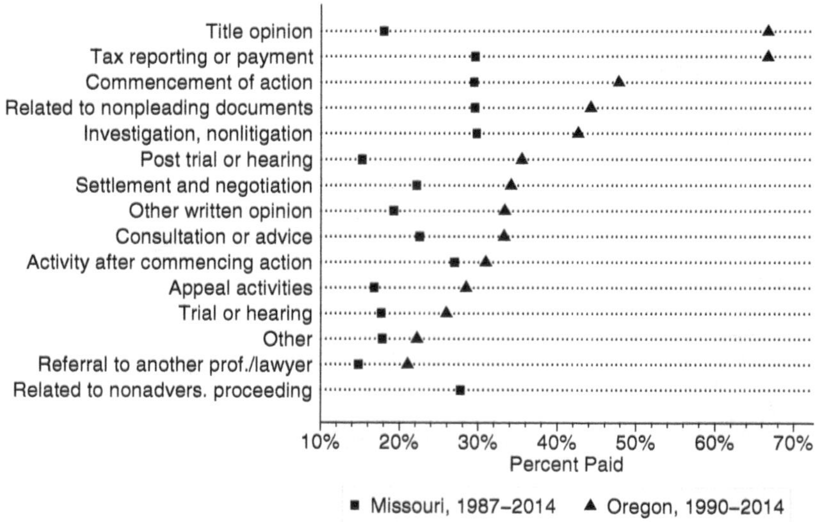

Figure 5.7 Claim Success by Activity Producing the Claim, Missouri and Oregon Data

or transmittal of documents, activities after commencing an action, and settlement or negotiation accounted for about 60 percent of the claims in Missouri and Oregon. Figure 5.7 shows how the success of claims varied depending on the activity alleged to lead to the error. Over 60 percent of Oregon claims arising from title opinions or tax-related activities resulted in some payment to the claimant, with between 40 and 50 percent of Oregon claims paid when the activity was commencement of an action, related to nonlitigation documents, or investigation outside of litigation. Although the success rates were much lower in Missouri, these same areas, except for title opinions, also produced the highest claimant success rates there. Three types of activities fell toward the bottom on success for both states: appeal activities and other post-trial activities. The differences in claim success depending on the nature of the activity leading to a claim cannot be attributed to chance (chi square = 81.20, $p < .001$, df = 14 for Missouri; chi square = 726.90, $p < .001$, df = 14 for Oregon).

A final potential predictor of claim success included in the Missouri data is the nature of the alleged error.[9] Figure 5.8 shows the variation in success by nature of the error, and this variation is both substantial and statistically significant (chi square = 302.03, $p < .001$, df = 21). The three errors at the top of the figure all relate to missing a deadline and resulted in success rates between 37.8 percent and 44.0 percent. The other errors with claimant success

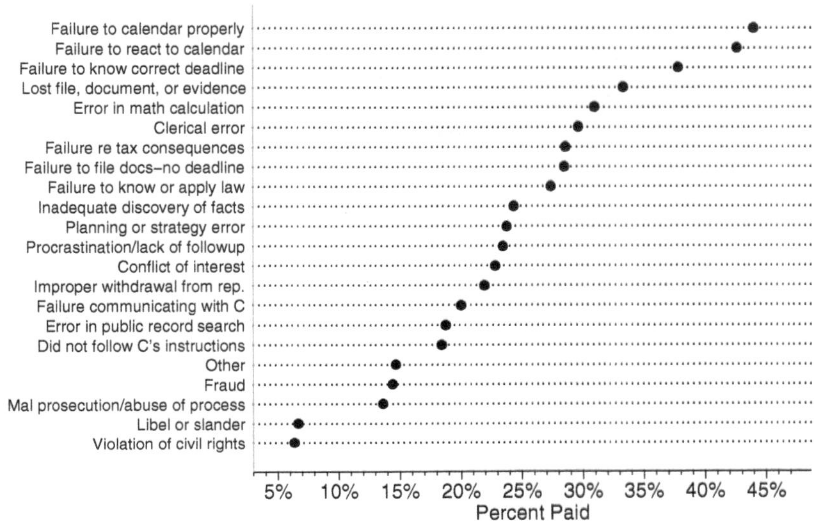

Figure 5.8 Claim Success by Alleged Error, Missouri Data

rates of 30 percent or more were errors in math calculations and losing a file or document, with clerical errors, failure to file a document, failure to know tax consequences, and failure to know or apply the law properly approaching 30 percent. The lowest success rates, under 15 percent, involved allegations of what constitute intentional acts: fraud, malicious prosecution/abuse of process, violation of civil rights, and defamation, the latter two having success rates under 7 percent.

AMOUNTS PAID TO CLAIMANTS

When a claim was successful, meaning that the claimant received some compensation, how much compensation did the claimant typically receive? One could use several different measures to describe the typical amount of compensation: the median amount paid, the mean amount paid, and the proportion paid exceeding some threshold. The discussion that follows relies primarily on the median (in 2010 dollars) and the proportion exceeding $100,000 (in nominal dollars). We use nominal dollars for the $100,000 threshold analysis because the SCLPL reports provided information based on categories, and there is no way to adjust those category amounts for inflation and still get a figure for the percentage of paid claims with an adjusted payment over $100,000.[10] We limited our use of the mean because it can be greatly affected by small numbers of outliers, and this was a problem when breaking the cases into categories, some of which have relatively small numbers of observations.

Payments and Policy Limits

For the Florida paid cases, information is available on the limits of the insurance policy. For the early data, the amount is for the "primary policy limits of the insured law firm"; for the later data it is the "insured per claim limit" and the "insured aggregate limit." Almost all claims (97.9 percent) were resolved for less than the policy limit. Fewer (1.4 percent) were resolved for the exact policy limit, and the remaining cases—a total of 29 out of 4,602, paid claims for which we have information on the policy limits—for more than the policy limits. Exactly what accounts for those over-limits payments is unclear.[11]

Similar information is available in the data we obtained from Oregon. One important difference is that this information only deals with the basic insurance coverage, which maxes out at $300,000; given this relatively low limit, one might expect limit payments to be more common. However, such payments were in fact less common in Oregon: in only 51 of 7,666 cases, two-thirds of 1 percent of paid cases, was the payment for the limit of the policy.[12]

It is worth comparing this result with what happens in medical malpractice cases. Hyman and colleagues examined the frequency of "at limits" payments in medical malpractice claims in Texas.[13] Limiting their analysis to cases with payments of at least $25,000, they found that 13 percent of physician-defendant claims settle at exactly the policy limits, and another 7 percent within 10 percent of the limits. In the Florida medical malpractice data provided by FLOIR, not limited to claims in which at least $25,000 was paid out, 18.1 percent paid limits and another 3.4 percent paid within 10 percent of limits (i.e., between 90 and 100 percent of limits). Clearly, limits payments are much less common in cases of LPL.

Concentration of Payments

The amounts paid in compensation to resolve LPL claims can be very large when the financial loss of the claimants is very large. For example, as noted in Chapter 1, in 2015 a Texas jury awarded $196 million in a case against Andrews Kurth.[14]

The result, even ignoring the extreme cases such as that involving Andrews Kurth, is that a small proportion of legal malpractice claims accounts for a very large proportion of the total damages paid out. Across the data from Missouri's DIFP, a total of more than $211.4 million (in 2010 dollars) was paid in compensation. As shown in Table 5.1, of that total, 29.1 percent was paid in the top 1 percent of all paid claims, 54.3 percent was paid in the top 5 percent of claims, and 77.1 percent in the top 10 percent; the bottom half of the claims received 5.8 percent of all compensation paid in legal malpractice claims in Missouri.

The picture in Florida is similar. Based on the FLOIR data, of the total of $690.8 million paid to claimants, 22.9 percent went to the top 1 percent of claims, 46.0 percent to the top 5 percent, and 60.9 percent of payments to the top 10 percent; the bottom half of claims received 6.1 percent of all compensation paid in Florida. The broad picture does not change in Oregon, where the limits of the policies offered by the PLF is only $300,000, although this does reduce somewhat the concentration because there are no very large payments. It is important to note that none of the claims in these data was a megacase such as Andrews Kurth; the largest amounts paid in Missouri and Florida were $11.5 million and $8.4 million (both in 2010 dollars).

Using similar data on medical malpractice claims from Missouri and Florida, it is possible to determine if the concentration of payments in a small fraction of paid claims is different between these two types of professional liability cases. As Table 5.1 shows, this is not the case. The concentration of payments is considerably greater than in medical malpractice cases from Missouri but less than the concentration in Florida. However, we do wonder if by being limited to examining data from these two states, we are underestimating the degree of concentration in legal malpractice cases nationally. The largest unadjusted payments in LPL malpractice cases in the two states were $8.8 million in Missouri and $9.0 million in Florida, which pale in comparison with some of the payments made by the Attorneys' Liability Assurance Society (ALAS) and Aon. As discussed in Chapter 4, Richmond identified 67 publicly reported verdicts and settlements in claims brought against lawyers or law firms from the mid-1980s through early 2015, with payments or verdicts exceeding $20 million and the largest verdict and largest settlement exceeding $100 million; another 70 cases had payments between $3 million and $20 million.[15] Across both Missouri and Florida, only 24 claims resulted in nominal payments of $3 million or more, and in only three of those cases was it likely that there would have been a public report.

Table 5.1: Concentration of Malpractice Claim Payments, Missouri, Florida, and Oregon Data

	Legal Malpractice			*Medical Malpractice*	
	Missouri *1987–2014*	*Florida* *1981–2014*	*Oregon*	*Missouri* *1990–2014***	*Florida* *1998–2014*
Total payments*	$211.4 million	$690.8 million	$230.8 million	$3.1 billion	$10.2 billion
Percent of total constituting:					
Top 1 percent	29.1%	22.9%	12.3%	15.5%	34.0%
Top 5 percent	54.3%	46.0%	40.2%	39.9%	51.4%
Top 10 percent	77.1%	60.9%	56.1%	54.5%	62.3%
Bottom 50 percent	5.8%	6.1%	7.4%	5.3%	6.7%

*2010 dollars

**Figures for Missouri medical malpractice cases provided by Brent Kabler, Department of Insurance, Financial Institutions, & Professional Registration.

Change in Amounts Paid over Time

Figure 5.9 shows the median payments (inflation-adjusted to 2010 dollars) over time based on the SCLPL reports and the claims data from Missouri, Florida, and Oregon. The line for the SCLPL data shows seven points as dots representing the seven reports. That line shows an initial drop, followed by a more modest pattern of increase until a sharp jump in the 2004–2007 period; the line drops for 2008–2011 back to a median that would suggest a pattern of linear increase starting with the 1990–1995 report, but then jumps again for the 2012–2015 report to the level in the 2004–2007 report. We do not have an explanation for this inconsistent pattern. At least some of the inconsistency probably reflects differences in the companies participating in the various reports.

The solid lines without dots in Figure 5.9 track the median payment in Missouri, with the heavier, smoothed line fitted using the LOWESS procedure. The Missouri median fluctuated greatly from year to year. As shown by the smoothed line, it seemed to hit something of a trough in the 2000s but has been rising in the years since then. What accounts for either the trough or the increase is unclear. The short-dashed lines track the medians for Florida. Although the figure shows substantial year-to-year variation, there was a clear upward pattern, with the inflation-adjusted median increasing from approximately $30,000 to about $50,000. A straight-line regression fitted to the annual

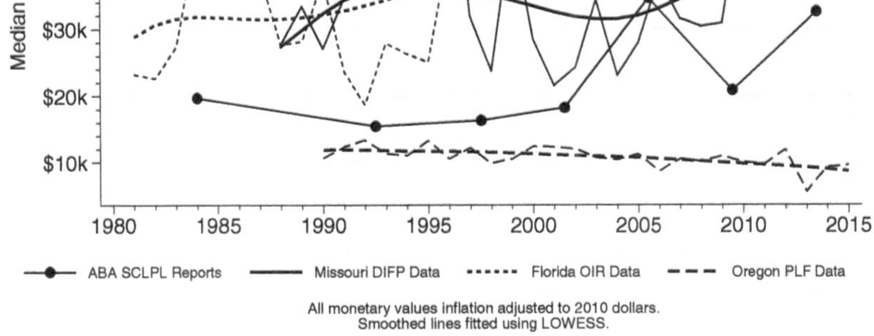

Figure 5.9 Median Payments to Claimants

Florida medians suggests a trend with the median increasing by $978 per year ($r^2 = .554$). The longer-dashed lines track the Oregon medians; they are much lower than any of the other sources, and the smoothed line suggests a pattern of slow decline with the median decreasing by about $125 per year ($r^2 = .348$).

The medians for both Missouri and Florida were generally higher that what was reported by SCLPL. The most likely explanation for this difference is that the SCLPL reports were dominated by information from insurers that focus on smaller firms and solo practitioners, where the severity of claims was less. As is shown later in this chapter, the typical size of indemnity payment was much greater for larger firms. However, that does not explain why the median payments were so much lower in Oregon. Even though the policy limit in Oregon is $300,000, that would not account for a lower median. It appears that Oregon's PLF is willing to pay small claims, whereas other insurers might resist them; this would be consistent with the overall higher rate of claims paid in Oregon.

Figure 5.10 tracks the percentage of payments exceeding $100,000 in nominal dollars. The heavier lines (solid for Missouri and short dashed for Florida) indicate that in both Missouri and Florida there were strong upward trends, increasing from on the order of 5 to 10 percent to 25 to 30 percent. The trend for Florida was quite linear, whereas in Missouri the trend plateaued from about 1995 to 2005 before resuming its upward movement, with Missouri hav-

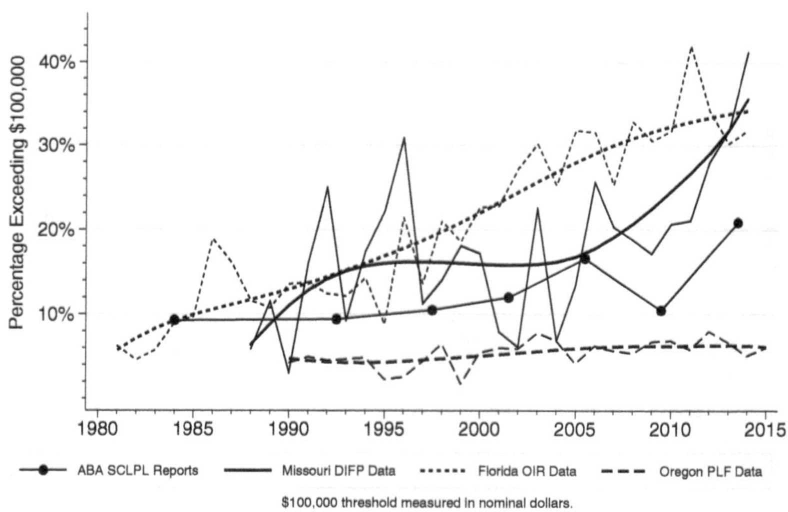

Figure 5.10 Percentage of Payments to Claimants Exceeding $100,000

ing particularly sharp increases for the last two years shown in the figure. The percentage of payments exceeding $100,000 in the SCLPL data started in the same range as for Missouri and Florida and has had a pattern of increase, but that increase has been much less, at least until the most recent (2012–2015) report, when 20.9 percent of payments exceeded $100,000. It is unclear why there was a drop in $100,000-plus payments in the 2008–2011 SCLPL report (only 10.5 percent of payments exceeded $100,000). Again, the best explanation for the differences between SCLPL and the figures based on the data from the two insurance regulators is the selective and changing nature of insurers participating in the SCLPL reports. However, this does not account for the much lower rate of over $100,000 payments in Oregon, which has never exceeded 10 percent and has shown little increase over time.

From the perspective of one seeking to understand claims and claims processing, the medians of the payments are most informative because they avoid distortion by a small number of extreme payments. However, from the perspective of the insurers making the payments and possibly the insureds paying premiums,[16] the mean payment is more important because it is based on the total amount of payments being made to claimants. It was not possible to compute means based on the SCLPL data because of the way payment information was presented in the reports.[17] Consequently, Figure 5.11 tracks the inflation-adjusted means for the Missouri, Florida, and Oregon data and

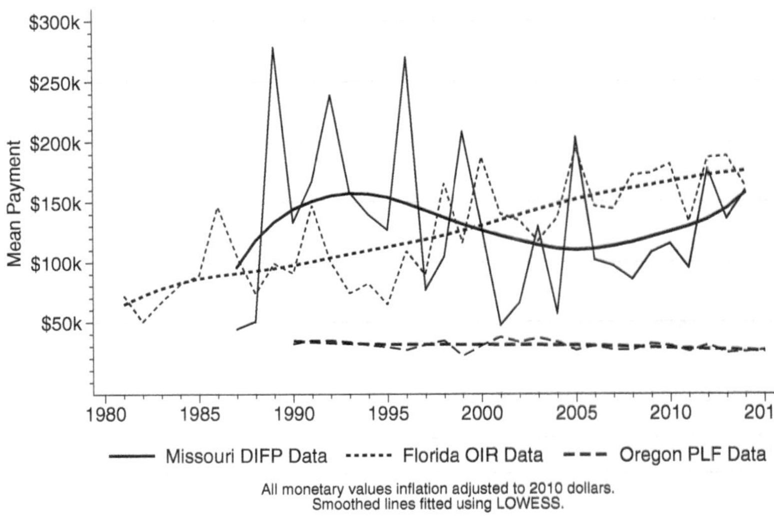

Figure 5.11 Mean Payments to Claimants, Missouri, Florida, and Oregon Data

shows very different patterns. As one would expect, there was a lot of year-to-year variation for Florida and Missouri but not for Oregon. The LOWESS lines help identify trends, and the line for Florida shows a strong linear trend, with the inflation-adjusted mean roughly tripling over the period, from about $65,000, to about $175,000. In contrast, the inflation-adjusted mean in the Missouri data has decreased over time, falling by about one-third before starting to rebound. Oregon shows much less variation generally but does appear to decline 10 to 20 percent over the period for which we have data. We have no explanation for why the patterns would be so different in the three states.

Amounts Paid by Large-Firm Insurers

In principle, the data collected by Missouri's DIFP and FLOIR include claims against very large firms as well as against lawyers in small firms or practicing solo. However, these are not states where major corporate firms, particularly very large firms, tend to be based. What can be distilled regarding payments using information from ALAS and Aon? Because of issues in the information from those two sources, that information is best used to provide a sense of magnitude rather than exact numbers.

Turning first to the ALAS figures, there are several caveats. First, ALAS did not report the number of claims closed with payment. Second, the figures were given as aggregations since the founding of ALAS rather than for a given year, and no adjustments can be made for inflation. Third, the figures given were for "gross incurred loss," which includes both actual payments and amounts reserved for paying claims currently pending, including payments made by reinsurers plus any defense expenditures. Fourth, although ALAS reported "gross incurred loss per claim," it did this by dividing the total gross incurred loss by the number of (real) claims including those (real) claims closed without payment. Fifth, although it is unclear whether the gross loss incurred included the self-insured retention (deductible) paid by the insured, most likely it did not. With those caveats, there are still some insights to be gained by looking at what ALAS reported if one is willing to make some assumptions we specify below.

The 2014 *ALAS Annual Report* showed the average per (real) claim "gross incurred loss" to be $409,200.[18] If one assumes that half of (real) claims incurred at least some loss, the average loss per paid claim exceeded $800,000. If one additionally takes into account the self-insured retention paid by the insured, which over the years averaged over half a million dollars, that would put the average incurred loss at well over $1 million. For purposes of comparison, we computed the equivalent figures for Florida and Missouri. The mean gross loss in Missouri was $49,877 and in Florida $52,926 (both inflation adjusted); these figures included both claims resulting in some loss and those with no loss (i.e., neither payment nor expenditures on defense).[19] Thus, the typical loss for ALAS's claims was an order of magnitude greater than what is found using the two state-level data sources.

As with ALAS, the information regarding Aon claims did not allow separating out payment to claimants from expenditures on defense.[20] Also, as with ALAS, the loss amounts Aon reported included both actual losses and amounts reserved for pending claims; this means that the figures slightly understated the amounts of loss associated with closed claims, but unlike ALAS the Aon amounts included what the clients paid as their self-insured retentions. Also, unlike ALAS, Aon provided information on the number of claims with a recorded loss, which allows computing a mean loss for only those claims; Aon also reported the median loss for claims with some loss, so that information is available as well. Lastly, the figures in the report were in nominal dollars rather than inflation-adjusted dollars, but that is less of an issue here because the information was limited to a 10-year period, 2004–2013, and if the loss amounts for each of these years were equal, the inflation adjustment to 2010 dollars would be only +2.9 percent.

With these caveats in mind, the mean loss reported by Aon was $1.58 million and the median was $190,800. In comparison, the means of loss for claims with at least some reported loss in Missouri and Florida for all years for which we have data were $99,328 and $143,263, respectively; the medians were $20,484 and $45,720, respectively. Limiting the Florida calculation to those years for all claims had to be reported, the mean and median are $90,927 and $29,287, respectively.[21] Here again, the Aon figures were approximately an order of magnitude larger.

Variations in Payments to Claimants

Variation by Firm Size. Because the Missouri data included information on firm size, one can look at whether and how payments varied by firm size. As shown in Table 5.2, the typical amount paid, measured both by the mean and by the median, did increase with firm size. The biggest jump was in the mean

Table 5.2: Firm Size and Claim Payments, Missouri Data, 1987–2014

Firm Size	*% of Claims*	*% Paid*	*N*	*Mean Paid*	*Median Paid*	*N*
Solo	26.5	25.9	1,706	$52,678	$24,351	442
2–5	40.0	264	2,578	$110,994	$34,034	681
6–30	28.7	21.5	1,850	$190,455	$49,620	398
> 30	4.7	18.2	303	$669,503	$135,301	55
All	100.0	24.5	6,437	$134,176	$34,750	1576
test statistic		22.48[a]		30.26[b]	54.73[c]	
p-value		< .001		< .001	< .001	

[a] Chi square (contingency table; df = 3)

[b] F statistic (one-way ANOVA); Kruskal-Wallis rank test, chi square = 90.72, p < .001

[c] Chi square (k-sample equality of medians test)

All monetary values inflation adjusted to 2010 dollars.

amount paid by firms with more than 30 lawyers, although, as the medians show, this reflected the skew in the payments by those firms. This is consistent with the much larger payments reported in the previous section by insurers for large firms, although here the amounts are limited to the payments made to claimants, and the claims are limited to those for which some payment was made. The pattern shown in Table 5.2 is also consistent with comments we heard from insurers to the effect that the likelihood of claims decreases as a firm size increases, but the "severity" of the claims increases.

Payments by Area of Practice. In 2010 dollars, the overall median indemnity payment in Missouri was $34,570, and the mean was $134,176; the comparable figures for Florida were $42,760 and $137,966; and for Oregon $10,868 and $30,110. In all three states the amounts paid varied substantially depending on area of practice generating the claim. Figure 5.12 shows median amounts paid in 2010 dollars for all areas of practice producing 10 or more paid claims; the squares represent medians for Missouri, the circles for Florida, and the triangles for Oregon. One adjustment to the plot is that the median for securities cases in Missouri was trimmed to reduce the plot scale; the actual median for that set of cases was more than $138,000. Consistent with the two hemispheres perspective, the areas toward the top of Figure 5.12 tend to be the areas of practice associated with corporate work—securities, business transactions,

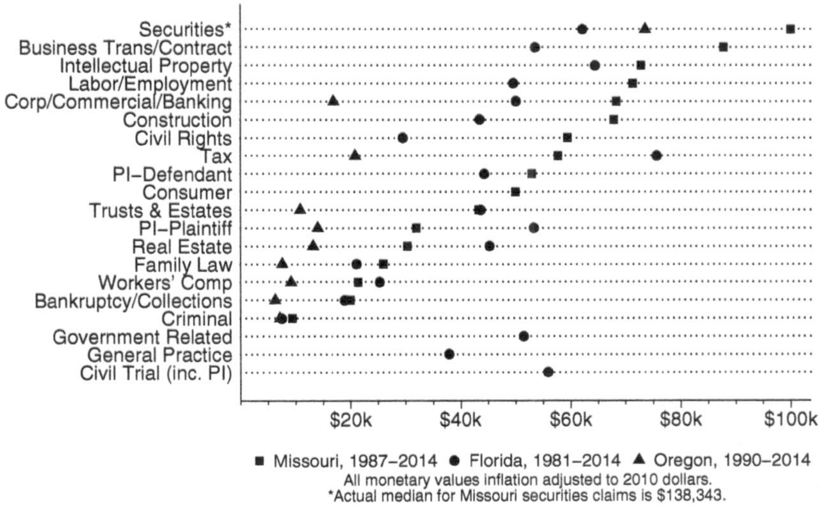

Figure 5.12 Median Payment by Area of Practice, Missouri, Florida, and Oregon Data

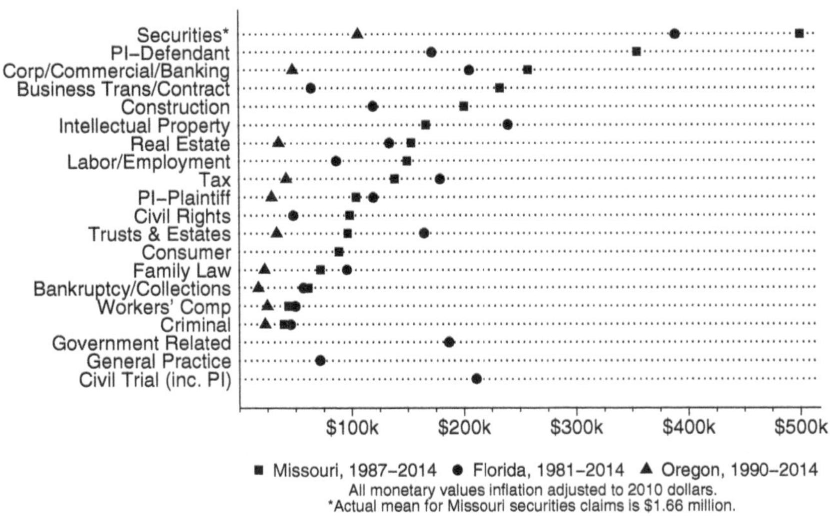

Figure 5.13 Mean Payment by Area of Practice, Missouri, Florida, and Oregon Data

corporate, and labor and employment—whereas those toward the bottom—criminal, workers' compensation, family, bankruptcy/collections—tend to be associated more with the personal services sector. Figure 5.13 shows the means by area of practice, and the pattern is generally the same. One exception is the

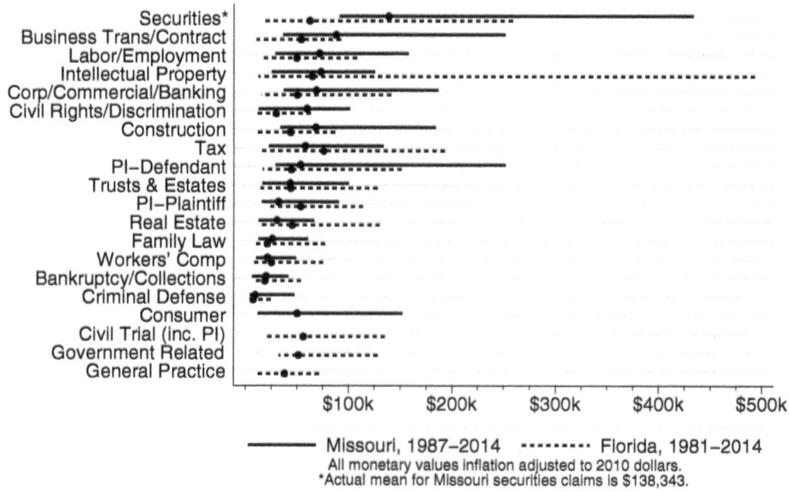

Figure 5.14 Midspreads and Medians in Payments by Area of Practice, Missouri and Florida Data

high mean for personal injury defense from Missouri, which reflected a small number of payments exceeding $1 million.

Figure 5.14 provides a sense of the variation in payments by area of practice in Missouri and Florida. We have omitted Oregon from this figure because there is so much less variation in Oregon, at least in part because of the low policy limit, that there would be relatively little to see if it were included in this graph.[22] Missouri is represented by the solid line and Florida by the dashed line. The lines represent the midspread, which runs from the first quartile (twenty-fifth percentile) to the third quartile (seventy-fifth percentile) and constitutes the middle half of the observations. The length of the lines is a measure of variation called the interquartile range. Also shown by the dot on each line is the median. As with the means and medians, variation tended to be the highest for areas of practice associated with the corporate hemisphere, with less variation in the areas associated with the personal services sector.

Payments by Alleged Error. Figure 5.15 is similar in format to Figure 5.14: the line represents the midspread and the dot the median. It shows that amounts paid also varied substantially by the nature of the error. Conflict of interest stands out as near the top both in terms of its median, right behind violation of civil rights. In contrast, the other intentional act categories, fraud and malicious

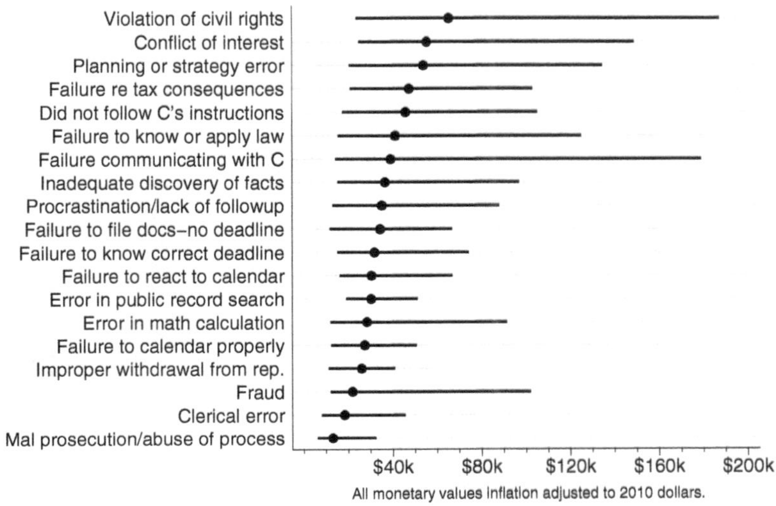

Figure 5.15 Medians and Midspreads in Amounts Paid by Type of Error, Missouri Data, 1987–2014

prosecution, fall at or near the bottom. The figure also shows that there is a lot of variation within many of the categories, although why some categories have a lot of variation and others do not is unclear.

Chapter 4 showed that the broad type of error leading associated claims differed by area of practice, with claims arising from plaintiffs' personal injury standing out as having over 50 percent of all of the claims involving a deadline-related issue. Using the Missouri data and the same set of summary categories for the errors (see Table 4.4),[23] Figure 5.16 shows the proportion of all damages paid (in 2010 dollars) by broad type of error for the same six areas of practice. Again, plaintiffs' personal injury stands out with more than half of all damages paid out involving deadline issues. For all of the other areas, substantive errors accounted for more than half of the damages, and this figure rose to over 70 percent for claims involving real estate and almost 67 percent for claims involving corporate or commercial matters. The largest percentages associated with client relations issues occurred with claims involving family law or bankruptcy/collection matters; both were about 19 percent of all damages paid. None of the areas of practice had a substantial proportion of loss attributable to intentional behavior, but this is highest for the corporate/commercial area, perhaps reflecting the "bad client" problem discussed in Chapter 4.

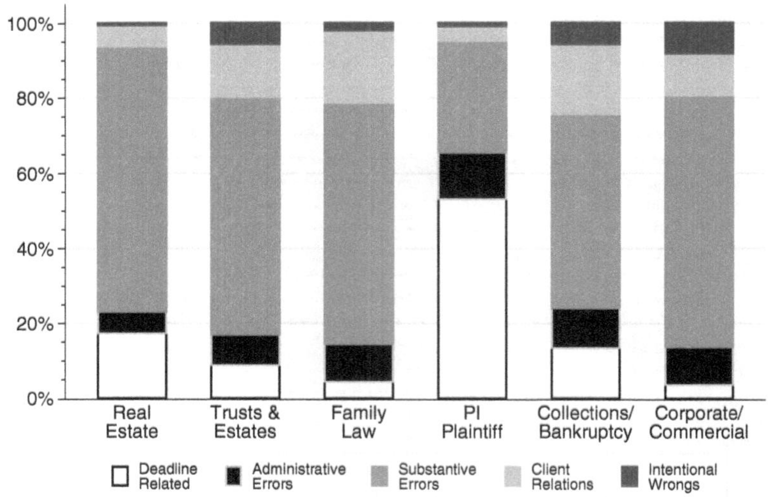

Figure 5.16 Total Payments by Broad Error Type, Selected Areas of Practice, Missouri Data, 1987–2014

Payments by ALAS and Aon. The information on payments from ALAS and from Aon are not exactly comparable to the other sources. As previously discussed, neither source provided information on indemnity payments but rather reported "incurred loss," which includes both indemnity payments and claim adjustment defense costs for defense counsel and other expenditures. Also, the information was not limited to claims in which indemnity was paid. In the case of ALAS, the information reported was the average incurred loss across all "real" claims, and those figures did not include the amounts paid by the insured to cover self-insured retentions. The figures from Aon, both means and medians, did include amounts paid by the insured ("ground up") but were based on all claims in which there was some loss expense or indemnity payment. Although the inclusion of the loss adjustment expense would tend to increase the mean and/or medians that were paid, the averaging across either all "real" claims or all claims with payments of either loss adjustment expense or indemnity payment almost certainly more than overcompensates for that.

Figure 5.17 shows the median amounts of ground-up incurred loss for Aon across areas of practice.[24] The areas that stand out are banking (1.4 percent of claims), tax (3.8 percent of claims), and securities (3.2 percent of claims). It is easy to see how these areas would be dominated by claims with large losses. Large banking claims and large securities claims probably resulted from

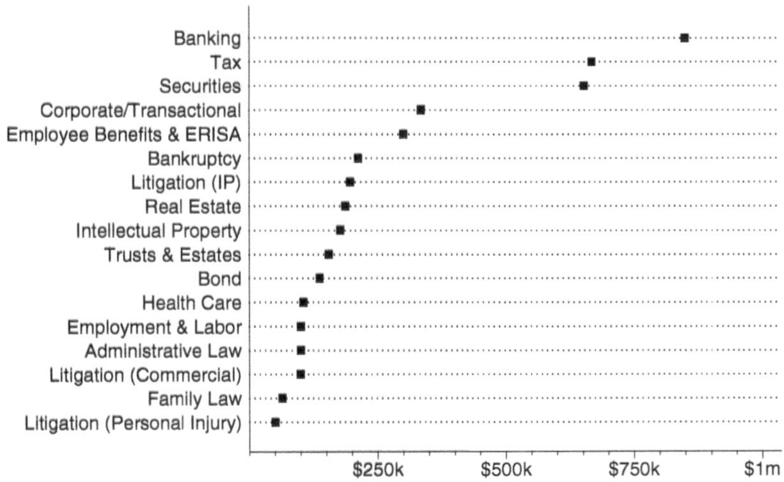

Figure 5.17 Median Ground-Up Incurred Loss by Area of Practice, Aon, 2004–2013

allegations from nonclients that the firm aided some activity of a client that resulted in significant damages to those nonclients; large tax-related claims probably reflected errors in advising corporate clients on the tax consequences of certain actions or errors in drafting agreements that led to large unexpected tax liabilities. Looking at the two areas representing the largest share of claims with losses, corporate/transactional (21.4 percent) and commercial litigation (25.0 percent), the former fell just below securities but was sharply less than securities and commercial litigation, which fell almost at the bottom, with only family law and personal injury litigation having lower medians.

Figure 5.18 shows mean loss by area of practice as reported by both Aon and ALAS. The two groups do not use identical categories, and hence for some categories the figure shows a mean for only one of the two sources. Perhaps the most striking aspect of the figure is the much lower means for ALAS. However, this reflects two factors noted previously. First, ALAS computed the averages across all "real" claims regardless of whether there was any incurred loss. Second, ALAS considered only amounts paid by ALAS, excluding any amounts paid by an insured as part of its self-insured retention, whereas Aon's amounts are "ground up." The latter factor is probably the primary driver of the differences between ALAS and Aon, given that the median firm insured through ALAS (as of January 2015) had a retention of $500,000 and the median lawyer insured through ALAS faced a $1 million retention.[25] The exclusion of the

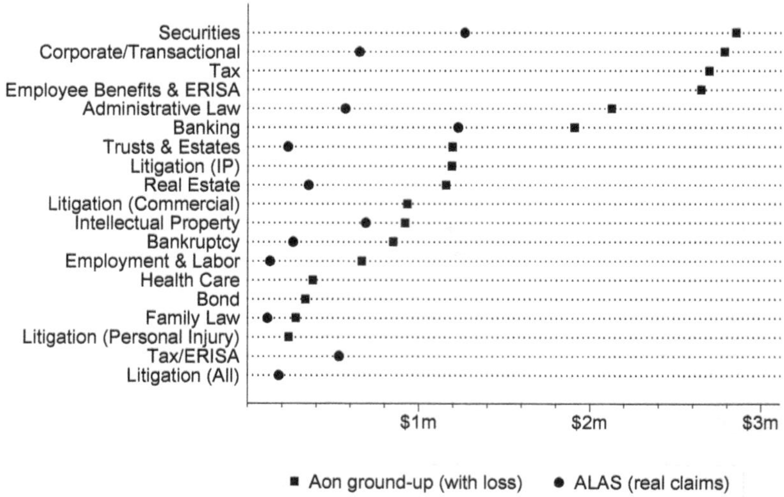

Figure 5.18 Mean Incurred Loss by Area of Practice, Aon and ALAS

retention amounts paid by the insured could readily account for the Aon-ALAS differences. More importantly, if this interpretation of the differences between the Aon and ALAS means is correct, it shows another aspect of the differences between the two hemispheres. Specifically, the deductibles for most lawyers working in the personal services sector are on the order of $1,000 to $5,000, 1 percent or less of what lawyers and firms working in the corporate hemisphere are likely to face.

Turning to a comparison of the specific means, for ALAS two areas, securities (4 percent of claims) and banking (2 percent of claims), stood apart with an average per-claim incurred loss exceeding $1 million. Four areas had average per-claim losses between $500,000 and $1 million: intellectual property (3 percent of claims), corporate/transactions (26 percent of claims), administrative law (1 percent of claims), and tax/ERISA (4 percent of claims). Litigation fell toward the bottom in terms of per-claim loss, less than $200,000 per claim, while accounting for the largest share of claims (39 percent). In looking at these figures, it is important to keep in mind that the "per-claim" calculation included both claims in which the claimant recovered and claims in which there was no recovery. There are some similarities in the ordering for the ALAS and Aon means: securities and corporate/transactional were toward the top for both Aon and ALAS. Banking was the second-highest mean for ALAS, and although it was the second highest *median* for Aon, the mean for that area of practice fell below several areas in the Aon claims. Although intellectual property (IP) was toward the top for ALAS, it fell toward the middle of the pack for Aon. Litigation in the ALAS figures fell toward the bottom, but for Aon some litigation (IP) was higher and some was lower (personal injury, presumably defense).

THE COSTS OF LAWYERS' PROFESSIONAL LIABILITY IN THE TWO HEMISPHERES

How do the total amounts paid out compare between the corporate and personal services sectors? Obtaining comprehensive information on the total amounts paid in LPL claims is not possible. However, the ALAS and Aon reports provide some information relevant to this question. In its 2014 annual report, ALAS showed figures for "net claims expense" of $278.0 million and $231.5 million for the 2013 and 2014 fiscal years, although, as previously discussed, the ALAS amounts do not include payments by insureds as part of the insured's self-insured retention (SIR).[26] For the ten-year period ending with 2013, Aon reported a total "ground-up" loss of $1,848.5 million, or an average of $184.8 million not taking into account inflation.[27] Using the average of the two years' data from ALAS, the corporate sector losses represented by these two sources totaled more than $439.6 million per year; if we assume that amounts paid as ALAS's insureds' SIRs amounted to about $45 million per year, estimated as $100,000 per claim with an average of 450 claims per year,[28] the total comes to about $485 million. This figure does not account for large firms that place their insurance with a broker other than Aon, or with one of the other large-firm mutuals that does not work with Aon. If we assume that ALAS and Aon combined provide insurance for 85 percent of large firm lawyers, and the claims experience of the remaining 15 percent are similar to the other 85 percent, the total comes to about $570 million.

Getting an estimate for the personal services/small-firm sector is difficult. However, extrapolating from our data for Missouri's DIFP, Levin estimated that the total indemnity payment for solo and small firm practitioners was $260 million.[29] To arrive at this figure, Levin used an earlier version of our Table 5.2 to compute the average annual amount paid out by insurers for solo practitioners and firms with 5 or fewer lawyer; she then converted the Missouri average to a national figure by assuming that 1.5 percent of all such practitioners in the United States were in Missouri. Her figure did not include claims expenses as do the ALAS and Aon figures. Using her methodology with more recent figures, and adding in claims adjustment expenses, we arrive at a total of $336.6 million; if we include all firms with fewer than 30 lawyers, the figure rises to $639.8 million.

Admittedly, these estimates are very crude. Still, these figures suggest that the share of payments in the solo and small-firm sector limited to firms with five or fewer lawyers is somewhere between 35 and 40 percent. This figure exceeds that sector's share of legal services revenue from individual clients as opposed to business clients, which is approximately 31.1 percent.[30] If we define the personal services sector to include firms of up to 30 lawyers, the legal malpractice cost for that sector is greater than in the corporate sector, constituting over half of the costs associated with LPL.

SUMMARY

This chapter has shown that there was substantial variation in the outcomes of LPL claims, both in terms of whether any payment or loss was incurred and in terms of the amounts of those payments or losses. The key areas of variation were along three dimensions: area of practice, type of error, and size/sector of practice. The first of these is correlated with the other two. Corporate sector firms tend to practice in areas in which, when an error occurs, the damages are larger than in other areas. Although we do not have any information on the size of the transaction or severity of loss for personal injury and property damage involved in the cases, corporate sector firms take on matters with greater amounts at stake, both in contentious matters and in transactional matters. Chapter 4 showed that the areas of practice producing claims varied substantially depending on the size/sector of the firm, with larger corporate sector firms more involved in commercial and corporate matters including securities and intellectual property, matters tending to involve substantial sums of money producing significant indemnity payments when errors occur.

Importantly, as shown in the last section of this chapter, lawyers/firms working in the corporate sector assume substantial risk themselves through the size of the self-insured retentions (SIRs) that are part of their insurance arrangements. This risk is shared by the firm, and probably not simply by the equity/share partners in the corporate firms because having to cover a large

SIR in case of a loss, or even in a case without any payment to the claimant in which a substantial amount had to be spent to defend the case, the amounts expended will reduce what is available to pay bonuses to other lawyers in the firm. Still, if the firm is quite large, a $1 million SIR when thought of on a per-lawyer basis might be less than the deductible a solo practitioner faces. When one combines this element with the very low per-lawyer claim rate in the corporate sector, lawyers working in that sector face a much lower risk than do lawyers in the personal services sector.

CHAPTER 6

Legal Malpractice Trials

One feature of the US civil justice system is that very few cases filed in court are ultimately resolved by trial. The most recent figures, based on courts from 10 counties around the country, show that 3 percent of tort cases and 4 percent of civil cases were "adjudicated."[1] Although some studies and reports single out medical malpractice trials as an object of study,[2] legal malpractice trials are either lumped together with "other professional malpractice" or put into the broad "other tort" category. Thus, trials involving lawyers' professional liability (LPL) have not been the subject of systematic empirical examination.

As with the analyses presented in Chapters 4 and 5, in this chapter we draw on a range of sources of information on trials involving legal malpractice and other types of professional liability that lawyers face. We consider two broad issues in the chapter: the incidence of trials involving LPL and the outcome of the trials that do occur.

DATA SOURCES ON TRIAL INCIDENCE AND TRIAL OUTCOMES

Parts of the discussion in this chapter draw on some of the sources used in Chapters 4 and 5 described at the beginning of Chapter 4. In addition to those sources, this chapter employs two sets of data on the outcomes of legal malpractice cases that reached a verdict or judgment at trial. The National Center for State Courts (NCSC) conducted a series of studies covering 1996, 2001, and 2005 on behalf of the US Justice Department's Bureau of Justice Statistics (BJS). The study involved collecting data on civil verdicts in a sample of the 75 largest US counties for the years 1996 (45 counties) and 2001 (46 counties); in 2005 the study was extended to include an additional sample of 110 less populous counties.[3] The three studies include a total of 54,494 verdicts from jury or bench trials; 34,613 of these verdicts involved tort trials. The coding of case type made it possible to zero in on legal malpractice trials, and the three studies included a total of 156 legal malpractice trials.

Subsequent to the BJS-sponsored studies, the NCSC conducted a study of civil litigation that was not limited to tried cases in 10 of the counties included in the BJS studies, covering cases disposed in those counties between July 1, 2012, and June 30, 2013.[4] Three of the courts in the study had case-type identifiers that permitted separating out legal malpractice cases.[5] The staff at NCSC provided some simple tabulation for those cases and for medical malpractice cases from those same counties.[6]

The second data source was limited to verdicts in jury trials. The publisher of the Illinois *Jury Verdict Reporter* (IJVR) made available summaries of all verdicts in legal malpractice cases reported to IJVR between 1988 and 2014.[7] This constituted a total of 105 verdicts.[8] Working from the published reports, we coded which side won, the area of practice producing the claim, the nature of the litigating parties, the nature of the alleged error or behavior, and the amount of any award, both before and after any offset. As with the other data reported in this book, unless otherwise noted, all dollar figures were adjusted to 2010 dollars.

For purposes of comparisons of trial rates, we also drew on statistical reports published by New Jersey's Administrative Office of the Court[9] and Texas's Office of Court Administration.[10] These reports contain detailed figures on the incidence of trial for various types of cases, including a "Professional Malpractice" category that lumps all professional malpractice other than medical malpractice into a single category.

INCIDENCE OF TRIAL

Very few legal malpractice claims proceed to a trial and verdict. Obtaining precise figures on the likelihood of a legal malpractice claim reaching a verdict at a trial is difficult. The ABA Standing Committee on Lawyers' Professional Liability (SCLPL) reports provide figures on the number of claims resulting in payment after a judgment for the plaintiff. These percentages range from 0.26 percent to 4.80 percent; aggregated across all the reports, 1.50 percent of claims resulted in payment for the plaintiff after a judgment.[11] If one assumes that plaintiffs and defendants each win about half of the trials, a pattern consistent with two of the other sources discussed below, then one would estimate that about 3 percent of claims result in verdicts. This is consistent with figures reported by the Oregon State Bar's Professional Liability Fund (PLF) showing that

3 percent of the claims it closed between January 1, 2004, and December 31, 2013, produced judgments for the plaintiff (1 percent) or the defendant (2 percent).[12]

The Florida Office of Insurance Regulation (FLOIR) codes disposition in a way that allows for a crude estimate of the occurrence of trials.[13] However, because FLOIR stopped requiring reports of all claims after 1997, and the reporting form changed after 1993, we can only use the FLOIR data to get estimates for 1981 to 1993. Slightly more than half of the 5,716 claims reported to FLOIR during this period (2,846) were in suit, but only 85 were recorded as either "judgment" or "judgment on appeal," with another 24 recorded as "directed verdict" and 166 as "summary judgment." Some of the "judgment on appeal" claims might have been appeals from summary judgment, but there is no way to determine whether this is the case.[14] Ignoring this latter issue, trials appear to have resolved at most 109 claims, or 1.9 percent of all claims and 3.8 percent of claims in suit.

The Attorneys' Liability Assurance Society (ALAS) reported the outcomes of cases reaching verdict at trial. Through November 30, 2014, 228 cases had reached verdicts, although 7 of those were settled before entry of judgment. During this same period, ALAS had handled, or was in the process of handling, 14,312 "real" claims, that is, those claims ALAS determined had at least minimal merit.[15] ALAS did not report the number of claims pending, but in recent years between 400 and 500 new claims were reported to ALAS. If one assumes that the average claim took two years to resolve, this would mean something on the order of 400 to 500 claims would be pending at any one time. Using 500 as the number of pending claims as of November 30, 2014, leaves 13,912 closed claims. Based on this figure, 1.6 percent of real claims against ALAS's insureds reached a verdict at trial.

Overall, we estimate that between 2 and 3 percent of LPL claims lead to trial verdicts. Is this figure high or low compared with other kinds of cases? Obtaining figures on the rate by which claims are resolved by trial is difficult because typically there is no information on the number of claims. Still, for Florida we can estimate the percentage of legal malpractice claims resolved by trial compared with the percentage of medical malpractice claims that led to trial verdicts. Using data from the FLOIR concerning 21,114 medical malpractice claims closed between 1976 and 1987, 5.0 percent were closed after trial.[16]

Estimating trial rates as a percentage of cases in suit is easier, and we had one source that provided this information. NCSC conducted a study of civil case dispositions in 10 counties around the United States covering the 12-month period starting July 1, 2012.[17] Three courts in those counties separately identi-

Table 6.1: Trial Rates for Various Types of Cases, New Jersey and Texas

	New Jersey		*Texas*	
	FY2004 (%)	*FY2014 (%)*	*FY2014 (%)*	*FY2004 (%)*
Auto personal injury	2.1	3.0	9.5	7.6
Product liability (nonasbestos)	3.1	1.4		6.4
Medical malpractice	8.3	9.2		9.2
Civil rights	3.3	2.0		
[Unspecified] personal injury	1.7	1.5		
Other injury or damage			10.7	8.2
Complex commercial	1.8	1.8		
Contract, non-debt-related				8.5
Tort other	2.1	1.9		
Professional malpractice	2.7	2.1		7.5

Sources: New Jersey, http://www.judiciary.state.nj.us/quant/index.htm; Texas, http://www.txcourts.gov/statistics/annual-statistical-reports.aspx.

fied legal malpractice cases: Cook County (Illinois) Circuit Court, Cuyahoga (Ohio) Court of Common Pleas, and Oahu County (Hawaii) Circuit Court.[18] Those three courts reported disposing of a total of 257 legal malpractice cases. Only 5 of those cases, 2.0 percent, were disposed of by a jury or a bench trial.[19] In contrast, there were 1,213 medical malpractice cases closed in these three counties, 67 (5.5 percent) of which were resolved by trial. The likelihood of a legal malpractice case being resolved at trial was slightly greater than two other types of tort cases: motor vehicle torts (1.5 percent of 17,382 cases closed) and product liability other than asbestos (1.3 percent of 395 cases closed).

As a further comparison, we located three sources that provided information on trial rates for professional malpractice without specifically separating out legal malpractice. NCSC provided figures on the percentage of all professional malpractice cases for 13 states reaching trial in 2012.[20] In total 6.3 percent of malpractice dispositions came at or after trial, with Florida having the lowest trial rate at 3.6 percent. The Administrative Office of the Court in New Jersey and the Texas Office of Court Administration published detailed figures on the incidence of trial for various types of cases, including a "Professional Malpractice" category that lumps all professional malpractice other than medical malpractice into a single category. Table 6.1 shows the percentage of suits terminated by trial for several categories of tort cases for the fiscal years 2004 and 2014.[21] If roughly the same percentage of professional malpractice lawsuits proceed to trial in New Jersey as in Florida, it is clear that such cases would not stand out regarding the likelihood of trial, although they would certainly be substantially less likely to result in a trial than medical malpractice lawsuits in New Jersey. The figure for Texas is considerably higher, but that largely reflects bench trials: 17 of 22 trials (77 percent) of other professional malpractice cases involved bench trials.

Importantly, as explained previously, the figures shown in Table 6.1 reflect only claims that led to a lawsuit being filed; we have no information on the number of claims resolved prior to a lawsuit being filed. This means that those figures overstate the percentage of *claims* proceeding to trial.[22] However, based on these comparisons, legal malpractice claims that reach suit do not stand out as either overly likely or overly unlikely to be terminated after a trial verdict has been rendered.

OUTCOMES OF LEGAL MALPRACTICE TRIALS

A prominent theory about the outcome of civil trials is that about half of the time the plaintiff should win and about half of the time the defendant should win because the cases that end up going to trial are those where the outcome is most uncertain.[23] One area that stands out prominently as deviating from what has been called the 50-percent rule[24] is medical malpractice, in which studies have consistently shown plaintiff win rates on the order of 20 to 30 percent.[25] What is the pattern for legal malpractice trials? Four sources allow us to look at this question along with the amounts of damages awarded.

Florida Office of Insurance Regulation

As noted previously, the FLOIR data we used in prior chapters provided indicators of whether a claim went to trial. Although the post-1997 data included only claims that resulted in a payment to the claimant or at least $5,000 in claim expenses, it is unlikely that many, if any, legal malpractice claims could be tried with less than $5,000 in defense costs. We identified a total of 190 legal malpractice claims between 1981 and 2010 that appeared to have gone to trial, and plaintiffs prevailed in only 39 (20.5 percent) of these trials.[26] Omitting 9 cases that settled postverdict,[27] the verdicts ranged from $3,345 to more than $4.4 million.[28] The mean and medians were $484,486 and $181,623, respectively.[29]

Table 6.2: Malpractice Trial Outcomes, BJS/NCSC Studies, 1996, 2001, and 2005

	Total Number	*Percent Bench Trials*	*Percent Plaintiff Verdicts*	*Percent of Awards Exceeding $1 Million (nominal)*	*Percent of Awards Exceeding $1 Million (2010$)*
Lawyers	156	38.5	48.7	15.5	15.5
Physicians	1,908	2.0	23.2	37.3	41.3
Dentists	136	5.9	27.9	5.1	7.7
Other	150	12.0	38.8	18.3	21.7
	Mean (2010$)	*Median (2010$)*	*Standard Deviation*	*First Quartile (2010$)*	*Third Quartile (2010$)*
Lawyers	$1,192,028	$108,328	$4,478,354	$27,800	$455,457
Physicians	$2,401,400	$695,000	$5,304,435	$245,398	$2,154,250
Dentists	$166,920	$102,518	$235,620	$26,979	$228,655
Other	$5,301,904	$274,775	$5,301,904	$76,938	$881,582

Bureau of Justice Statistics Civil Verdict Studies

The three studies conducted on behalf of the US Justice Department's Bureau of Justice Statistics (BJS) by the NCSC included a total of 54,494 verdicts from jury or bench trials; 34,613 of these verdicts were from tort trials. The coding of case type made it possible to separate out legal malpractice trials for comparison with medical malpractice trials. Table 6.2 displays a range of statistics for the professional malpractice cases included in the three BJS/NCSC studies.

As noted above, the combined studies included data on a total of 156 trials involving claims of professional malpractice by lawyers. In comparison, the data included 1,908 cases of professional malpractice by physicians, 136 by dentists, and 150 by "other" professionals.[30] Perhaps most striking is the fact that 38.5 percent of legal malpractice trials were conducted without a jury. In contrast, only 2.0 percent of physician malpractice trials were bench trials. The plaintiff prevailed in 48.7 percent of cases involving lawyer-defendants compared with 23.2 percent involving physicians, 27.9 percent involving dentists, and 38.9 percent involving other professionals. In looking at the size of awards in cases where the plaintiff prevailed, the median award in legal malpractice trials was a bit over $100,000 compared with almost $700,000 for awards against physicians; the median award against dentists was slightly lower than that against lawyers. As one would expect the means tended to be much higher, although this was not true for awards for dental malpractice. The first and third quartiles give a sense of variation. In absolute terms, the difference between the quartiles was greatest for physician malpractice. However, the relative variation for legal malpractice was greater than in any of the other categories, using two different measures: the ratio of the third to first quartile were 16.38 for legal malpractice compared with 8.78 for physician malpractice, 8.5 for dentist malpractice, and 11.48 for other types of professional malpractice; the relative interquartile range, computed as the difference between the first and third quartiles divided by the median, was 3.95 for legal malpractice, 2.75 for physician malpractice, 1.97 for dental malpractice, and 2.93 for other professional malpractice. Nominal awards exceeding $1 million occurred in only 15.5 percent of cases of legal malpractice compared with 37.3 percent of physician malpractice; the comparable numbers for dental malpractice and other professional malpractice were 5.1 percent and 18.3 percent, respectively.[31]

The fact that almost half of legal malpractice trials in the BJS/NCSC studies did not employ a jury raises the question of whether the choice between a jury trial and a bench trial was associated with any difference in the outcome, either who won or the amount of damages awarded when the plaintiff won. Note that we speak here of association rather than causation because we do not have information on factors influencing the decision by both parties to forgo a jury trial. Plaintiffs were about 10 percentage points more likely to win before a jury (53 percent) than before a judge (43 percent), but the small sample size does not permit a conclusion that this difference is more than what reasonably could be produced by a random process (chi square = 1.42, p = .233). However, we can conclude that there were differences not attributable to random variation in the amounts awarded when the plaintiff prevailed. With a jury the median award was $194,878 compared with $39,249 for bench trials (Kruskal-Wallis test chi square = 8.09, df = 1, p = .0028), 22 percent (11 of 50) of the jury awards exceeded $1 million compared with only 4 percent (1 of 26) of the bench awards (chi square = 4.24, p = .039). Comparing these results with those of medical malpractice trials, in which only 2 percent of trials were without a jury, we find that medical malpractice plaintiffs were more likely to win before a judge than with a jury (38 percent versus 23 percent, chi square = 5.13, p = .024), but the median award of juries was higher than the median award of judges ($695,000 versus $347,3800) (Kruskal-Wallis test chi square = 6.15, df = 1, p = .0131); 38 percent of the jury awards exceeded $1 million compared with no million-dollar awards by judges (chi square = 9.017, p = .003).

Very few of the plaintiffs who prevailed in professional malpractice cases were awarded punitive damages. Nonetheless, such awards were most likely in legal malpractice cases in which such awards were made in 3.1 percent cases won by plaintiffs. For the other types of professional malpractice, punitive awards were made in 0.4 percent of physician malpractice cases, 0.7 percent of dentist malpractice, and 2.0 percent of other professional malpractice. The number of cases is too small (five lawyers, eight physicians, one dentist, and three other professionals) to compute any meaningful statistics, but it is perhaps worth noting that the largest punitive damage award against a lawyer was $15 million ($16.8 million when adjusted to 2010 dollars) compared with $3 million ($3.48 million adjusted) against a physician. However, the second-largest award against a lawyer was only $75,000 ($104,250 adjusted), whereas the second-largest punitive damage award against a physician was $2.5 million ($3.35 million adjusted).

The BJS/NCSC data included information on the type of parties involved in the case. For our purposes, there are four relevant categories: individuals, insurance companies, hospitals and clinics, and other businesses; we combined the three latter categories under the label "business." The data provided information on how many of each party type were included among the plaintiffs.[32] This means that there could be only individuals, only businesses, or a combination of the two as the plaintiffs in a case. However, when there are both businesses and individuals as plaintiffs, it might be that the business is actually just an extension of one or more individuals.

For example, one of the cases coded as both business and individual was the lawsuit described in some detail in Chapter 2, filed by Scottie Pippen and Air Pip, Inc.; Air Pip was a corporation Pippen formed in connection with the purchase of a partial interest in a Gulfstream II jet airplane. Although technically the case involved both an individual and the corporation, the latter was simply an extension of the former created to hold certain assets. Although the BJS data do not include case identifiers such as docket numbers and case names, we did match information regarding 10 of the 12 cases coded as having both businesses and individuals as plaintiffs through online searches of dockets and similar materials; 9 of the 10 cases were effectively brought by individuals, and 1 was essentially brought by a business. It is possible that many of the cases coded only as having businesses as the plaintiff involved personal

Table 6.3: Trial Outcomes by Type of Plaintiff, BJS/NCSC Studies

	Number of Trials	*Number of Plaintiff Verdicts*	*Percent Plaintiff Verdict*[a]	*Percent \$1 Million or More*	*Median Award (2010\$)*
Individual(s)	127	63	50	16	\$141,050
Business(es)	27	12	44	17	\$18,754

[a]Chi square = 0.24, df = 1, p = .626

corporations similar to Air Pip, Inc.; however, when we sought to track down information about those cases, we found information for only 3 cases, and hence we treated all of them as businesses. After making adjustments based on the information found on the 10 cases, we had 127 (81.4 percent) cases that involved only individual plaintiffs, 27 (17.3 percent) that involved only business plaintiffs, and 2 (1.3 percent) for which we were not able to locate information to clarify the nature of the plaintiff.

Table 6.3 provides information on the outcomes of legal malpractice trials controlling for type of plaintiff except for the two cases for which we could not determine whether they were individual or business cases. As the table shows, there was little difference in the likelihood of a plaintiffs' verdict between individual and business plaintiffs. The percentage of plaintiffs receiving awards of \$1 million or more was essentially the same for the two types of plaintiffs. However, interestingly, the median award for successful individual plaintiffs was substantially greater (\$141,050) than the median award for successful business plaintiffs (\$18,754).[33] The patterns regarding type of plaintiff were quite different in the source of data discussed next.

Illinois Jury Verdict Reporter *(IJVR)*

Turning to the legal malpractice verdicts reported in the IJVR, plaintiffs obtained favorable verdicts in 58 (56 percent) cases. Individuals were the plaintiffs in 67 (65 percent) of cases; businesses, including banks and insurance companies, were the plaintiffs in the remaining cases.[34] Individual plaintiffs won 54 percent of their cases, whereas businesses won 61 percent; however, this difference is likely to represent nothing more than random variation given the small number of observations (chi square = 0.52, p = .472). The awards in the Illinois cases were higher than those in either the BJS/NCSC or the FLOIR data. The median award (2010 dollars) was $477,650 (mean $2,049,915); the first and third quartiles were $132,390 and $2,462,000. The medians differed sharply between cases brought by individuals for whom the median award was $229,877 compared with $1,399,585 when the plaintiff was a business—the reverse of the pattern in the BJS/NCSC data.[35] Awards of $1 million or more were made in 36 percent of cases won by plaintiffs.[36] Half of the awards obtained by business plaintiffs exceeded $1 million compared with about a quarter for individual plaintiffs.[37]

Table 6.4 shows a range of statistics controlling for area of practice. The areas that stand out in the Illinois verdicts were corporate/commercial (16.5 percent), family (11 percent), real estate (16.5 percent), and tort injury (19.5 percent). As one might expect, the pattern differed depending on whether the plaintiff was an individual or business. For individuals, the most prominent areas of practice were family (16.4 percent); plaintiff's tort cases (16.5 percent); and, interestingly, corporate/commercial (11.9 percent). Real estate constituted only 7.5 percent of malpractice trials with individuals as plaintiffs. On the business side the largest proportion of trials involved real estate (33.3 percent) followed by corporate/commercial (25.0 percent).[38] No other area of practice accounted for more than 7.5 percent, either overall or within either category of plaintiffs. Substantial differences in the likelihood of a plaintiffs' verdict occurred in these four areas, the only areas that had more than 10 cases (the minimum we use when computing percentages), with plaintiffs' verdicts most likely in real estate cases (71 percent), followed by plaintiffs' tort cases (65 percent), corporate/commercial cases (35 percent), and family cases much lower (18 percent). The only two areas with more than 10 plaintiffs' verdicts were real estate and plaintiffs' tort, and in those two areas the awards exceeded $1 million in 83 percent of the former and 77 percent of the latter.

For purposes of analysis, the nature of the alleged error or behavior was collapsed into six categories plus an "Other or Unclear" category.[39] Table 6.5 provides a summary of the patterns related to the nature of the defendant's alleged malpractice.[40] As the table shows, the most common alleged error concerned inaction or nonappearance, followed by missed deadlines. Individual plaintiff's complaints were most likely in cases alleging missed deadlines, followed by inaction/nonappearance. Substantial variation occurred in the likelihood of plaintiffs prevailing in cases; it was most likely when the defendant was alleged to have missed a deadline (81 percent), followed by conflict of interest/breach of fiduciary duty (73 percent). Plaintiffs' verdicts were least likely in areas in

Table 6.4: Outcome by Area of Practice, Illinois Verdict Data

Area of Law	*Number of Cases*	*Percentage of Cases in Area of Practice*	*Number with Individuals as Plaintiffs*	*Percentage of Cases with Individual Plaintiffs**	*Number of Plaintiffs' Verdicts*	*Percentage Plaintiffs' Verdicts**	*Number of Awards $1 Million or More*
Bankruptcy	7	7	5	71	3	43	
Civil rights/discrimination	3	3	3		3		
Construction	1	1	1		1		
Contract	2	2	0		2		
Corporate/commercial	17	17	8	47	6	35	
Criminal	1	1	1		0		
Employment	2	2	2		0		
Family	11	11	11	100	2	18	
Government	1	1	0		1		
Intellectual property	2	2	0		0		
Immigration	2	2	2		1		
Legal malpractice	1	1	1		1		
Trusts and estates	2	2	2		0		
Real estate	17	17	5	29	12	71	10
Securities	3	3	2		3		
Tort defendant	4	4	0		4		
Tort plaintiff	20	19	19	95	13	65	10
Other litigation	1	1	0		1		
Workers' comp/disability	3	3	3		3		
Other	3	3	2		2		
Total	103	102**	67	65	58	56	

*Percentages computed only if based on 5 or more cases.

**Percentages total exceeds 100% due to rounding.

Table 6.5: Outcome by Alleged Error, Illinois Verdict Data

	Number of Trials	*Percentage of Each Type of Error*	*Number with Individuals as Plaintiffs*	*Number with Plaintiff Verdicts*	*Percentage Plaintiff Verdicts*	*Number of Awards > $1 Million*
Bad advice	13	13	7	4	31	1
Conflict of interest/ breach of fiduciary duty	11	11	5	8	73	3
Missed deadline	16	16	14	13	81	11
Document/drafting error	11	11	7	5	45	3
Inaction/nonappearance	20	19	16	13	65	12
Investigation/discovery	11	11	6	3	27	2
Other/unclear	21	20	12	12	57	7
Total	103	101*	67	58	56	39

*Percentages total exceeds 100% due to rounding.

which the defendant could potentially defend on the basis of the alleged error representing a matter of professional judgment that turned out to be wrong, bad advice (31 percent plaintiffs' verdicts), and investigation/discovery (27 percent plaintiffs' verdicts). The number of plaintiff verdicts associated with each error was small, with only two types of errors having more than 10 plaintiffs' verdicts: missed deadlines and inaction/nonappearance. As shown in Table 6.5, for both of those two errors a large proportion of awards exceeded $1 million.

ATTORNEYS' LIABILITY ASSURANCE SOCIETY VERDICTS

Finally, what about the outcomes of trials involving law firms insured by ALAS?[41] Recall that ALAS reported that over its history through November 30, 2014, only 228 cases had reached a trial verdict. Of those, 162 (70.1 percent) resulted in a finding of no liability and another 10 resulted in a damage award lower than the final settlement demand. Of the 66 cases producing a verdict in favor of the plaintiff, 18 were reversed on appeal or by post-trial motion (in another two cases, an appeal was still pending). Taking these figures from the plaintiff's perspective, plaintiffs won a favorable verdict in 29.9 percent of trials, but in the end prevailed in only 21.1 percent of the cases tried after accounting for appeals and post-trial motions.[42] Unfortunately, we are unable to extend our analysis of verdicts in ALAS cases to a consideration of the amounts awarded at trial because that information is not available.

JURIES AND LAWYERS

The above analysis of the NCSC data included a comparison of outcomes in bench versus jury trials. That analysis showed that plaintiffs fared better in jury trials than in bench trials, although chance could not be ruled out as accounting for the difference given the small number of LPL trials. Because there was no information on why the parties opted for a bench trial over a jury trial, there is no way to determine if the difference was a result of which cases were selected for one type of trial or the other, or whether juries and judges tended to decide cases of legal malpractice differently. Some authors have claimed that judges are biased in favor of lawyer-defendants in such cases.[43] Alternatively, if there are differences, it might be that juries tend to disfavor lawyers when they appear as defendants in professional liability trials.

Chapter 5 briefly discussed a situation observed by the first author in a prior unrelated study in which a law firm was facing a potential malpractice claim arising from a late court filing that resulted in a case being dismissed. The firm worked hard to get the case reinstated and eventually succeeded in its efforts at claim repair (although the case was eventually voluntarily dismissed for unrelated reasons). One point of conversation in the office was a perception that if a legal malpractice claim proceeded to trial, the lawyer-defendant would be disadvantaged because the jury would look more favorably upon the plaintiff than in a trial of the underlying case (i.e., the case within the case). As discussed in Chapter 3, a central issue in a legal malpractice claim is what the outcome of the underlying matter would have been but for the lawyer's negligence, and in a case of a missed deadline, the only real issue at a legal malpractice trial would be the outcome of the case within the case. The lawyers working in that office had the perception that not only would they face a greater likelihood of losing at trial than would the original defendant but also that the jury would award a larger amount in damages than would a jury trying the original case. During the interviews discussed in the next chapter, several respondents mentioned this same concern: juries are biased against lawyer-defendants in a legal malpractice trial.

An ideal test of this argument would be to match legal malpractice cases going to trial in which the only issues concerned the case within the case with cases similar to the case within the case going to trial; that would allow a determination of whether there were systematic differences in the outcomes depending on whether the defendant was the former lawyer or the original alleged tortfeasor. Accomplishing this type of matching would be extremely difficult, if not impossible. Also, even if it could be accomplished, there would be problems raised by the selectivity of which cases reached trial rather than being settled pretrial or being resolved by summary judgment. As discussed in Chapter 3 and illustrated by the first case summarized in Chapter 1, in many states a legal malpractice claim is unlikely to get past summary judgment if there is significant doubt about what the outcome would have been in a trial of the original case. More generally, as discussed earlier in this chapter, it is well established that the cases that make it to trial are a highly selective subset of cases, in which typically there is substantial uncertainty about liability and/or damages.

One way to get around these problems is to use simulated juries. Although this is less than a perfect approach because of the uncertainty of whether the simulated juries accurately reflect how actual juries would decide cases, jury simulations can shed some light on the question, particularly if the effects in the real world are very strong. Exactly this kind of experiment is reported in detail elsewhere.[44] Here we briefly summarize how the experiment was carried out along with the results obtained.

Summary of Experimental Design

The experiment used three different cases, one involving an auto accident, one a premises liability issue, and one a claim of medical malpractice.

In the auto case, the issue was limited to the amount of damages because the negligence of the other driver, an elderly man, was undisputed. He had turned left in the face of oncoming traffic to enter a parking lot. The damages issue turned on the question of whether an injury to the female plaintiff's knee was caused by the accident or by something such as lifting her young child. The complication in the case was that, although the plaintiff had seen medical providers immediately after the accident and then again a week later for an unrelated matter, the first reference to any issue with her knee in the medical records did not appear until a third medical visit two weeks after the accident.[45] There was also some question as to whether the mechanics of the accident could have produced the kind of injury the plaintiff contended she had suffered.

In the premises case, the plaintiff had tripped over a raised portion of the sidewalk. The plaintiff hit his head when he fell and claimed that his head injury resulted in an inability to work for an extended period. In this case, there were disputes regarding both liability and damages. The liability issue was whether the defect in the sidewalk was sufficiently bad that the homeowner defendant had been negligent in not repairing it, or if the accident was simply a result of the plaintiff's inattention. The damages issue concerned the amount appropriate for the plaintiff's pain and suffering.[46]

In the medical malpractice case, there were also issues of both liability and damages. The physician-defendant had failed to accurately diagnose the plaintiff's spinal condition. The issue was whether the physician had violated the standard of care when he had not ordered a specific diagnostic procedure when the plaintiff first saw the physician; that procedure would have revealed the condition. The delay in diagnosis resulted in injuries that could not be treated as successfully as would have been the case if the condition had been identified when the plaintiff initially saw the defendant. The primary damages issue was the amount of compensation appropriate for the additional pain and suffering experienced by the plaintiff.[47]

For each of the three cases, two different versions were prepared: one that just presented the original case and a second version that presented the claim in the context of a lawyer who had missed the filing deadline and was sued for negligence (the fact that the lawyer had missed the deadline was not contested). Thus, the experimental condition was when the lawyer had been negligent and was the trial defendant who would have to pay any damages; the control condition was the original case in which the defendant who would have to pay damages was the driver, homeowner, or physician. For the experimental condition, the mock jurors were told that the lawyer admitted missing the deadline and that the only issue the jurors were to decide concerned the case within the case; this point was emphasized both at the start of the case and again in the judge's instructions at the end of the presentation of the case. All references to the lawyer-defendant were omitted for the control condition jurors; otherwise the experimental and control versions of each case were identical.

The experiment was conducted over the Internet using a commercially obtained Internet survey panel. Participants were screened for jury eligibility by asking if they were either currently registered to vote or were eligible to register to vote. Only those indicating that they were currently registered or eligible to register to vote were retained as participants. Each participant was assigned randomly to one of the six conditions. The case was presented textually through a series of screens. At the conclusion of presentation of the case and the judge's instructions, the participants were asked how they would decide the case. For the auto case, the only decision participants made was the amount of damages, but for the other two cases they first determined whether there was liability, and if there was, then set a figure for damages. For the experimental condition, a manipulation check was included to test whether the participant understood that the lawyer was the defendant who would pay any damages awarded; only those passing the manipulation check were included in the analysis. Oversampling of the experimental conditions was done to obtain roughly equal numbers of experimental and control participants for each of the three cases, although the numbers for each case varied. There was a total of 1,157 participants who produced usable responses; the minimum number for any combination of case and condition was 173, and the maximum was 203. The median time to complete the experiment was 20 minutes.

Summary of Results

The analysis employed both simple tests comparing the experimental and control conditions and multivariate analyses that included additional control variables. For the premises and medical malpractice cases, the first question was whether jurors were more likely to find for the plaintiff in the experimental condition compared with the control condition. There was no effect for the medical malpractice case; in fact, a higher proportion of participants in the control condition found liability than in the experimental condition.[48] For the premises case, there was a statistically significant ($p = .042$, one-tailed) difference: experimental 42 percent liable, control 34 percent.

The analysis of damages was complicated by two factors. First, there was some skew in the responses, which significantly affected the means and resulted in large standard deviations. Second, for the premises and medical malpractice cases the damages question was asked only if the participant had found liability; this meant that for these two cases there were fewer observations for the damages analyses, between 57 and 82 participants. Only for the premises case did the statistical test produce consistent evidence that the awards were higher for the legal malpractice condition.[49]

The multivariate analyses included controls for demographics (gender, education, and household income), political ideology, personal experience in a civil case (serving on a civil jury, as a plaintiff, or as a defendant in a lawsuit other than divorce), and whether a member of the participant's immediate family was a lawyer or was currently in law school. For the medical malpractice case, a control was also added for whether any member of the participant's immediate family was a physician or was currently in medical school. Logistic and linear regression models tested whether including these variables modified the results concerning the experimental manipulation, but no modifications were found.

TRIALS: SUMMARY

This chapter considered two broad questions regarding trials alleging that a lawyer or law firm was liable for negligence, breach of the lawyer's fiduciary duty or some intentional act. Regarding frequency of trials, our findings are reasonably consistent across data sources: about 2 to 3 percent of LPL claims reach a trial verdict. The likelihood of an LPL claim reaching trial is not greatly different from that in most other areas of tort law. An LPL claim might be more likely to reach trial than the most routine tort claims, such as those arising from traffic accidents, but that likelihood does appear to be lower than the likelihood of a medical malpractice claim reaching trial.

However, as is true with much of the rest of our analysis, there are inconsistencies in the findings regarding trial outcomes. Two data sources showed that plaintiffs and defendants were about equally likely to prevail. For two other data sources, plaintiffs obtained favorable verdicts in only about a quarter of the cases that proceeded to trial. The reason for this inconsistency is not obvious. It might reflect differences in the norms affecting decisions to take cases to trial: norms that are local in nature (Florida versus Illinois) or norms that reflect difference in the practices of insurers.

As for the amounts awarded at trial, there were again some differences among data sources. The medians in the Florida data and in the BJS/NCSC data were roughly comparable; in contrast, the median verdict in the Illinois data was substantially higher. This might reflect general tendencies of Illinois juries to behave differently (particularly those in Cook County, where Chicago is located) compared with juries in other locations, or it might just be chance that the figures from Florida and the BJS/NCSC studies were similar, or perhaps cases in areas with substantial numbers of large corporations tend to be different from other areas.

One interesting difference regarding trial outcomes concerned bench versus jury trials. Only the BJS/NCSC data allowed this hypothesis to be examined. Those data did show that the LPL plaintiffs tended to do better in the cases decided by a jury rather than by a judge sitting alone. To further explore one explanation for this finding—that juries disfavor lawyer-defendants—we described an experiment we conducted that sought to test the hypothesis of juror hostility; the results of the experiment were inconsistent, but even where there was evidence that lawyers fared poorly, the effects were modest.

In this chapter, there were at best glimpses of the two hemispheres of legal malpractice. Consistent with what was discussed in Chapter 5 concerning the size of losses, the report from ALAS shows that the amounts awarded when a corporate firm loses a liability case at trial are much greater than the amounts awarded to individual and small-business plaintiffs. The specific data from the IJVR confirmed this conclusion: the typical award to a business plaintiff is substantially larger than that received by an individual plaintiff. However, the BJS/NCSC data showed that business plaintiffs were less likely to win at trial, and when they did win, the median damage award was much smaller. There is some uncertainty in those data regarding coding of the type of plaintiff, but it is unlikely that difference fully accounts for why the pattern in those data was so different from the IJVR data.

CHAPTER 7

Processing Lawyers' Professional Liability Claims

How are lawyers' professional liability (LPL) claims actually handled by lawyers and insurers working in this area? This chapter addresses that question by relying on a series of interviews with practitioners and representatives of several LPL insurers. The interviews initially focused on practitioners in Minnesota, North Carolina, and Wisconsin, producing 11 interviews with plaintiffs' lawyers who handle LPL cases and 9 interviews with insurance defense lawyers who handle LPL cases; this first set of interviews was completed in 2011–2012. Potential respondents were identified largely through a snowball technique, starting with names suggested by people at insurance companies plus contacts with members of the bars in the three states; only two lawyers contacted in this first round of interviews did not respond or declined a request for an interview. These interviews were conducted either by telephone or in person; several were recorded, but for the most part detailed notes were taken and then expanded soon after the interview was completed.[1] The interviews typically lasted from 30 to 40 minutes.[2]

What we found in those interviews was that with one possible exception, none of the plaintiffs' lawyers had a practice dominated by LPL cases. In addition, no one contacted in these three states could identify any plaintiffs' lawyer who might have such a practice. This led us to conduct 12 additional telephone interviews in 2015 with practitioners around the country including in California, Connecticut, Florida, Illinois, Michigan, and Texas. With one or two exceptions, these lawyers could be called specialists in LPL. Most of the lawyers interviewed were identified by first reviewing published information on jury verdicts, and then checking each lawyer's website to obtain a sense of how prominent LPL was in the lawyer's practice. A few such lawyers were suggested by an insurance company representative. We contacted a total of 18 lawyers via letter; 6 never responded to subsequent phone messages. All interviews were recorded and subsequently transcribed.

Finally, we had conversations or substantive e-mail exchanges with representatives of five different LPL mutual insurers around the country. These exchanges varied in content but mostly focused on the process of handling claims. We also sought to determine from the conversations or exchanges exactly what the insurers designated as a "claim" for counting purposes. Some of these conversations or exchanges occurred in 2012 and others in 2015 or 2016. None of these conversations were recorded but involved taking detailed notes later expanded and transcribed.

THE PLAINTIFFS' BAR

One might think legal malpractice would draw interest from many plaintiffs' lawyers. In fact, as noted above, finding lawyers who have a significant legal malpractice caseload is not easy. If one does a Google search for "legal malpractice attorney," one does get a large number of hits (more than 100,000 as of December 30, 2016). However, how many of those hits represent law firms actually seeking LPL clients is unclear, and even if an attorney is seeking such clients, that does not mean the attorney actually does a lot of LPL work.[3] For example, the State Bar of California, with over 180,000 active members,[4] has a program to certify lawyers in legal malpractice. The website listing those lawyers showed a total of 90 lawyers, but only 16 who, according to their websites, devoted their practice to plaintiffs' legal malpractice; most of the rest handled the defense side.[5]

Another indication of the absence of a substantial number of plaintiff-side practitioners handling LPL cases came during our interviews of defense-side practitioners. When we asked them for names of lawyers who regularly brought legal malpractice claims on behalf of plaintiffs, we heard comments such as:

> I really don't see the same people a lot.
>
> I don't think there are a lot of plaintiffs' lawyers who do a lot of this kind of work.
>
> Insurers are dealing with a relatively small market of lawyers who are willing to sue other lawyer, number one, and who are themselves comfortable in terms of having the technical skill and ability to try a legal malpractice case.
>
> There aren't a lot of plaintiffs' lawyers I see over and over again.

> There is not a regular plaintiffs' bar; it's catch as catch can. There is a high dismissal [including summary judgment] in legal malpractice because lots of plaintiffs' lawyers don't know the area and aren't discriminating in the cases they take.

> There is no established plaintiffs' bar for legal malpractice, and that means lots of the plaintiffs' lawyers who take legal malpractice cases are not that good.

The defense-side lawyers had to struggle to name more than one or two plaintiff-side lawyers with a reputation for handling LPL cases.

One might speculate that the limited size of the specialist plaintiffs' bar handling LPL claims was because of concern about approbation by other lawyers. Interestingly, although this might deter some lawyers from taking on LPL cases, at least some of the specialists with whom we spoke had a very different view:

> If it's a very strong case, and it's a lawyer we know, quite frankly the lawyer that we know would prefer we handle it rather than someone who doesn't know what they're doing.

> I don't feel like I'm hated for taking on legal mal cases. That's because I am particular about the cases that I take.

Of the 23 respondents on the plaintiffs' side, 11 could be characterized as having practices that consisted primarily of plaintiffs' LPL cases, another 3 had practices that were a third to a half plaintiffs' LPL, with the remaining 9 spending no more than 20 percent of their time on LPL and many considerably less. Equally interesting, those specializing in LPL tended to carry small caseloads; 1 lawyer reported only handling one or two cases at a time. Only 3 lawyers reported typically having more than 20 LPL cases open at any one time. Almost all of the lawyers whose practices were either primarily LPL or who had a heavy component of LPL worked either solo or with only 1 or 2 other lawyers; 9 of the 15 in this subset were solos, 1 had been in solo practice but subsequently moved to a firm of 40 (none of the other lawyers at the firm handled LPL cases), 3 had 1 or 2 associates or partners, and 1 was in a firm with 4 other lawyers. The firm setting varied more for the lawyers for whom legal malpractice was a relatively small part of their practices: only 1 practiced solo, 2 with a second lawyer, and the rest in firms ranging in size from 6 to more than 50.[6]

For the lawyers for whom plaintiffs' LPL was a small part of their practices, that work was combined with other types of litigation, most often various kinds of traditional plaintiff-side work but also sometimes with business litigation. Lawyers whose practices focused on LPL often combined that work with work concerning other issues in the broad area of the law of lawyering and/or work assisting other lawyers and their firms in developing risk-management procedures. There also tended to be some differences in how these two groups came to be handling plaintiffs' legal malpractice. For many in both groups, a first case came along in a somewhat happenstance way; however, within the group of specialists, several started out doing the defense side of professional malpractice, often medical malpractice defense, and subsequently switched over to handling the plaintiffs' side of legal malpractice. A common experience across both specialists and nonspecialists was that after one had handled a case or two, the word got around that this was the kind of case that lawyer would consider taking.[7]

For all but one of the lawyers, the dominant source of contacts was referrals from other lawyers, who usually made those referrals without any expectation of a referral fee. Only one lawyer reported that his online presence was the dominant way by which potential clients found him. Other than this one lawyer who relied strongly on the Internet, those who obtained significant traffic from their web pages reported that the good cases, the ones they were likely to take, came not from that source but as referrals. The lawyers varied in how selective they were in accepting cases. The most selective tended to be those who fell at the specialist end of the spectrum, with several accepting less than 1 percent and only one accepting more than 10 percent. These figures are similar to the selectivity one finds in medical malpractice.[8] Among the nonspecialists, selectivity varied more widely, with the lawyers reporting accepting from a low of 1 percent of potential cases to as high as one-third.

The procedures for screening potential cases varied substantially. About half of the lawyers reported that they essentially did all the screening themselves. For some of them this was because they worked entirely alone, but for others it was because they felt they could do it more effectively themselves than by relying on a staff person or associate. Interestingly, the specialists were more likely to do the screening themselves than were the nonspecialists. The lawyers who relied on staff varied in their exact procedures and in how quickly they became involved in reviewing cases. Some allowed the staff to make the first cut, often based simply on whether it was the kind of case the lawyer would even consider, whereas others simply had the staff collect information and either complete a form or a prepare a short memo that went to the lawyer, who then decided whether to move to the next step, which could either be collecting records or possibly bringing in the potential client for a meeting.

All of the lawyers shied away from or avoided entirely certain categories of cases. Most commonly avoided or automatically rejected were cases related to criminal defense. In significant part, this reflects the requirement in many states that a plaintiff in such cases prove actual innocence (discussed in Chapter 3),[9] but it also reflects the problem of the absence of clear economic damages. Immigration is a second category avoided or rejected by most lawyers, presumably in significant part because of the problem of damages. Beyond those two categories, the most frequent type of underlying case the lawyers shunned was family law, essentially meaning divorce cases. This reflects two concerns: first, reluctance to work with clients in such cases who are often very unhappy people, and second, even if the former lawyer had failed to get the level of support payment the client was entitled to or had failed to correctly determine marital assets, in most cases the amounts involved were too small for the case to be worth pursuing, either on a contingency-fee basis from the lawyer's perspective or on an hourly fee basis from the potential client's perspective.[10] Workers' compensation–related cases constituted another category the lawyers avoided, again because of the limited damages. Beyond these more common areas of avoidance, there were individual differences. Some lawyers avoided patent cases because of their concern about the very technical nature of such cases. Others avoided medical malpractice because of their own lack of expertise and the costs associated with proving the case within the case (i.e., proving that the potential lawyer-defendant would have won the underlying case and would have collected damages for the client). However, some took the opposite view, usually because they had previously defended medical malpractice cases and felt comfortable with the area.

As one might expect for lawyers who, as will be discussed shortly, tend to work on a contingency-fee basis, the amount of potential damages was an important criterion in decisions whether to accept a case. Most of the lawyers had a nominal potential damages threshold for what they would seriously consider handling; those thresholds ranged from a low of $100,000 to a high of $5 million. There was an indication from some of the lawyers with whom we spoke that under certain circumstances they might take a smaller case. Typically, this would be a situation in which liability and damages were very clear, and they believed the case would settle quickly, such as when there was a missed filing deadline in a pedestrian-injury case or there were no case-within-the-case problems such as failing to note a significant property lien when doing a title opinion. In the words of one lawyer, "That [kind of] situation is a little different. Somebody would settle that case rather fast . . . [although] there are very few of those, but there are some."

There were two considerations regarding the potential lawyer-defendant that played a role in the decision whether to take a case. First, several lawyers noted that they would not take cases against lawyers whom they viewed as friends or good professional colleagues; for example, "I know the lawyer really well." Second, our respondents reported being very reluctant to pursue a claim against a lawyer they knew to be uninsured. This was because they were concerned about, or had actual experience with, collectability problems, as well as problems during the litigation, because often the uninsured defendant represented himself: "If the attorney is representing himself, you are running into a real hardscrabble guy, and he's desperate, and he wants to avoid paying . . . just not a pleasant situation all around. And if you are successful, you're not likely to get much." The uninsured defendant was more of a dilemma for lawyers in some states than in others because of variation in the requirement that lawyers reveal whether they had LPL insurance, either through the lawyers' annual registration or through communicating that fact directly to their clients.

Of course, a major issue for all of the lawyers was the quality of the case against the potential defendant. Interestingly, many respondents indicated that the issue of whether the potential defendant's work had fallen below the standard of care (i.e., whether the defendant had breached his or her duty to the client), a prima facie element if the claim is one of negligence, was often not the key question. In the words of several respondents:

> A fair number recount stories that if true, you wonder if the law firm did or didn't do something they should have.

> Most of the time the client is coming because there is some viable screw up by the lawyer.

> More often than not there was some breach of the standard of care.

In a good percentage there was malpractice.

[In] about half the cases there was malpractice.

In the vast majority of calls the lawyer did something wrong; most of the time there is malpractice by the lawyer.

It's pretty rare that I felt that there was no malpractice.

In the majority [of declined cases] there is malpractice.

[No negligence is] a smaller percentage than you might expect. . . . [F]or the most part people who call can identify a departure from good and accepted practice.

In only 50 percent of those I reject was there no malpractice.

For most of the lawyers the bigger issue was whether there were any damages attributable to what was or was not done, the "but-for" cause issue or the "case-within-the-case" issue that arises in LPL claims (discussed in Chapter 3). That is, although the potential lawyer-defendant might have been negligent, there was the issue of whether that negligence caused any actual damage to the client.

Finally, some lawyers mentioned a factor not related to the merits of the case or the potential lawyer-defendant: Was the potential client someone with whom the lawyer felt comfortable working?[11] One respondent mentioned that he would be concerned if he were the fourth or fifth lawyer the potential client had approached regarding the alleged malpractice. Another simply said he rejects about 5 percent of potential cases because he "doesn't like the plaintiff profile."

We asked the lawyers what the area of practice was in recently closed cases; some were asked about the most recent three cases and some just the most recent case. No one type of area of practice dominated as indicated by the following breakdown:

7 trusts and estates
6 personal injury (one of which was medical malpractice)
6 corporate/commercial (including sales of businesses)

4 real estate
3 divorce
3 litigation other than personal injury
3 employment
2 tax
1 patent
1 construction lien

About two-thirds of the cases listed above would probably be characterized as transactional rather than litigation. It might be that lawyers are more willing to take transactional cases, assuming sufficient damages, because the case-within-the-case issue would be less likely to be problematic. One lawyer observed, "Transactional cases are much easier to prove." Finally, the recoveries in these cases mostly involved at least six figures, although they ranged from as low as $40,000 to as much as $33 million.

There was a surprising amount of variation in the fee arrangements the lawyers reported employing. One might expect LPL to be similar to medical malpractice, with almost all cases being handled on a contingency-fee basis. Although it is likely that a majority of cases had at least a significant contingency element, most of the lawyers reported that their fee arrangements varied, with some cases on a straight percentage basis; some on a straight hourly basis (two lawyers reported that *all* of their legal malpractice cases were handled on an hourly basis); some on a hybrid percentage-hourly; some on what they called a "cap convert" basis, which switches from an hourly to a percentage after some hourly cap is reached; and some on a percentage plus retainer with the retainer credited toward the percentage fee if there was a recovery. A lot of this variation reflects the fact that many of the clients in legal malpractice cases are corporations or other forms of businesses, and they bring a measure of sophistication to working out a fee arrangement. Some of the straight contingency fees were based on a single percentage, mostly one-third of the recovery but a few up to 40 percent. Many of the percentage arrangements reported by the lawyers involved a sliding percentage, most often based on the stage of resolution but sometimes tied to the amount recovered. These arrangements typically started at 25 percent and could go as high as 50 percent, although most topped out at 40 percent. The hourly rates mentioned ranged from $250 to $600.

For most of the lawyers with whom we spoke, few of their LPL cases fail to get into suit. A typical comment was that only one or two of the LPL cases the lawyer had handled since starting to handle such work were resolved short of filing suit. Two lawyers mentioned that the one kind of case that they frequently settled without filing suit was a blown deadline case. One lawyer did report that about half of the cases he had closed in the previous year were closed without filing suit; another estimated that he resolved about 30 percent of his cases without having to file suit. However, these two lawyers clearly stood out in comparison with the other respondents. It is worth noting here that reports based on insurance company data discussed in Chapter 4 showed that a quarter or more of cases in which payments were made did not get into suit.

Although the lawyers with whom we spoke reported large proportions of cases getting into suit, none of them reported large numbers of trials reaching a verdict. About a third of the lawyers reported having tried one or zero LPL cases to verdict during their entire professional careers. Less than a quarter had tried a case in the previous year, and less than half had tried one or more cases in the previous five years. One lawyer did say that he tried one or two a year. These figures seem consistent with the very small number of LPL verdicts we located in the two sources we used for the analysis in Chapter 6. Although we do not have numbers, our impression is that a larger number of cases were settled during trial than reach an actual verdict. As one lawyer noted:

> When you go on trial, after a day or so the insurance company figures out that they don't want to run the risk, and we do too. We assess, "how's it going?" So they get settled frequently after [the trial] starts. . . . If it's going to get settled after you picked a jury, it's going to be while the plaintiff's case is going on. It's rare that it's after the plaintiff has rested, and while the defense is putting on its case that it gets settled.

Given that our analysis of various sources of insurance company data (see Chapters 4–6) showed that even those cases that become lawsuits result in payment only about half of the time, the lawyers with whom we spoke were remarkably successful in the cases they handled. Three respondents reported that no recovery was obtained in 20–25 percent of their cases; another reported his nonrecovery rate as somewhere between a third and 40 percent. For the other respondents, lack of success was a rare event, with the majority reporting no nonrecoveries in the previous year and many reporting only one or two in the previous five or ten years. One possible reason for the apparent inconsistency in the statistics regarding claim outcome is that we spoke only with lawyers who handled LPL claims with some regularity. It seems clear from our conversations with insurers and defense lawyers that a large proportion of LPL claims is brought by lawyers who lack expertise in the area, thinking such cases are no different from the other kind of negligence cases they handle. Some of the plaintiff-side lawyers we interviewed made specific comments about this issue:

> There's a number of lawyers and law firms who are handling these cases infrequently and don't do a very good job. . . . There are lawyers who get knee-deep into it, and all of a sudden it gets close to trial, and they truly realize they don't know what the heck they're doing.
>
> [Regarding lawyers who get burned after trying to do a legal mal case] I get referrals from a lot of those lawyers.
>
> I will get calls where people [i.e., lawyers lacking expertise in legal malpractice] are a month out from trial, and they will ask me for my expert. And I have to tell them, "Every case has a different expert." It's not like I have some little guy in the backroom.
>
> [When asked about other lawyers in his city who specialized in legal malpractice] Most of the cases are one-offs.

Given the absence of trials and the apparent fact that most of our respondents seldom lost at the summary judgment stage, what does the resolution process look like? Several respondents emphasized that cases were rarely settled quickly. It is not that settlements never occurred quickly or before a ruling on summary judgment; it might be that discovery turned up something akin to a smoking gun. One lawyer reported that his most recent case had been settled early: "The defense lawyer was a lawyer I know very well. He and I attended a document inspection together. We had a conversation for a couple of hours over the file, and we were both on the same page from very early in the case."

However, for many cases in suit, the plaintiff must prevail on an almost inevitable motion for summary judgment. To get to this stage, discovery related to both the claimed negligence or improper behavior and the case within the case normally must be completed. This relates to what some respondents described as the time required for the lawyer-defendant to accept that he had made a serious error that had harmed the client. It also is consistent with what some saw as the need of insurance defense firms, at which the lawyers are paid hourly, to put in time to bill.[12] Most lawyers reported that settlement negotiations tended to begin after the defendant had lost a motion for summary judgment: "Once summary judgment has been denied to the defendant, [the insurer is] prepared to offer enough money that it is too tempting to resolve the matter for the plaintiff, because very few of these cases are so clear-cut in all four aspects of legal malpractice that one can refuse a reasonable settlement with impunity."

After an unsuccessful motion for summary judgment was when mediation would tend to take place, often producing a settlement. However, a few lawyers reported some differences among insurers, with one singled out (Insurer Y) as not taking settlement seriously until trial was rapidly approaching:

> [Insurer Y] fights to the bitter death.
>
> Every case is fought; every case goes down to the wire. They don't have any interest in anything until you are actually on the courthouse steps.
>
> I've found that the insurance company is usually the one that digs in its heels, and it doesn't really care about the insured's reputation or anything like that.

Other than with this one carrier and the Attorneys' Liability Assurance Society (ALAS), which we discuss below, lawyers did not see substantial differences in how they handled cases depending on the insurer. Rather they saw the differences as depending more on who the defense lawyer was, noting that insurers might differ regarding how much they deferred to their outside counsel.

As indicated above, in settlement the insurer is the dominant concern, not the lawyer-defendant, even though most legal malpractice insurance policies have a consent-to-settle clause. As one lawyer observed, "My case is against the insurance carrier. The law firm and defendant-lawyer are just speed bumps for me. Except in the rare consent policy, the defendant doesn't really play much of a role in the settlement process. It's simply the insurer." More generally, we did not get a sense that the specialists with whom we spoke always held the lawyers they were suing in particularly high regard. As one lawyer commented, "Lawyers make the worst witnesses. Taking their deposition is just a joy. It's very rare that you have to tease information out of lawyer-witnesses. They want to talk. They want to tell their story. They try to advocate. They trip over their own feet." At the same time, another lawyer did comment in comparing medical and legal malpractice cases, "There's a big difference between doing a legal malpractice [case] and a med malpractice [case]. Lawyers don't hold it nearly as personal, take it nearly as personal. Doctors, it doesn't matter what they do, they get pissed at anyone who sues them, and they never admit that they screwed up, never." Alternatively, as stated in a somewhat more cynical fashion by another specialist, "I don't sue doctors anymore. Some days it's like shooting fish in the barrel with some of these lawyers."

Given the relatively unique nature of ALAS and the kinds of firms it insures, we were interested in whether plaintiffs' lawyers found dealing with cases involving ALAS different. Two lawyers mentioned ALAS without our prompting; we asked most of the others whether they had had any cases involving ALAS. A significant proportion of respondents had not heard of ALAS. However, seven of our respondents had dealt with cases in which the defendant was insured by ALAS. Their views of ALAS varied somewhat, as reflected in the following comments:

> [ALAS insured firms] hire law firms that look like themselves that may or may not have any particular experience in legal malpractice defense. And they process the cases differently than the typical insurance defense law firm.

> In every one of the ALAS cases I've had, the firms are more than willing to spend their deductible to fight the case. In all of those cases the damage claim has been greatly in excess of the deductibles.

> I would say those cases are more likely to settle earlier on than [those of Insurer Y].

> They probably settled with greater difficulty, but in the end for more money. What happens is you go to mediation, and they adjourn the mediation because they have to go to the next level of insurance, and you have to convene again.

> [ALAS is] real difficult to deal with. . . . The only advantage you have when you are suing [an ALAS insured] is that a Mayer Brown & Platt will be defended by Jenner & Block, and Jenner & Block by Jones Day. The good thing about that is that the expenses, the attorneys' fees that are charged, are outrageous. The managing member of the firm that's defending the case might only be charging $1,200 per hour, but every time they have a meeting, three lawyers are in attendance, and they are all charging. So what ends up happening is at some point in time when they can't get out of the case, and they see they've got a problem, they are willing to talk to you about settling.

> ALAS cases tend to involve very highly qualified defense firms, and the culture at ALAS seems to be, "We're not going to resolve the case until we turn over every stone," and so they become labor-intensive cases, but they have generous coverage and they pay generously.

Finally, we were initially curious about the relationship between seeking compensation through an LPL claim and filing a disciplinary complaint against the lawyer-defendant. In our first round of interviews, we asked whether the LPL claims the lawyers handled were frequently accompanied by an ethics complaint to the regulatory authorities. The responses indicated that some of their claims did raise ethical issues, but they typically told clients to hold off on filing a complaint until the LPL claim had been resolved. As one lawyer explained, this was for strategic reasons: "I tell them not to [file an ethics complaint] while they're in the case because I think if you start going after a guy's license, he tends to fight a little harder."

Before turning to the defense of LPL claims, it is important to reiterate the limitations of the portrait we have presented. Our focus is on lawyers who can be characterized as either specialists or semispecialists in LPL cases on behalf of claimants. All the evidence we found regarding the lawyers who bring LPL claims is that the majority, probably the vast majority, of claims is brought by lawyers who have little experience or expertise in handling such claims.[13] The nonspecialists, those lacking significant experience prosecuting LPL claims, often have problems understanding what such a claim involves, particularly regarding the issue of causation: whether the alleged negligence actually produced any harm, and the nature of the evidence needed to survive a summary judgment motion regarding causation. Given that the specialists with whom we spoke generally have fairly high potential-damage thresholds for the claims they will take on and that, as discussed in the previous chapter, about three-quarters of paid cases involve payments of $50,000 or less (half of those for $10,000 or less), we do not have a clear picture of how the more run-of-the-mill cases, prosecuted by nonspecialist plaintiffs' lawyers, are handled.

THE INSURERS

All of the insurers with whom we spoke focus primarily on small firms, with the average number of lawyers on a policy something less than two. Some of the insurers explicitly limit the size of the firms they cover, whereas for others it reflects a combination of the size of firms existing in their coverage areas and the preference of larger firms for dealing with different insurers. Some of the insurers with whom we spoke specifically excluded some areas of practice from what they would insure. Typically, these were securities and intellectual property, with the explanation that the size of potential losses in these areas of practice was greater than what the insurer wanted to risk. In the words of one insurance claims manager, "We've gotten beaten up pretty badly on patent claims." The policies most of these insurers write had deductibles ranging from $1,000 to $100,000 or more. Some of the insurers' policies included a "consent-to-settle" clause, but even those insurers who did not have such clauses as part of their policies reported that they "work[ed] with [their] insured to reach settlements that [were] mutually acceptable." Premiums were generally a function of area of practice, years of experience, and past claims experience.

The insurers reported that they opened files either after being notified by an insured of a possible problem or after receiving an inquiry or claim from a client or a client's new lawyer. One insurer observed, "Claims usually come in as a call from our policyholder." As discussed in Chapter 4, some of the insurers distinguished between opening a file and an actual claim; others treated all files as claims for counting purposes. At all of the insurers, claims were immediately referred to in-house "claims attorneys" who functioned as the equivalent of the claims adjuster in other kinds of insurance settings.

The claims attorneys sought to obtain information, either from the insured or the claimant,[14] regarding the nature of the underlying matter, the outcome of the representation, the nature of the alleged problem, and the nature and magnitude of the alleged or possible harm suffered by the client. Based on this information, the claims attorney would try to quickly assess whether the claim had any validity. If it involved allegations of negligence, and it was not clear whether the insured's action fell below the standard of care, the insurer retained or consulted an expert in the relevant area of practice.[15] Based on the information collected, the claims attorney determined whether there was some basis for the claim, and if there were, the attorney would make a judgment as to whether claim repair might be possible. If there were an opportunity to cure the problem, the claims attorney would advise and work with the insured or bring in an outside lawyer to assist in the repair attempt. One insurer estimated that their claims attorneys devoted 50 percent of their time to claim repair. One insurer reported that about 12 percent of the prior year's claims had been closed after a successful claim repair.

If, after evaluating the claim, the insurer determined there was no negligence or no harm, the insurer notified the claimant, assuming there had been contact with a claimant about the matter, that it was denying the claim. Most of the insurers with whom we spoke asserted that if their claims attorney concluded that there was negligence resulting in damages, they tried to settle the claim. The insurer assessed the damages, obtained consent from the insured, and made a settlement offer to the claimant. As one insurer with whom we spoke put it, "If possible, we will avoid having to hire a defense lawyer or getting into suit." That person went on to say:

> We are proactive. . . . We don't wait to see if [the] claimant can prove it. We don't wait to see if there's going to be a claim made if [the] lawyer reports a mistake. If we think it's just a matter of time, we're not going to just sit on it. We do not go out to the potential claimant and tell them they should make a claim, but we are proactive in doing the investigation. We want to be ready to move fast if a claim does come because claims grow over time.

That same insurer described how the claims attorney worked with the insured if an actual claim had been made (noting that the insurer's policy gave the insurer the right to control the defense):

> We involve the insured lawyers from the start. We see them as our first expert, and we tell them that in [the] first conversation. We also seek to reassure them by telling them, "We think you're a good lawyer." We have the right to choose the defense lawyer, but we give the insured a short list and let them pick from the list.

> We find that if the lawyer has been involved in this way, we have very little trouble getting consent when we believe it's appropriate to settle.

That insurer's policy included both a consent-to-settle clause and a "hammer" clause that put the insured at risk for damages and expenses above the amount of a settlement the insurer had deemed appropriate if the insured refused to consent to the settlement. The insurer reported that reminding the insured of the hammer clause ("We have taken it out and waved it around a couple of times") usually solved the problem of an insured who did not want to go along with a settlement the insurer thought was appropriate. Our contact at another insurer whose policies contained a hammer clause confirmed this pattern but went on to describe a case in which the lawyer firmly believed he had done nothing wrong and "wanted his day in court" but that the insurer wanted to settle for $1,000. The lawyer initially held to his position even after the claims attorney explained the hammer clause; however, eventually the lawyer was convinced he should accept the claims attorney's judgment that it was best to settle the claim.

The effort by insurers to work with their policyholders when a claim is made raises some challenges for the insurer and the lawyers they retain to defend claims. First, "they [the insureds] are devastated and livid when they are challenged. They are like cornered raccoons when confronted with a claim. . . . They don't want to be second-guessed on their professional judgment. We have to work to set the insured's expectations and unset the wrong expectations." A further complication is that "most lawyers don't do litigation, and they don't know what to expect when they are sued"; often the insurer or the defense lawyer has to explain the litigation process to the lawyer-defendant.

In contrast with the plaintiffs' lawyers who reported that almost all of their cases involved filing suit, all of the insurers with whom we spoke insisted, consistent with various statistics we found, that half or more of their claims were settled with payment, without a suit having been filed, although one informant also said, "Not a whole lot of the cases that are settled with payment are handled entirely in-house." The insurers and plaintiffs' lawyers were consistent regarding the infrequency of trial. One respondent reported that his company was involved in less than one trial per year; another said that in recent years his company had closed perhaps half a dozen cases in which a trial had at least started. For the cases that proceeded to suit because of conflicting views on the merits of the case,[16] summary judgment was a crucial decision point for the insurers: if the defense lost at summary judgment, the insurer then would try to settle the case.

It was clear from the interviews that probably somewhat more than half of the *actual* claims result in payment of some damages. Obtaining exact figures is difficult because most of the representatives with whom we spoke were not able to clearly distinguish between cases in which an actual claim (i.e., a demand for payment) was received and those in which the insurer was on notice regarding a possible problem but never received an actual claim. One insurer reported that 75 percent of its files close with no actual claim being received.[17]

A couple of other issues we explored with one or more of the insurers are worth comment. First, we asked how the risk of claims varied with the size of firms the company insured. The responses were consistent with the statistics from Missouri presented in Chapter 6: although the frequency of claims decreased as the firm size increased, the severity of the claims increased with the firm size. In a sense, the insurers seemed to be saying that the risk, measured as the expected loss (probability of a paid claim *times* the cost of the claim), might not vary that much as the size of the firm increases.

A second question we explored concerned real estate claims. The simple explanation for the high frequency of such claims discussed in Chapter 4 is the large numbers of real estate transactions, that such transactions are document intensive, and that usually significant amounts of money are involved. The document-intensive nature of the work creates many opportunities to make mistakes. Moreover, in some states an attorney is required to sign off on all real estate transactions, which in turn increases both the volume and the risk because at least some attorneys will be tempted to function as signers only, giving little attention to what they are signing particularly if they receive only a minimal fee for each signing. A significant proportion of real estate work is conducted by nonspecialists, which probably adds to the risk of error.[18] Finally, a documentation error and the associated harm are much easier to prove than is a claim of negligence and harm in litigation.

Finally, as mentioned earlier in this chapter, we asked several of the insurers to name the attorneys who regularly handled legal malpractice cases on the plaintiffs' side. One of our contacts observed, "We don't see the same lawyers popping up." This helps to explain the disconnect between what the plaintiffs' lawyers described as high success rates and the much lower success rates reported by insurers and found in the claims. Specifically, specialists are probably adept at screening out most cases that will not be successful, but the nonspecialists who might only ever handle one or two legal malpractice cases probably bring many, or even most, of the cases that ultimately are unsuccessful. This does not necessarily mean that all of those with expertise in the area are equally skilled at identifying good cases. This was made clear by another of our contacts, who named two local lawyers who regularly brought claims. The first was described as "not screening his cases well," although "every once and a while he has a decent case." In contrast, the other lawyer named "looked at [his] cases very closely," and "when [this lawyer] calls us up, we will pay attention to it."

THE DEFENSE BAR

Interviews were completed with nine lawyers who regularly handled the defense of legal malpractice cases. All of these lawyers were in Minnesota, North Carolina, or Wisconsin. The percentage of their time devoted to this work ranged from 10 percent to 75 percent, with most between one-third and two-thirds. The balance of their work tended to be other types of insurance defense, although one reported that a measurable part of his work was plaintiffs' medical malpractice. The majority worked in firms of 30 or more, the largest with more than 100 lawyers. One worked in a firm of 4, where 2 lawyers did various forms of insurance defense work and 2 did plaintiffs' work. Caseloads varied from as low as 1 a year to as high as 30, with most in the 10 to 20 range. Hourly billing rates (as of 2012) ranged from $160 to $275 with 1 lawyer, who handled some cases for firms insured by ALAS, reporting a range from $250 to $400.

Most of the lawyers received some cases before suit as well as after the plaintiff had filed suit. Two lawyers reported that half of their legal malpractice cases were received presuit. Some of the presuit work involved assessing whether a claim had merit, and some involved claim repair. One lawyer who reported that "perhaps half" of the cases opened presuit were claim repair commented, "I'm retained to come in and try to fix it." The lawyer who also handled plaintiffs' medical malpractice observed regarding claim repair that in contrast to medical malpractice, "In legal malpractice one often has the ability to mitigate the loss by getting a ruling reversed or by appealing something like a tax decision or assessment."

One consistency between the plaintiff-side and defense-side lawyers was the infrequency of trials. Few of the defense-side lawyers with whom we spoke reported doing as many as one trial a year, and several had tried only one or two over the entire time they had been handling legal malpractice cases. One defense lawyer reported that, although he had handled more than 100 trials over the years across all areas of his practice, only 2 or 3 were legal malpractice; this lawyer reported opening 10 to 15 legal malpractice cases a year, although some of those involved only a question about whether an LPL policy covered a particular claim. One lawyer did report having tried numerous legal malpractice cases, perhaps 40 over his career, but he clearly was an outlier among our respondents.

Not surprisingly, summary judgment stood out as more important than actual trials. One lawyer commented that although he had handled few trials, he had had many appeals related to summary judgment. Although it was hard to get a figure on success at summary judgment from many of the respondents, most of the actual in-suit claims referred to defense counsel and then resolved without payment involved a successful motion for summary judgment. One defense lawyer estimated that half of his cases were won at summary judgment.

When we asked what proportion of the cases they handled was resolved without payment to the plaintiff, we got very inconsistent answers. One lawyer said that in 80 percent of his cases no payment was made, whereas another said no payment occurred in "very few" of his cases. Some of this variation might reflect which cases a lawyer received or how the referring insurer handled cases. Some insurers might make a greater effort to settle cases presuit than do others, and for those insurers the cases that get to outside defense counsel might be the most problematic for the plaintiff.

We asked the lawyers who primarily controlled the defense, the insured or the insurer? Several commented that formally it was the insurer, although one made clear that he viewed the insured as his client and looked to the insured as being in control. However, most said that decisions regarding defense were largely consensual. Generally, they did not see a lot of conflict between the insurer and the insured over strategy or tactics, even when the insurance policy formally granted the insurer control. Things might be different when the insured had a high self-insured retention (SIR), which might give the insured both the power to select defense counsel (perhaps subject to approval by the insurer) and control of the defense because the insured is effectively paying the cost of defense. More generally, regarding selection of defense counsel, this too was largely a consensual process involving insured and insurer, with one or the other making a suggestion or providing a list of options and the other acceding or making a selection.

One area in which conflict might arise between the insurer and the insured is in deciding whether to settle.[19] Many LPL insurance policies include a "consent-to-settle" clause that is likely to be accompanied by the "hammer clause" previously described. As observed by one lawyer:

> The most typical example is where the attorney defendant insured says, "No way do I want to settle. I didn't do anything wrong." Of course, we have to follow the directive of our client; the attorney is our client, and so we have to follow those directives. Most of the insurance policies also have a provision in them where the carrier believes a settlement is appropriate where there is a definite settlement proposal on the table from the plaintiff: "We will take $10,000," and if the attorney refuses that settlement and the case goes to trial and the damages come in in excess of the $10,000 offer, then the attorney becomes self-insured for anything above that $10,000. That is colloquially referred to as the "hammer clause." [laugh]

Another respondent commented that he had never had an insured reject a settlement after he had explained the import of the hammer clause. Another respondent said bluntly, "The hammer clause is pretty persuasive."

As discussed in Chapter 3, an additional factor potentially putting pressure on an insured to agree to a settlement is that many of the insurance policies lawyers purchase include the cost of defense within the policy limits, sometimes providing a separate amount for defense costs so that costs deplete the amount available to pay a claimant only after that separate amount has been expended. This means the more that is spent defending the case, the less there is available to pay any award or settlement. Costs within limits will cause a lawyer to think twice about how hard he or she wants to fight the claim if the alleged amount of damages is substantial. This issue can cut both ways because it can also increase pressure on the insurer to act under its duty to settle to avoid expending so much on defense, leading to an overlimits outcome that might raise issues of good faith.[20] Failing to settle within the amount of insurance available can open the insurer to liability for much higher amounts than the policy limits; this was what happened in the case of *Insurance Commissioner of Indiana v. Fillenwarth et al.*, discussed in Chapter 3.

There are other situations in which an insured might want to settle a claim the insurer prefers to defend. This might occur simply because a lawyer prefers for the matter to be resolved quietly or to get it over quickly in order to avoid having to devote significant time to dealing with the matter.

> I think what is a bigger motivator to settle is as one moves closer and closer to trial, legal malpractice cases tend to be complex enough that it's not going to be a two- or three-day trial. This is going to be two weeks, minimum. And the idea of sitting in a courtroom, without a great deal of control, in their home county [laugh] tends to be a bigger motivator for most attorneys, if they're on the fence, if they're on the fence.

One lawyer described the following experience:

> In the case, the insured and the plaintiff knew each other very well. The insured did not take much interest in the case until about a week before it was set to go to trial. It involved a transactional matter. The day we were to go to trial, I suggested that the plaintiff and the insured meet and talk about a number to settle the case. They did. They agreed on a number. I called the insurance company, and told them what had happened, and the insurance company said they would not settle on that basis, but they wanted to go through traditional negotiations, where you start far apart and move to the center. That didn't happen. The case went to trial, and the verdict was about three times what it would have settled for.
>
> It may have been over limits. The number it could have settled for was 150; the verdict was 350 or thereabouts, and I think limits were 300, but I didn't know that for sure.
>
> We ended up negotiating a settlement that resolved the case short of the appeal, and I think probably the insurance company paid something over their limits to get it done. It was not a good decision on the insurance company's part.

Many of the defense lawyers we interviewed were derisive regarding the plaintiffs' lawyers they tended to see on the other side:

> I'm never sure what motivates plaintiff lawyers to bring legal malpractice actions, especially those that have not made an investigation of what the applicable law is.

> It is quite often the case that no critical examination has been made before a case has been filed.
>
> There is a high dismissal [including summary judgment] in legal malpractice because lots of plaintiffs' lawyers don't know the area and aren't discriminating in the cases they take.
>
> Lots of the plaintiffs' lawyers who take legal malpractice cases are not that good. . . . The plaintiffs often stumble on causation: Did the negligence produce the negative outcome, or would that have happened even in the absence of negligence?

One respondent talked about the plaintiffs' lawyers bringing legal malpractice cases who do not understand what they must prove:

> They don't get it. The classic is the conflict of interest. They catch your client in an obvious, clear conflict of interest, and they think they have a slam dunk, and they lose because they don't even realize all the hoops they have to jump through, frequently don't realize all the hoops they have to jump through in order to prove that had that conflict of interest been handled differently, a different result would have been obtained. . . . They tend to miss it a lot, and not perceive the problems in legal malpractice causation and damages. So, it is very few cases where there isn't a significant causation and damage issue.

Another observed:

> I don't think there are a lot of plaintiffs' lawyers who do a lot of this kind of work, and it's one of the significant advantages that the defense lawyers have is that, I don't care who I'm up against in the case, I will always have handled at least 5, probably 10, maybe 20 times more cases, even for someone who does some significant plaintiffs' malpractice work, I will have handled 10 or 15 times more cases than they have, every time.

One lawyer described the problem by giving a hypothetical:

> Imagine some lady who has been playing bridge and drinking at the country club who gets behind the wheel of her Land Rover, is driving home from the club under the influence of alcohol, and smacks a school bus discharging people. She

> goes to a lawyer and the lawyer says, "Oh, you've got a great case, we're going to sue the school system, and we'll get you a whole lot of money." The foolish lawyer who said that then neglects to bring a lawsuit in a timely fashion, allowing the statute of limitations to run. There are people who will bring a malpractice claim against the foolish lawyer, saying, "Well, you promised you were going to get some money for this woman, you didn't, and now you have to pay." That's not what the law is in any state. The law is that the plaintiff has to demonstrate that there's a valid case within a case; the plaintiff has to demonstrate that had the case against the school system been properly handled, the drunken lady would have gotten some money. I don't think there's any place in the country where you can recover money for rear-ending a stopped school bus; we see cases almost that silly. And you want to say, what on earth are you thinking? But folks continue to bring cases like that, and we continue to defend them.

Another question we explored with the defense lawyers was whether they found any differences in handling cases depending on which insurer was involved. One lawyer who had handled cases for ALAS and for the Lloyd's syndicate saw differences between those insurers and others, describing ALAS and Lloyd's as typically being more hands off. In our question, we tried to draw a distinction between the mutual insurers that specialized in lawyers' professional liability and general insurers who wrote LPL policies as one of many types of insurance they offered. A majority of respondents did not see a difference because the generalist insurers had specialized departments handling legal malpractice claims. However, one respondent did see a subtle difference between the generalist insurers and the NABRICO[21] mutuals: "I think the specialist insurers [i.e., mutuals] are a little more sensitive to the culture of their insureds, and to their insureds interests. . . . I think they're more in touch." Regarding the mutuals, another observed: "They know the law firms and the lawyers . . . or know they will be running into them in the future."

Another commented on the difference between the insurance claims staff with whom he dealt on legal malpractice claims and the claims staff handling more routine matters: "The differences are that all the claims people who handle legal malpractice cases are much more, I'll use an inappropriate term that I think gets the idea across, touchy-feely about their lawyers than by and large people handling automobile and product liability and homeowner claims are with regard to their insureds, because the cases are different; they just are."

Finally, in response to our "did I miss anything important" question, a couple of respondents commented on what it was like working with the lawyer-defendants they were representing:

> The most interesting thing about doing legal mal defense is how cooperative my clients are. . . . Always hear how terrible lawyers are as clients, but I haven't found that to be true.
>
> The best and the worst clients are lawyers. The worst part, any lawyers would understand it, who would want to represent people like us? And so there's a lot of second-guessing and there's a lot of very emotional sorts of aspects to it, but I understand that. I don't mean to sound critical. It's some of the hard parts of it. The rewarding part of it is that when you get good results for them, when they know you're doing a good job. . . . It's very seldom that in a litigation practice that you get what's a really heartfelt thank you from somebody when the case is over. . . . I don't get gifts from clients very often; 75% easily, maybe 90% of all the gifts I've ever gotten in 37 years of practice are from lawyers who I represented who wanted to make sure that I knew how much they appreciated what I did for them. They realize all the vagaries of this, and they're very appreciative, and I enjoy it.

The perspective of the defense lawyers with whom we spoke aligns well with what we heard from the insurers. Although the plaintiffs' lawyers had little concern about claim repair, this is a significant part of the work of at least a portion of the defense lawyers. Defense lawyers vary in their reported likelihood of success in defending claims, with some reporting a high level of success and others a low level; this probably reflects differences in how the insurers deal with cases prior to their being referred to defense lawyers. On two points there is strong agreement among all three sets of respondents: summary judgment is a pivotal point in legal malpractice suits when there is an issue of causation,[22] and trials reaching verdict are rare in legal malpractice cases.

CONCLUSION

This chapter draws on our interviews with those involved in prosecuting and defending legal malpractice claims. The major limitation of the discussion above is that the plaintiffs' lawyers with whom we spoke were specialists or semispecialists in legal malpractice, yet most LPL claims are prosecuted by lawyers who have little or no experience in handling such cases. This is in contrast to medical malpractice, in which a large percentage of cases are brought by lawyers with substantial experience in handling such cases.[23] It is clear from our interviews that both the insurers and defense counsel take advantage of the lack of experience of a plaintiffs' lawyer. What is unclear is whether this reflects cases that an experienced lawyer recognized as not winnable or that the inexperienced plaintiffs' lawyers tend to make mistakes of judgment in how they handle their LPL cases.

Despite the lack of experience of many lawyers handling LPL cases, insurance data indicate that a significant proportion of such claims does lead to the payment of compensation, albeit the typical amounts paid tend to be low. Clearly, it is not the case that lawyers inexperienced in legal malpractice cannot bring successful claims. We do suspect that, as with the specialists and semispecialists we interviewed, most plaintiffs' lawyers turn away most potential LPL cases, and many nonspecialists simply will not consider taking such cases.

Finally, the fact that the experienced plaintiffs' lawyers with whom we spoke reported seeing malpractice in a large proportion of cases they declined is consistent with the broad theme of this book: large numbers of persons harmed by the actions of their lawyers are denied access to justice. There are several reasons for this finding, ranging from the modest size of many claims to legal and procedural issues that create problems somewhat unique to LPL claims. In Chapter 8, we turn to possible ways of improving access for those who have suffered harm.

CHAPTER 8

Improving Access to Justice for Those Harmed by the Actions of Their Lawyers

As the preceding chapters make clear, there is substantial variation in the characteristics of claims involving lawyers' professional liability (LPL). Arguably, the variation in this area of professional liability is greater than in the most visible area, namely negligence of physicians and surgeons. The dimensions characterizing LPL are more extensive than those characterizing the liability incurred by medical professionals, and the issues that arise differ in important ways depending on those dimensions. Moreover, as noted in Chapter 1, the costs, based on expenditures on liability insurance, to legal professionals of liability claims exceeds the costs to medical professionals when measured relative to revenue.

One of the key dimensions in LPL is the two hemispheres of practice described in Chapter 1 and referred to throughout this book. In the introductory section, we foreshadowed our findings by pointing to what Heinz and Laumann labeled the "two hemispheres" of the bar.[1] The analyses in Chapters 4 and 5 make it clear that there are "two hemispheres of lawyers' professional liability." The frequency of LPL claims, the areas of practice producing claims, the kinds of errors asserted in claims, the amounts at stake in the claims, and the ultimate amounts paid out to resolve the claims all differ depending on whether one is looking at the kinds of legal practices that serve primarily individuals and small businesses or those that serve large corporations. Fundamentally, this reflects the differences in the kinds and scale of legal work conducted on behalf of individuals compared with the work conducted for corporations.

Corporate firms do appear to face fewer claims, at least as measured on a "per-lawyer" basis. However, this might be something of a measurement artifact because it does not account for the number of lawyers who worked on a matter that produced a claim. Still, it is likely that even accounting for the use of teams of lawyers, the team approach builds in checks of various types to catch errors before those errors cause harm. Interestingly, we heard from at least one source that insurers of large law firms have seen an increase in the proportion of claims arising from "substantive errors" as compared with "administrative errors," and the speculation we heard is that this might be because of large firms coming under pressure to reduce costs, which they probably accomplish by reducing the amount of review and cross-checking of work products.

Even as large, corporate firms might be able to limit the frequency of the claims they face, when they do have a claim it is likely to be much more severe in terms of the potential loss involved. For the largest firms these losses can be several times the largest losses in medical malpractice. The magnitude of these risks is such that single insurers are generally unwilling to underwrite insurance policies covering those risks. As discussed in Chapter 3, for the largest firms, this means arranging a tower of insurance with multiple layers and multiple insurers sharing the risk at each layer. One large-firm insurer, the Attorneys' Liability Assurance Society (ALAS), does offer limits as high as $75 million per claim, but it is unique in offering this level of coverage. The largest firms insured by ALAS probably secure additional layers of insurance on top of that provided by ALAS.

A key element in the difference between the two hemispheres is the ability of clients to obtain redress when an error has caused some loss. First, it is probable that corporate clients are less likely to face a loss caused by their law firms. However, just as important, in the situation when a loss does occur, corporations know that the firms they employ have insurance that can be the source of compensation for the loss. In contrast, the lawyers used by individuals and/or small businesses have a significant likelihood of not being insured—except in the state of Oregon—and, as discussed in Chapter 7, lawyers experienced in prosecuting LPL malpractice cases seldom will take on a case if the lawyer-defendant is uninsured. Moreover, many of the losses experienced by individuals or small businesses, although significant in terms of the resources of the potential claimant, are relatively small in relation to the costs of prosecuting an LPL liability claim, and this further limits the willingness of knowledgeable lawyers to take on a claim.

Thus, there is a real dilemma for clients in the personal services sector of the legal market. They face a greater likelihood of a lawyer making a costly error, and they face greater limitations in securing the kind of assistance needed to prosecute a claim against the negligent lawyer. This is an access-to-justice problem as well as a potential image problem for the legal profession. There are partial solutions, but the likelihood that many of those solutions will be implemented is small.

Unfortunately, as discussed in Chapter 4, we have no way to ascertain the frequency of legal malpractice akin to the research conducted in the medical area based on a review of medical records. However, it does seem highly likely that only a relatively small proportion of valid legal malpractice claims results either in claims filed or in redress obtained.[2] The result is significant harm to the clients of lawyers, and the absence of this avenue of redress might contribute to the low esteem in which lawyers are held.

There is a variety of reasons for the inability of victims of legal malpractice, or other forms of behaviors by lawyers that produce liability, to obtain redress. One argument is that the courts have effectively stacked the rules in favor of lawyers and that judges tend to give lawyers the benefit of the doubt.[3] As we will discuss below, we believe this is in part true, but other factors limit the ability of aggrieved clients to obtain redress. As discussed above, two major factors are: first, the failure of large numbers of lawyers to be insured, resulting in the unwillingness of lawyers with experience and expertise in LPL claims to represent claimants against uninsured lawyers; and second, a large proportion of errors by lawyers causes relatively modest harm to the client in absolute terms, although that harm can be significant to the client. Furthermore, in cases such as those involving issues including child custody and visitation, the errors that might be most harmful do not produce a financial loss, and in LPL cases damages are generally not available for nonfinancial harm. Individuals harmed by their lawyers seldom have sufficient resources to pay another lawyer to pursue an LPL claim and must rely on lawyers' willing take the case on a contingency-fee basis; however, experienced lawyers will only accept cases on a contingency-fee basis if the damages reach some threshold, often a high threshold. In the remaining pages, we suggest several changes that would help enable those harmed by their lawyers to obtain some type of redress.

INSURANCE

Calls to require lawyers representing private clients to carry some level of professional liability insurance are by no means new.[4] Why is Oregon the only jurisdiction in the United States that requires such insurance?[5] Interestingly, in Oregon the authority to require insurance was granted by the legislature to the state bar. It was not imposed either by the legislature itself or by the state supreme court. Presumably in most, if not all, other states the state supreme court, as the ultimate regulator of legal practice in the state, could impose such a requirement. Why that has not happened can only be a matter of speculation.[6]

Mandatory Insurance

Most other major democratic countries require that legal professionals carry professional liability insurance. The only major common-law country where this is not the case is New Zealand.[7] Among the 28 members of the European Union, at least 19 require LPL insurance, and most of the exceptions are in Southern Europe (Spain, Portugal, Italy, Greece, and Malta).[8] Other major countries not requiring insurance include Japan (*bengoshi*), Israel, Brazil, India, and China.[9]

In many US states the legislature could impose a mandatory insurance requirement on lawyers much as it does on many other professionals. Some state supreme courts might throw out such a law, arguing that under separation of powers they, not the legislatures, are the regulators of the legal profession. Some observers would probably argue that state legislatures have not moved to impose such regulations because of the combination of lawyers constituting a significant portion of the membership of state legislatures (and controlling legislative committees that would review relevant legislation) and the generosity of lawyers as campaign contributors. However, it is not clear that this would explain the inaction given that the majority, often the vast majority, of lawyers in a state does carry insurance, and one might expect them to want to force other lawyers to bear that cost so that uninsured lawyers do not have a competitive cost advantage.

Regardless of the reasons for inaction, it borders on scandalous that only Oregon requires lawyers to have professional liability insurance. The much higher rate of claims per 100 insured in Oregon compared with what we found for other insurers of small to medium-sized practices clearly indicates that the absence of required insurance discourages claims.[10] Lawyers might oppose required insurance, arguing that it would increase costs for all lawyers because those lawyers most likely to be subject to claims are currently the least likely to carry insurance. Some of this can be mitigated by setting rates based on risk, area of practice, and past claims experience.

Some opponents might argue that this will disadvantage general practitioners, who might be subject to higher rates because they do not have the same degree of expertise as do specialists. It is not clear, however, that such a requirement is necessarily a bad thing. One defense-side respondent made the following observation: "I think the reason personal injury law pops up so much and real estate law pops up so much is that there are lots of people who do that work as a sideline to their principal business. Lots of general practitioners handle real estate matters and handle personal injury cases, and because they don't do a lot of them they tend to make more mistakes."

Importantly, there are types of situations in which the general practitioner, particularly the small-town general practitioner with a modest practice, might commit errors that have large financial consequences. In the words of another defense-side respondent:

> There are a lot of small law offices in rural communities that are underinsured, and those small-time solo practitioners or two-man office-sharing arrangements can get themselves in just as much trouble as big city firms, clearly not on patent or that kind of thing, but you've got a situation where some farmer comes into the small-town lawyer's office in his coveralls with manure around his boots and says, "Draw me up a will; I don't want to pay much money for it," and you charge 100 bucks and you draft the will. Well, the guy could be working $5 or $10 million in multiple farms, and maybe he's carving one kid out of the will; the lawyer's sitting there with a $100,000 policy and it's going to be expensive to defend.

Although this lawyer was thinking about the problem of low-limit policies, what the story also suggests is that the hypothetical lawyer probably did not do the kind of investigation or have the knowledge to get the will prepared in the right way to avoid the kind of claim the respondent mentioned.

Insurance Disclosure Requirements

If a state supreme court and state legislature are unwilling to require coverage, at a minimum there should be ways to provide information to potential clients on whether a lawyer has insurance and simultaneously create additional incentives for lawyers to carry insurance.

Require Reporting Lack of Insurance Coverage to Regulators. One type of solution is to require that lawyers report to the state regulatory body whether they have insurance and any changes in their insurance situations. Some states require such reporting at the time a lawyer renews his or her license to practice; there should also be a requirement that a lawyer who reports having insurance inform the regulator if that insurance has lapsed. As discussed in Chapter 3, some states make information on a lawyer's insurance status easily accessible to the public, but others do not. For a reporting requirement to be useful for potential clients, information on the lawyer's coverage status must be easy to check on a website accessible to the public. Furthermore, there should be efforts to inform the public on how to access the information. State bars should periodically undertake a public service announcement campaign alerting residents to the ready availability of this information. Another possibility would be a regulation that required lawyers taking on a new client or taking on new matters for an existing client to provide the client a single-page notice about the availability of the information. There might be exceptions in situations in which the firm is required to be insured, such as in states where LLPs or similar structures must carry insurance. There might also be exceptions for firms exceeding a certain size, on the assumption that all such firms could be assumed to carry liability insurance.

If lawyers are not required to report lapses in insurance, insurers could be required to notify the regulatory authority of any lapse in coverage because of nonrenewal or cancellation. Members of the public might be given the option of having the online system automatically notify them if the insurance coverage for a specific lawyer lapsed. Any such notification request should be active for some stated time period, with the requester also being notified shortly before the request expires and an easy way to have the request renewed.

The system described above would involve some implementation costs, but that implementation could be funded by a onetime surcharge on lawyers' registration fees, with the annual cost covered by some modest increase in the annual registration fee.

Require That Clients Be Informed Whether the Lawyer Is Insured. As discussed in Chapter 3, some states have a requirement that lawyers notify their clients regarding whether they carry professional liability insurance. In some states the requirement is to inform the client if the lawyer is uninsured, as is the case in California, and in other states the notice requirement covers both the presence and the absence of coverage. Typically, the lawyer must include the required information in a retainer agreement or letter of engagement, that is, at the start of representation. As noted in Chapter 3, South Dakota has the most stringent requirement: lawyers who do not have at least $100,000 in LPL coverage must include on their stationery and in all written communications with the clients an explicit statement that the lawyer or firm "is not covered by professional liability insurance."

There are at least two problems with many of the current requirements as they exist. First, the notice is usually included in the retainer agreement or letter of engagement. It is likely to be merely one of many points in the agreement, and many clients probably fail to notice it just as they fail to notice many details in legal documents. Although a requirement such as that in South Dakota would be ideal, there are other options. One way to highlight the information might be for the lawyer to be required to give each client at the start of representation a short pamphlet on potential avenues of redress if the client is dissatisfied with the lawyer's services in any way, including but not limited to negligence. This would include prominently on the cover a box for the lawyer to check indicating whether he or she is insured, plus contact information for the state regulatory authority and a lawyer referral service for additional assistance. Alternatively, the lawyer might simply be required to provide the client a copy of the fully executed retainer or letter of engagement with a cover sheet prominently indicating whether the lawyer is insured. Some lawyers might object that this would create a disincentive for potential clients to retain a lawyer who was not insured, but that is in fact one of the goals because it would further incentivize lawyers to have liability insurance.

The second problem, identified by a plaintiff-side lawyer in California with whom we spoke, is that a lawyer's insurance might lapse after the start of the representation, and there is no requirement that the client be informed of that lapse. The South Dakota requirement comes close to doing this, but there could be some time gap between when the insurance lapsed and the next written communication with one or more clients. Lawyers should be required to notify all active clients of any lapse in their LPL insurance with severe sanctions should they fail to do so. An effective sanction might be a one-year suspension from practice if any claim were filed that turned out not to be covered by insurance because of a lapse of which the client was not informed. A more draconian sanction would be to impose a suspension regardless of whether any claim of negligence had been filed but simply if a client learned that a lawyer's insurance had lapsed and the client had not been informed. There are practical issues here regarding the form of the required notice and how a lawyer could establish that notice was sent, but these can be overcome and themselves might serve to encourage lawyers to take extra care their insurance is maintained.

Should There Be Consequences for Failing to Have LPL Insurance?

If a lawyer never faces a potential malpractice claim, the sole consequence of going bare is to save on the cost of insurance unless there is a rigorous requirement to inform potential clients regarding the lack of insurance, which might discourage some potential clients from retaining the lawyer. However, the primary effect of forgoing insurance is probably to prevent harmed clients from bringing actions against the lawyer because of potential problems of collecting any judgment. As discussed in Chapter 7, few knowledgeable plaintiffs' lawyers with expertise in LPL cases will pursue a claim against an uninsured lawyer.

Surprisingly, there seems to be little in the way of consequences for lawyers who fail to pay an LPL judgment.[11] Although there are aspects of the rules governing lawyers' professional conduct that would seem to apply, finding examples in which they were applied is difficult; this might simply reflect that few claims are pursued against uninsured lawyers. There are at least two sections of the Model Rules of Professional Conduct that would apply: "Rule 3.4(c): knowingly disobey an obligation under the rules of a tribunal except for an open refusal based on an assertion that no valid obligation exists [and] Rule 8.4(d): engage in conduct that is prejudicial to the administration of justice."[12] However, both of these rules as applicable to failing to pay a judgment suggest a conscious decision not to pay; the rules might not apply if the issue were an inability to pay.[13]

One possible way to encourage lawyers to carry liability insurance short of requiring it would be to impose automatic disbarment or suspension for failing to pay a malpractice judgment or settlement. Although this would be unlikely to incentivize lawyers who are experienced at prosecuting LPL claims to take cases in which the lawyer-defendant lacked insurance, it would provide a tool to encourage uninsured lawyers to pay a judgment in a case prosecuted by a lawyer who took on the case without knowing about the lack of insurance. Most importantly, even the *potential* loss of the license to practice would serve to encourage lawyers to avoid practicing without insurance.

ALTERNATIVES FOR REDRESS

A very different approach to increasing options for clients who have suffered harm because of the negligence or other actions of their attorneys would be to move away from having to pursue claims through the courts by filing a tort or contract suit. A range of dispute-resolution mechanisms could serve this function.

A Legal Ombudsman

One option might be some type of legal ombudsman with the power to recommend, or even impose, resolutions in claims brought against lawyers. England has a legal services ombudsman (LeO) to deal with claims related to legal services.[14] The LeO's remit is to resolve disputes between legal services providers and their clients, and it can require a provider to compensate the client as much as £30,000.[15] Although formally the LeO does not have jurisdiction when the issue is negligence on the part of the provider,[16] in practice it does deal with many claims that arguably arise from negligence on the part of practitioners.[17]

In principle, there is no reason an ombudsman service might not be allowed to deal with negligence claims involving claimed damages below some moderate limit. It is worth noting that, according to the 2012–2015 ABA Standing Committee on Lawyers' Professional Liability report on legal malpractice claims, 75 percent of paid claims provided no more than $25,000 in compensation, and 86 percent provided no more than $50,000 (in nominal dollars).[18] The data from the Oregon State Bar's Professional Liability Fund (PLF) are very similar: in 89 percent of paid claims, the payment (in nominal dollars) was $50,000 or less, and in 78 percent of claims it was $25,000 or less. An even larger proportion of all claims would probably be less than $25,000 or $50,000 if an ombudsman-type system were available because such programs are designed to allow a claimant to proceed without professional representation.[19]

Some might argue that although an ombudsman-type scheme might work for claims related to quality of service, such schemes have no place when the problems involve judgments about professional decisions. Potentially, claims could be excluded if the issue were whether the lawyer properly exercised professional judgment. However, many, possibly even most, claims involve something other than issues of questionable judgment, and in the United States it is already the case that we ultimately empower laypeople to decide whether a lawyer was negligent provided certain conditions are met. Hence, although the formal exclusion of negligence might make sense in England, where trials of cases alleging negligence are heard by professional judges without a lay jury, that argument cannot be sustained in the United States, where cases do go to lay juries.

The ombudsman service we have in mind as a potential model is the Financial Ombudsman Service (FOS) in England.[20] The FOS has jurisdiction over complaints with banks, insurance companies, and other financial service providers such as stockbrokers. The FOS deals both with problems related to poor service and problems of the kind that can lead to lawsuits (e.g., failure to inform as required by law, misrepresentation of the terms of a product, etc.).

After receiving a formal complaint, FOS conducts an investigation and makes a determination as to whether the complaint has validity.[21] If that body determines that a claim is not valid, the FOS will dismiss it, advising the complainant that he or she may initiate formal legal action if the complainant is not satisfied with the FOS's decision. If FOS does find the complaint is valid, it tries to broker a resolution between the complainant and the company. If that attempt is not successful, FOS makes a formal determination and issues an order for compensation up to as much as £150,000.[22] If the complainant is dissatisfied with the amount of compensation, he or she can go to court. However, the company is bound by the ombudsman's decision and may not go to court if it is dissatisfied with the outcome. One important aspect of what the FOS does is that it employs an inquisitorial-style process in which the burden is on the FOS to assemble relevant information.[23] This means that a complainant normally does not need legal representation.

Beyond the issue of whether an ombudsman service modeled on the FOS would work for claims of legal negligence in the United States, something that cannot be determined without trying such a system, a couple of practical issues should be addressed regarding such a system for legal negligence or other professional liability claims. The ombudsman services in England and Wales, and there are several others in addition to the LeO and FOS, serve a population of 57 million people.[24] They have substantial volumes of claims, 73,000 in the first two years of the LeO[25] and more than half a million in 2014 for the FOS.[26] This kind of volume allows for the development both of expertise among investigators and of systems for dealing with claims. The two most populous states in the United States, California and Texas, have populations of 37 million and 27 million, respectively. These states could probably support their own ombudsman service, as could New York and Florida, each having about 20 million residents. However, for many states, there would not be a sufficient volume of complaints to have a viable operation. A solution to the problem of volume could be for several states to form a joint service, with investigators assigned to one or two specific states in order to have adequate knowledge about any state-specific legal issues.

The second issue concerns whether a system that denied the lawyer respondent the option of going to court if the respondent were dissatisfied with a negative outcome would run afoul of the civil jury, due process, or equal protection clauses of the federal or state constitutions. The argument that it would not violate constitutional protections would be that there is no right to practice law, and the state has the power to impose a requirement that practitioners accept a negative decision by the ombudsman as a condition of being granted a license to practice in the state or as a condition of being admitted *pro hoc vice.*[27]

Regarding the second issue, it is also worth noting that an ombudsman service has value not just to the complainant but also to the respondent. The forerunner of the English FOS was a similar service established by a group of major insurance companies in the 1970s. The independent Insurance Ombudsman Service (IOS) operated in ways similar to the FOS, including the power to order an insurer to pay compensation.[28] One of the payoffs from the industry's viewpoint was that even a decision by the IOS denying the claim usually mollified the complainant, and the industry came to realize that this kind of dispute-resolution mechanism was a useful way to deal with unhappy consumers who refused to accept the company's own rejection of their complaints.[29] It is also noteworthy that in FOS cases, although a complainant retains the right to go to court but the responding company does not, the company may introduce the negative decision of the FOS as part of its defense in any lawsuit.[30]

Other Dispute Resolution Mechanisms

In Australia, the legislation regulating lawyers provides a right for consumers to seek redress for a "consumer dispute" in an administrative tribunal. One such tribunal is the Victoria Civil and Administrative Tribunal, which operates a "legal practice list" to deal with disputes between consumers and their lawyers when clients allege that their lawyers caused them to suffer a financial loss. The tribunal can hear disputes arising under the Legal Profession Uniform Law (Victoria), Legal Profession Act 2004 and Fair Trading Act 1998, or the Australian Consumer Law and Fair Trading Act 2012.[31] Compensation is limited to AU$25,000. Over a three-year period ending with 2014–2015, about 200 cases were handled through the legal practice list,[32] although there is no information on how many of those cases involved claims of negligence or other kinds of LPL.[33]

In the Netherlands, the Dutch Bar Association established a Consumer Complaints Board (CCB) to handle matters involving a maximum claim of €10,000. The volume handled by the CCB has been quite small, well under 100 cases per year for the three-year period 2011–2013. How many of the matters involved allegations of negligence or related issues is unknown.[34]

Under the Federal Lawyers' Act in Germany, regional bar associations are required to offer a dispute-resolution mechanism to deal with disputes between a lawyer and a client. These programs are binding only if both parties agree. The programs were not established with negligence issues in mind but might be used for such issues. Regardless of the basis of the dispute, the programs are generally limited in the compensation they can confer; for example, the program run by the Federal Bar Association has a limit of €15,000.[35]

Finally, in Israel, the disciplinary tribunal can order a lawyer to provide a limited amount of compensation to an aggrieved client when a disciplinary violation caused harm to the client. The maximum compensation is 25,000 NIS (about $6,500).[36]

ONE-WAY FEE SHIFTING TO MAKE SMALLER CASES ECONOMICAL

A major issue for a large proportion of potential LPL claims that involve relatively modest damages is obtaining legal representation. The amount of potential damages is too small for a knowledgeable lawyer to be willing to handle the case on a contingency-fee basis; in addition, it is not feasible to pursue the claim paying a lawyer on an hourly basis because the costs of representation would exceed or consume much of the damages that might be recovered.

The problem of obtaining representation in modest but otherwise meritorious claims arises because of the general rule in US civil procedure that each side bears its own litigation costs. However, there are some exceptions. Alaska has a general, but partial, two-way fee shifting rule,[37] and there are a range of state and federal statutory provisions imposing a one-way fee shift on a losing defendant.[38] The various one-way rules have been adopted specifically to facilitate access to justice by plaintiffs who otherwise would have difficulty obtaining representation. In one state, New Jersey, the state supreme court in *Saffer v. Willoughby* imposed a one-way fee shift on lawyers found liable in legal malpractice cases, stating, "A negligent attorney is responsible for the reasonable legal expenses and attorney fees incurred by a former client in prosecuting a legal malpractice action. . . . [These] are consequential damages that are proximately related to the malpractice."[39]

Meritorious but modest legal malpractice claims would be facilitated by some type of provision requiring a lawyer found liable or who otherwise agrees to pay compensation to pay the reasonable fee of the claimant's lawyer. For such a rule to be effective, the fee shift would have to apply in cases resolved by settlement. An issue would be on what basis to compute a fee shift, and whether the fee shift should include an enhancement for the claimant's lawyer having taken the risk of no fee if the claim were unsuccessful. The fee payable by the lawyer-defendant would have to be computed on some type of time/hourly basis rather than as a percentage of any recovery. The threat of no fee in an unsuccessful case would provide an element of control on the plaintiff's lawyer spending a lot of unnecessary time on a case in order to build up the potential fee, and the plaintiff's lawyer could be required to provide an accounting of his or her time that would be subject to objection from the defendant or the defendant's insurer. The hourly rate could be based on the prevailing local hourly rate for insurance defense multiplied by some enhancement factor; that is, it could be what is commonly referred to as a lodestar fee in the context of class actions.[40] Several decisions by New Jersey appellate courts applying the *Saffer* decision found that a lodestar approach was the appropriate way to calculate the fee payable by the losing defendant.[41]

The goal here is to make handling smaller cases financially viable. Hopefully, this would lead more practitioners to develop sufficient expertise to efficiently and appropriately handle such kinds of cases.

ALLOW NONECONOMIC DAMAGES FOR NONFINANCIAL HARM

As noted previously, one problem in some cases of LPL, particularly when it takes the form of negligence, is that there is real harm, but that harm is not financial in nature. This is most likely in the context of family law, in which a lawyer made errors affecting court decisions about child custody, visitation, and/or parental rights. The law governing negligent infliction of emotional distress (NIED) developed largely in the context of personal injury, with a focus on the emotional impact of injuries to a close family member or close calls directly experienced by the plaintiff him- or herself (e.g., almost being run down because of the negligent operation of a motor vehicle). One of the major challenges in deciding how to deal with NIED claims is a concern that many claims will be brought when the distress involved is no more than what one normally expects to experience as part of life and/or that claimants will exaggerate the emotional impact in order to obtain compensation.

It seems obvious that emotional distress resulting from a lawyer's negligent handling of issues such as child custody or parental rights is real harm and is harm beyond what one expects might be experienced in the normal course of life.[42] However, there is still the problem of how to value that kind of distress. This might be one type of harm regarding which the only practical way is to set amounts of financial compensation through a schedule of damages established by the legislature or by some type of administrative body; any such schedule should have provisions to ensure adjustments for inflation. Exactly how the amounts would be determined, and what factors would be deemed relevant in setting the amounts (e.g., number of children, age of children, etc.) would have to be worked out.

A counterargument to this proposal is that most errors of the type referenced in this section should be amenable to claim repair, that is, they are correctable. However, even if the errors are corrected, the nature of the emotional distress caused by the errors should be compensable, particularly if the correction takes time to be implemented. Furthermore, any expense involved in correcting the errors should be compensable. Arguably, this is also the kind of claim that would be made more feasible by the availability of fee shifting.

APPLY THE LOSS-OF-CHANCE DOCTRINE TO LPL CASES

One of the major challenges facing plaintiffs in LPL cases is proving that the lawyer's action caused the plaintiff financial harm. This is analogous to a situation common in medical liability in cases arising from the death of a patient.

The problem is that in many such cases the error was one of a missed, and hence delayed, diagnosis of what turned out to be a fatal condition. If the condition had been diagnosed when it should have been, the probability of survival would have been higher than when the condition was finally diagnosed. The issue in such cases is that even if the condition had been diagnosed earlier, the patient might not have survived.

For purposes of discussion, we define "full damages" as the amount a tortfeasor who was 100 percent responsible for someone's death would in theory owe, even if the amount paid were limited by the tortfeasor's ability to pay and/or the limits of the tortfeasor's insurance policy. With this in mind, consider two situations of medical negligence in which the patient died. In the first situation, the patient would have had a 60 percent chance of survival, but by the time of the actual diagnosis the survival chance was only 20 percent. In the second situation, the initial chance of survival was only 40 percent, with a survival chance again reduced to 20 percent. Following the normal "more likely than not" standard for civil cases, the claim on behalf of the now-deceased patient would be for full compensation in the first situation, but no compensation would be available in the second situation. In the first situation it was more likely than not that the patient's death was because of the provider's negligence, whereas that was not the case in the second situation. This is essentially the standard analysis for liability in a civil claim.

An alternative approach exists for medical negligence claims that involves the "loss of chance doctrine."[43] Under the loss of chance doctrine, the amount of the claim is for full damages times the reduction in the loss of chance attributable to the negligence; this applies even if the initial chance of survival were less than 50 percent. Consequently, in the first situation, the claim would be for 40 percent (60–20) of the full damages, and 20 percent (40–20) in the second situation.[44] There are two hybrid approaches. First, a successful claim involving a patient who had greater than an initial 50 percent chance of survival receives damages proportional to the loss of chance, but no damages are payable if the initial chance of survival had been less than or equal to 50 percent.[45] Second, full damages are payable in a claim in which the original chance of survival was greater than 50 percent, with the proportional approach used only for claims in which the original chance of survival was 50 percent or less.[46]

Turning back to the LPL context, the clearest analogous situation involves cases arising from unsuccessful litigation in which the plaintiff lost or was denied the opportunity to proceed with a claim because of an error such as the lawyer missing an important deadline that barred the case from proceeding. Short of a situation in which the defendant in the underlying case had acknowledged liability, there is no way to know with 100 percent certainty that a trial in the underlying case (the case within the case) would have resulted in a verdict for the plaintiff. The uncertainty over what might have happened at trial in the underlying case within the case can be resolved at a trial of the legal LPL by having a trial within the trial. However, the issue of concern is getting beyond a summary judgment because, as discussed in Chapter 3, some states require the plaintiff to produce an expert who will testify that the plaintiff would have won at trial, and absent that testimony the defendant will win the summary judgment motion, ending the case. Applying the loss-of-chance logic would be a way of getting around that issue.

This change, which to date courts have rejected,[47] would be significant because it is likely one could find experts able and willing to testify to the probability of a claim succeeding at trial even if it is not possible to find someone willing to testify to some standard of certainty that a case would have been successful at trial. Of course, it is likely that there would be differences between the testimony of the plaintiff's expert and the defendant's expert, but this is simply part of the adversarial process and is no different from experts providing conflicting testimony as to the chances of survival in a medical malpractice case. Such a system could incorporate a threshold rule of some sort whereby no recovery would be allowed unless the plaintiff's chance of success in the case within the case were to be found to meet or exceed the required threshold; one such threshold could be 50 percent, which would correspond to the "more likely than not" interpretation of the preponderance of the evidence standard in civil litigation. We note also that something akin to this type of loss-of-chance computation would potentially work well with an ombudsman-type arrangement.

STATUTE OF LIMITATIONS PROBLEM

A final area for potential reform that would allow more victims of legal malpractice to seek redress concerns the statutes of limitations. For claims involving LPL, the statutes of limitations vary from as little as one year in some states (e.g., Kentucky[48] and Louisiana[49]) up to six years in other states (e.g., Hawaii[50] and Wisconsin[51]). As also discussed in Chapter 3, the length is not the only problem; there is also the issue of when the statute of limitations starts to run.

In some states the statute of limitations runs from when the act or error occurred regardless of when the claimant became aware, or reasonably could have become aware, of the lawyer's error or behavior. In other states the statute of limitations does not start until the damages accrue regardless of when the claimant becomes aware of the harm. In still other states either of these rules is modified so that they depend on when the claimant became aware of the error or harm, or reasonably could have learned of the error or harm.[52] For example, if a lawyer tells his client that he made an error that could lead to greater tax liability because the tax authorities might treat some issue differently than intended but that they will not know for some time how the tax authorities will in fact treat it, the client might think it is best to just wait and see what the tax authorities do, and then pursue a claim only if and when it becomes clear that the outcome is negative. It might turn out that before the tax issue is resolved, the statute of limitations has run out, and any claim against the lawyer who made the error producing the negative tax consequence is time-barred.[53]

The statute of limitations problem was an issue raised by several of the plaintiffs' lawyers with whom we spoke. They reported that it was not unusual to have an otherwise good claim that was time-barred because the potential claimant did not realize that the statute of limitations clock started running as soon as the former lawyer informed the client of a possible problem. The plaintiffs' lawyers also reported that they sometimes must rush to initiate a lawsuit if the clock was getting close to the buzzer, although they had had situations where an insurer was willing to toll the statute while it conducted its own investigation with an eye to possibly settling the claim without a suit being filed.

There is an inconsistency with the requirement that a claimant might have suffered some actual financial harm and having the statute of limitations start running while the harm is only possible and has not actually occurred. Resolving this inconsistency, and retaining the requirement that there must be actual harm or loss, one of the cornerstones of the law of negligence, would seem to dictate that the statute of limitations cannot start until the harm has occurred.

REDUCING THE ACCESS TO JUSTICE PROBLEM

This chapter has discussed a range of possible changes to the current law and procedures governing LPL that would reduce the problems of individuals and small businesses in obtaining redress for harm caused by the negligence or other actions of their lawyers. Critics of these proposals will raise several objections.

First, some will say that making it easier for disgruntled clients to pursue claims against lawyers will encourage frivolous claims. Anything that makes bringing claims easier will encourage both meritorious and nonmeritorious claims. The lawyers who would probably be most adamant regarding the risk of frivolous claims are members of the plaintiffs' bar. Any cries of concern about frivolous claims coming from that sector of the profession would be ironic given its opposition to changes that would make it more difficult to pursue claims against physicians, hospitals, and manufacturers.

Second, some will argue that changes such as requiring private-practice lawyers to have LPL insurance will increase the costs of legal services, which in turn would reduce access to justice by making those services less affordable to the very group such a requirement would protect. However, the $300,000 base coverage in Oregon costs only $3,500 per year, probably less than many lawyers pay for auto insurance. Moreover, assuming a lawyer delivers 1,400 hours of professional services in a year, at $3,500 per year the cost of insurance is $2.50 per hour, a figure unlikely to significantly affect affordability. The requirement would be a problem for those working part-time or exclusively handling pro bono matters or matters such as *guardian ad litem* work for the family court; however, special arrangements for such situations are possible.

Third, for some lawyers, LPL insurance might be considerably more expensive than what it costs in Oregon, either because of the kind of work they do or because of their past claims experience. This could certainly be true in the absence of a program such as that in Oregon, which insures all comers at a fixed rate. It is even possible that some lawyers would be denied insurance in the commercial market.[54] If the cost of insurance were such that a lawyer with a bad claims record would be forced out of practice, that might be a positive. The cost of insurance might be high for some specific areas of practice, pushing up the cost of legal services for that type of work; however, this is no different from the issue faced by physicians and surgeons working in high-risk areas (e.g., obstetrics or neurosurgery) or a manufacturer who produces something that has a high risk of leading to liability claims while also having substantial utility.

Fourth, some would argue that requiring uninsured lawyers to inform clients of their lack of insurance will discourage potential clients from retaining the uninsured lawyers. That is in fact a positive because the goal is to make it less likely that a lawyer will choose to practice without insurance. This is evident from the low percentage of uninsured lawyers in South Dakota, where uninsured lawyers are required to include on their stationery and with every written communication to their clients a statement to the effect that they lack insurance.

In summary, although objections might be raised to many of the proposals discussed in this chapter, those objections serve to highlight the problems of the current system more than they represent strong arguments against the proposals.

Notes

CHAPTER 1. INTRODUCTION

1. *McKnight v. Dean*, 279 F.3d 513, 518 (2001).

2. *Hall and Hall v. Fedor*, 561 S.E.2d 654 (2002 S.Car. App.).

3. Gordon Gibb, "Legal Malpractice Verdict against Largest Law Firm on Planet," November 12, 2010, https://www.lawyersandsettlements.com/articles/legal-malpractice/legal-malpractice-law-12-15382.html, accessed February 17, 2016.

4. *Baker & McKenzie LLP v. Evans*, 123 So.3d 386 (Miss., 2013). Our discussion provides only a highly simplified version of the background of this case; the Mississippi Supreme Court decision provides a detailed discussion of that background.

5. Douglas Richmond to Herbert Kritzer, e-mail, February 17, 2016.

6. The major treatise on legal malpractice is Ronald E. Mallen and Jeffrey M. Smith with Allison D. Rhodes, *Legal Malpractice: Liability, Prevention, Litigation, Insurance* (Edina, MN: Thomson Reuters, 2017). A short treatment of the law of legal malpractice can be found in Vincent R. Johnson, *Legal Malpractice Law in a Nutshell* (St. Paul, MN: West, 2011); see also Susan Saab Fortney and Vincent R. Johnson, *Legal Malpractice Law: Problems and Prevention* (St. Paul, MN: Thomson West, 2008).

7. See http://selectusa.commerce.gov/industry-snapshots/professional-services-industry-united-states.html, accessed June 13, 2015. The Commerce Department reported revenue for five service subsectors: accounting, architectural services, engineering services, legal services, and management consulting. The next highest subsector was engineering services at $184.1 billion.

8. Centers for Medicare & Medicaid Services, National Health Expenditure Projections 2012–2022, http://www.cms.gov/Research-Statistics-Data-and-Systems/Statistics-Trends-and-Reports/NationalHealthExpendData/downloads/proj2012.pdf, accessed June 13, 2015. The other two components of health-care expenditures, hospitals and prescription drugs, totaled $892.4 billion and $260.8 billion, respectively.

9. See, for example, Eugene F. Sanger, "Malpractice," *Transactions of the Maine Medical Association* 6 (1879): 360–382. For academic discussions of the early development of medical malpractice litigation, see Charles J. Weigel III, "Medical Malpractice in America's Middle Years," *Texas Reports on Biology and Medicine* 32, no. 1 (Spring 1974): 191–205; James C. Mohr, *Doctors and the Law: Medical Jurisprudence in Nineteenth-Century America.* (New York: Oxford University Press, 1993); and Robert I. Field, "The Medical Malpractice Crisis Turns 175: What Lessons Does History Hold for Reform?" *Drexel Law Review* 4, no. 1 (2011): 7–39.

10. See Tom Baker, *The Medical Malpractice Myth* (Chicago, IL: University of Chicago Press, 2005), or Nora Freeman Engstrom, "A Dose of Reality for Specialized Courts: Lessons from the FICP," *University of Pennsylvania Law Review* 163, no. 6 (2015): 1644–1647, for good summaries of what is known about the incidence of medical malpractice. See Bernard Black, Charles Silver, David A. Hyman, and William M. Sage, "Stability, Not Crisis:

Medical Malpractice Claim Outcomes in Texas, 1988–2002," *Journal of Empirical Legal Studies* 2, no. 2 (2005): 207–259; and David A. Hyman, Mohammad Rahmati, Bernard Black, and Charles Silver, "Insurance Crisis or Liability Crisis? Medical Malpractice Claiming in Illinois, 1980–2010," *Journal of Empirical Legal Studies* 13, no. 2 (2016): 183–204, for evidence that the system of redress for medical malpractice has remained reasonably stable over a period of 25–30 years. For a discussion of how juries deal with medical malpractice cases, see Neil Vidmar, *Medical Malpractice and the American Jury: Confronting the Myths about Jury Incompetence, Deep Pockets, and Outrageous Damage Awards* (Ann Arbor: University of Michigan Press, 1995).

11. William C. Redington Sr., PowerPoint accompanying keynote address at Ninth Annual Errors and Omissions Liability Insurance ExecuSummit, Ucasville, Connecticut (June 16–17, 2016); William Redington to Herbert Kritzer, e-mail, May 16, 2016. For the medical arena, Redington provides separate figures for "claims made" policies (insurance covers all claims made during a time period regardless of when the alleged injury occurred) and "occurrence" policies (insurance covers claims when the injury occurred regardless of when the claim was made), but breaks out physicians and surgeons only for "claims made" policies; we arrived at the estimate of $5.6 billion for physicians and surgeons by assuming that the proportion of "occurrence" policy premiums attributable to physicians and surgeons was the same as the proportion for "claims made" policies. Note that the figures for the legal profession are almost certainly an understatement of the total expenditure on liability claims because most liability insurance for lawyers includes some form of deductible, often quite sizeable, whereas few medical malpractice policies have deductibles.

12. See John P. Heinz and Edward O. Laumann, *Chicago Lawyers: The Social Structure of the Bar* (New York: Russell Sage Foundation, 1982), 319; see also Alfred Z. Reed, *Training for the Public Profession of the Law* (New York: Carnegie Foundation for the Advancement of Teaching, 1921); Jerome E. Carlin, *Lawyers on Their Own: A Study of Individual Practitioners in Chicago* (New Brunswick, NJ: Rutgers University Press, 1962); and Erwin O. Smigel, *The Wall Street Lawyer: Professional Organization Man?* (Bloomington: Indiana University Press, 1964).

13. A replication of the study in 1995 found that the corporate sector's share of legal effort was up to 64 percent from 53 percent 20 years earlier, whereas the personal services sector's share was down to 29 percent from the previous 40 percent; see John P. Heinz, Robert L. Nelson, Rebecca L. Sandefur, and Edward O. Laumann, *Urban Lawyers: The New Social Structure of the Bar* (Chicago, IL: University of Chicago Press, 2005), 42.

14. Robert L. Nelson, Rebecca L. Sandefur, John P. Heinz, and Edward O. Laumann, "United States: From Professional Dominance to Organisational Dominance—Professionalism, Inequality, and Social Change among Chicago Lawyers, 1975–1995," in *Reorganisation and Resistance: Legal Professions Confront a Changing World*, ed. William L. F. Felstiner (Oxford, UK: Hart, 2005), 320.

15. Brenda Sapino Jeffreys, "Andrews Kurth Hit with Nearly $200M Verdict," *Texas Lawyer* (November 19, 2015); http://www.texaslawyer.com/id=1202742916570/Andrews-Kurth-Hit-with-Nearly-200M-Verdict?slreturn=20160106111130, accessed February 6, 2016. Several months after the verdict, and after post-trial mediation ordered by the trial judge, the

parties settled for an undisclosed amount; see Michelle Casady, "Settlement Reached in $200M Andrews Kurth Malpractice Suit," https://www.law360.com/articles/759999/settlement-reached-in-200m-andrews-kurth-malpractice-suit, accessed April 17, 2017.

16. The discussion in this paragraph draws heavily on National Legal Aid and Defender Association, "History of Legal Aid," http://www.nlada.org/About/About_HistoryCivil, accessed February 4, 2016.

17. Reginald Heber Smith, *Justice and the Poor* (New York: Carnegie Endowment for the Advancement of Teaching, 1919). Smith drew in part on a report from Los Angeles that discussed civil legal aid provided through the public defender's office; see Walton J. Wood, "Necessity of Public Defender Established by Statistics," *Journal of the American Institute of Criminal Law & Criminology* 7, no. 2 (1916): 230–244.

18. Charles E. Clark and Emma Corstvet, "The Lawyer and the Public: An A.A.L.S. Survey," *Yale Law Journal* 47 (1938): 1272–1293.

19. Barbara A Curran, *The Legal Needs of the Public: The Final Report of a National Survey* (Chicago, IL: American Bar Foundation, 1977); Rebecca Sandefur, "What We Know and Need to Know about the Legal Needs of the Public," *South Carolina Law Review* 67, no. 2 (2016): 443–460.

20. Eric H. Steele, "The Historical Context of Small Claims Courts," *American Bar Foundation Research Journal* 1981, no. 2 (1981): 293–376.

21. Charles E. Clark and Richard D. O'Connell, "The Working of the Hartford Small Claims Court," *Connecticut Bar Journal* 3 (1929): 123–129. Later studies usually reported the same pattern; see Barbara Yngvesson and Patricia Hennessey, "Small Claims, Complex Disputes: A Review of the Small Claims Literature," *Law & Society Review* 9, no. 2 (1975): 235–243.

22. Paul F. Douglass, *The Justice of the Peace Courts of Hamilton County, Ohio* (Baltimore, MD: Johns Hopkins University Press, 1932); Paul F. Douglass, *The Mayors' Courts of Hamilton County, Ohio* (Baltimore, MD: Johns Hopkins University Press, 1933).

23. Mauro Cappelletti, ed., *Access to Justice,* 4 vols. (Milan, Italy: Sijthoff and Noordhoff-Alphenaandenrijn, 1979); Bryant G. Garth and Mauro Cappelletti, "Access to Justice: The Newest Wave in the Worldwide Movement to Make Rights Effective," *Buffalo Law Review* 27, no. 1 (1978): 181–292.

24. There is substantial variation around the world as to whether some type of aggregate procedure is available, along with variation in the specific nature of the procedures that do exist; see Deborah R. Hensler, Christopher Hodges, and Magdalena Tulibacka, "The Globalization of Class Actions," *Annals* 622 (March 2009): entire issue.

25. *AT&T Mobility LLC v. Concepcion,* 563 U.S. 333 (2011); *American Express Co. v. Italian Colors Restaurant,* 133 S. Ct. 2304 (2013).

26. See Jessica Silver-Greenberg and Robert Gebeloff, "Arbitration Everywhere, Stacking the Deck of Justice," *New York Times,* October 31, 2015; Lauren Guth Barnes, "How Mandatory Arbitration Agreements and Class Action Waivers Undermine Consumer Rights and Why We Need Congress to Act," *Harvard Law & Policy Review* 9, no. 2 (2015): 329–354.

27. *2007 Texas Liability Insurance: Closed Claim Annual Report* (Austin: Texas Department of Insurance), 21, 25, http://www.tdi.texas.gov/reports/pc/documents/taccar2007.pdf,

accessed February 3, 2016. After 2007, the reporting rules changed such that the split was at $25,000 rather than $10,000.

28. See Ronald J. Bacigal, *The Limits of Litigation: The Dalkon Shield Controversy* (Durham, NC: Carolina Academic Press, 1990); Richard B. Sobol, *Bending the Law: The Story of the Dalkon Shield Bankruptcy* (Chicago, IL: University of Chicago Press, 1991).

29. See Jonathan Harr, *A Civil Action* (New York: Random House, 1995).

30. See Joseph Sanders, *Bendectin on Trial: A Study of Mass Tort Litigation* (Ann Arbor: University of Michigan Press, 1998).

31. Other types of contingency arrangements are sometimes used; see Herbert M. Kritzer, *Risks, Reputations, and Rewards: Contingency Fee Legal Practice in the United States* (Stanford, CA: Stanford University Press, 2004), 40.

32. See Stella Yarrow, *The Price of Success: Lawyers, Clients, and Conditional Fees* (London: Policy Studies Institute, 1998); Virginia G. Maurer, Robert E. Thomas, and Pamela A. Debooth, "Attorney Fee Arrangements: The U.S. and Western European Perspectives," *Northwestern Journal of International Law and Business* 19, no. 2 (1999): 307–316.

33. Jon Robins, "The Price of Success," *Law Society Gazette* (January 7, 1999): 14–15; Ed Gretton, "Jackson—an Overview," *Law Society Gazette* (March 25, 2013), http://www.lawgazette.co.uk/analysis/jackson-an-overview/70126.fullarticle, accessed February 5, 2016. For a history of the rise and fall of the "recoverable conditional fee," see John Peysner, *Access to Justice: A Critical Analysis of Recoverable Conditional Fees and No-Win No-Fee Funding* (Houndsmills, UK: Palgrave Macmillan, 2014).

34. Eleni Skordaki and Danielle Walker, *Regulating and Charging for Legal Services: An International Comparison* (London: Law Society, 1994), 26.

35. See Hazel Genn, *Hard Bargaining: Out of Court Settlement in Personal Injury Actions* (Oxford, UK: Oxford University Press, 1988), 109–110.

36. See Frederick H. Zemans, ed., *Perspectives on Legal Aid: An International Survey* (Westport, CT: Greenwood, 1979).

37. See Alan Paterson, "Legal Aid at the Crossroads," *Civil Justice Quarterly* 10, no. 2 (April 1991): 124–137.

38. Herbert Jacob, Erhard Blankenburg, Herbert M. Kritzer, Doris Marie Provine, and Joseph Sanders, *Courts, Law, and Politics in Comparative Perspective* (New Haven, CT: Yale University Press, 1996), 139–141.

39. Michael Zander, "The Government's Plans on Legal Aid and Conditional Fees," *Modern Law Review* 61, no. 4 (1998): 538–550.

40. Thomas D. Rowe Jr., "The Legal Theory of Attorney Fee Shifting: A Critical Overview," *Duke Law Journal* 1982, no. 4 (1982): 651–680.

41. See Thomas D. Rowe Jr., "Predicting the Effects of Attorney Fee Shifting," *Law and Contemporary Problems* 47, no. 1 (Winter 1984): 139–172.

42. Werner Pfennigstorf, "The European Experience with Attorney Fee Shifting," *Law and Contemporary Problems* 47, no. 1 (Winter 1984): 37–124.

43. Susanne Di Pietro and Teresa W. Carns, "Alaska's English Rule: Attorney's Fee Shifting in Civil Cases," *Alaska Law Review* 13, no. 1 (1996): 33–93.

44. Susan M. Olson, "How Much Access to Justice from State 'Equal Access to Justice

Acts'?" *Chicago-Kent Law Review* 71, no. 2 (1994): 547–582; Susan Gluck Mezey and Susan M. Olson, "Fee Shifting and Public Policy: The Equal Access to Justice Act," *Judicature* 77, no. 1 (1993): 13–20.

45. Gretton, "Jackson—an Overview."

46. Lowell E. Baker, "Reforming the Equal Access to Justice Act," *Journal of Legislation* 38, no. 1 (2012): 38, 62.

47. See *Saffer v. Willoughby*, 143 N.J. 256 (1996).

48. Bennett J. Waserman, "Recovering Damages in Legal Malpractice Cases," *New Jersey Law Journal* (January 21, 2013): 3; http://www.legalmalpracticelawreview.com/wp-content/uploads/sites/271/2013/02/2013-Wasserman-1_21_13.pdf, accessed February 6, 2016.

49. William L. F. Felstiner, Richard L. Abel, and Austin Sarat, "The Emergence and Transformation of Disputes: Naming, Blaming, Claiming . . ." *Law & Society Review* 15, no. 3 (1980–1981): 631–654; Neil Vidmar and Regina A. Schuller, "Individual Differences and the Pursuit of Legal Rights," *Law and Human Behavior* 11, no. 4 (1987): 299–317; Herbert M. Kritzer, "Propensity to Sue in England and the United States: Blaming and Claiming in Tort Cases," *Journal of Law and Society* 18, no. 4 (1991): 400–427.

50. Ellen Berrey, Robert L. Nelson, and Laura Beth Nielsen, *Rights on Trial: How Workplace Discrimination Law Perpetuates Inequality* (Chicago, IL: University of Chicago Press, 2017), 46.

51. Tom Baker, *The Medical Malpractice Myth* (Chicago, IL: University of Chicago Press, 2005), 22–36.

52. In the United Kingdom, there has been a movement to use a system of peer review of solicitors' files to assess the quality of representation; see Avrom Sherr, Richard Moorhead, and Alan Paterson, "Assessing the Quality of Legal Work: Measuring Process," *International Journal of the Legal Profession* 1, no. 2 (1994): 135–158; Avrom Sherr and Alan Paterson, "Professional Competence: Peer Review and Quality Assurance," *Alberta Law Review* 45, no. 5 (2008): 151–168. Generally, this type of assessment has been limited to solicitors paid through legal aid and required to consent to such reviews in order to handle legal aid clients. Even so, this approach has been used in only a very limited way to identify harmful errors, similarly that in the medical arena. Sherr reports that one assessment found that 6.6 percent of files reviewed in criminal matters showed that errors by solicitors had caused harm to their clients; Sherr to Herbert Kritzer, e-mail, February 3, 2016.

53. Robert MacCoun, "Blaming Others to a Fault?" *Chance: New Directions for Statistics and Computing* 6, no. 4 (Fall 1993): 31–33, 18; Jeffrey O'Connell and C. Brian Kelly, *The Blame Game: Injuries, Insurance, and Injustice* (Cambridge, MA: Lexington, 1987); Janice Nadler, "Blaming as a Social Process: The Influence of Character and Moral Emotion on Blame," *Law & Contemporary Problems* 75, no. 2 (2012): 1–32.

54. Baker, *Medical Malpractice*, 90. The American Medical Association published an advertisement in 2012 in support of a proposal before Congress, the Medical Liability Reform Act (H.R. 5), that would limit liability in the case of injuries sustained during medical treatment; in that advertisement "frivolous" lawsuits were driving up health-care costs, http://www.scjusticereport.com/2011/05/myths-vs-facts-the-american-medical-associations-numbers-dont-add-up.shtml, accessed February 5, 2016. The assertion that frivolous

medical malpractice lawsuits are common is a standard part of the campaign for limitations conducted by the American Tort Reform Association; see http://www.atra.org/newsroom/frivolous-lawsuits-undermine-healthcare-system-and-hurt-patients-according-new-survey, accessed February 5, 2016.

55. Several articles on lawyers' professional liability in countries other than the United States appeared in the *International Journal of the Legal Profession* 24, no. 3 (2017). These articles are based on papers presented at the Workshop on Consumer Redress When Lawyers Are Negligent, International Institute for the Sociology of Law, Oñati, Spain, July 9–10, 2015.

56. Leslie C. Levin, "Lawyers Going Bare and Clients Going Blind," *Florida Law Review* 68, no. 5 (2016): 1281–1331.

57. Leslie C. Levin, "Regulators at the Margins: The Impact of Malpractice Insurers on Solo and Small-Firm Lawyers," *Connecticut Law Review* 49, no. 2 (2016): 553–612.

58. Tom Baker and Rick Swedloff, "Liability Insurer Data as a Window on Lawyers' Professional Liability," *UC Irvine Law Review* 5, no. 6 (2015): 1273–1316; Tom Baker and Rick Swedloff, "The Organization of Lawyers' Liability Insurance Companies: Mutual and Stock," paper presented at Workshop on Consumer Redress When Lawyers Are Negligent, International Institute for the Sociology of Law, Oñati, Spain, July 9–10, 2015 (revised version available at SSRN, https://ssrn.com/abstract=2820654); Rick Swedloff and Tom Baker, "Insurers as Bumblebees in the Garden of Law Firm Norms," paper presented at Workshop on Consumer Redress When Lawyers Are Negligent, International Institute for the Sociology of Law, Oñati, Spain, July 9–10, 2015.

59. Werner Pfennigstorf, "Types and Causes of Lawyers' Professional Liability Claims: The Search for Facts," *American Bar Foundation Research Journal* 1980 (1980): 253–302.

60. Duke Nordlinger Stern, "The West Virginia Legal Malpractice Experience," *West Virginia State Bar Journal* 1978 (1978): 135–139, 161; the three other extant reports of this study are Duke Nordlinger Stern, "Lawyers' Professional Liability in Kentucky," *Kentucky Bench & Bar* (October 1978): 14–15; Duke Nordlinger Stern, "Legal Malpractice in Tennessee," *Tennessee Bar Journal* 14, no. 4 (November 1978): 19–24; and Duke Nordlinger Stern, "Causes of Attorney Malpractice Claims," *Professional Liability Reporter* 3 (June 1979): 199–200.

61. Other articles about legal malpractice during this period also refer to an increasing incidence of claims during the 1970s and then extending into the 1980s; see, for example, Fredric L. Goldfein, "Legal Malpractice Insurance," *Temple Law Review* 61, no. 4 (1988): 1285–1299; George M. Cohen, "Legal Malpractice Insurance and Loss Prevention: A Comparative Analysis of Economic Institutions," *Connecticut Insurance Law Journal* 4, no. 1 (1997): 306–351. By the mid-1980s rising claim volume, rising claim payouts, and rising malpractice premiums produced a crisis for firms seeking legal malpractice coverage; see Mary Ann Galante, "Malpractice Rates Zoom," *National Law Journal* (June 3, 1985): 1, 25–26; Mary Ann Galante, "Lawyers Face New Fights on Malpractice Coverage," *National Law Journal* (September 2, 1985): 3, 9; and Mary Ann Galante, "Insurance Costs Soar: Is There Any Way Out?" *National Law Journal* (March 10, 1986): 1, 7–8.

62. William H. Gates, "Lawyers' Malpractice: Some Recent Data about a Growing Problem," *Mercer Law Review* 37, no. 2 (1986): 559–567. See Richard L. Abel, *American Lawyers*

(New York: Oxford University Press, 1989), 154–155, for a brief summary of these findings and some other early statistics on legal malpractice claims.

63. Standing Committee on Lawyers' Professional Liability, *Characteristics of Legal Malpractice: Report of the National Legal Malpractice Data Center* (Chicago, IL: American Bar Association, 1989). Summaries of the reports (through the 2008–2011 report) can be found in Mallen and Smith with Rhodes, *Legal Malpractice, 2016 Edition: Liability, Prevention, Litigation, Insurance* (Eagan, MN: Thomson Reuters, 2016) section 1.6; note that this and future citations to this treatise reference section numbers rather than page numbers because the former will work for later and electronic editions of the treatise.

64. Standing Committee on Lawyers' Professional Liability, *Profile of Legal Malpractice: A Statistical Study of Determinative Characteristics of Claims Asserted against Attorneys* (Chicago, IL: American Bar Association, 1990). According to the report, the analysis was based on individual reports of 29,227 claims from January 1983 through the end of September 1985 (3).

65. Manuel R. Ramos, "Legal Malpractice: The Profession's Dirty Little Secret," *Vanderbilt Law Review* 47, no. 6 (November 1994): 1657–1750; Manuel R. Ramos, "Legal Malpractice: No Lawyer or Client Is Safe," *Florida Law Review* 47, no. 1 (1995): 1–62.

66. Ramos coded information about the 42 cases using the same form used in the original SCLPL study.

67. As will be explained in Chapter 3, PLF is the provider of the mandatory LPL insurance in Oregon.

68. Neil Vidmar and Mirya Holman, "Legal Malpractice: Ordinary Claims, Mega-Payments, and Punitive Damages," paper presented at 2010 Law and Society Association Annual Meeting, Chicago, Illinois, May 26–29, 2010.

69. Florida Statutes, 627.912(1)(c)4.

70. Lori Andrews, "Studying Medical Error in Situ: Implications for Malpractice Law and Policy," *DePaul Law Review* 54, no. 2 (2005): 357–392.

CHAPTER 2. ILLUSTRATIVE CASES OF LAWYERS' PROFESSIONAL LIABILITY

1. In fact, for several reasons there is no way to draw a random sample of legal malpractice claims or even legal malpractice lawsuits. Regarding locating lawsuits, although state courts generally identify which lawsuits involve claims of medical malpractice, we could not find any states that single out legal malpractice as a category, although some do have a broad "professional" malpractice category.

2. See Gregg Stevens and Lorin Subar, "Confidentiality in Settlement Agreement Is a Virtual Necessity," *GP Solo* 29, no. 6 (November/December 2012): 24, 28–29, http://www.americanbar.org/publications/gp_solo/2012/november_december2012privacyandconfidentiality/confidentiality_settlement_agreements_is_virtual_necessity.html, accessed August 5, 2016.

3. This contrasts in part to claims brought against physicians; all such claims that involve payment must be reported to the National Practitioner Data Bank. One state, Missouri, does require that all legal malpractice claims received by insurers be reported to the state insurance authorities; however, the information reported is limited, and no information is available that would make it possible to potentially obtain more detailed information about individual cases.

4. *Kranendonk v. Gregory & Swapp*, 2014 UT App 36, http://www.utcourts.gov/opinions/appopin/kranendonk21314.pdf, accessed August 10, 2016; S. P. Bailey, "Jury Trial: *Kranendock v. Craig Swapp and Associates*" (March 10, 2015), http://spbailey.net/blog/2015/10/5/jury-trial-kranendonk-v-craig-swapp-and-associates, accessed August 10, 2016; "Ogden Woman's Malpractice Lawsuit Against Law Firm to Continue," *Ogden Standard Examiner* (March 28, 2014), http://www.standard.net/Local/2014/02/17/Ogden-woman-s-malpractice-lawsuit-against-law-firm-to-continue, accessed August 10, 2016; "Malpractice Lawsuit Against Salt Lake City Firm Ends, Awards Ogden Woman $4.7M," *Ogden Standard Examiner* (April 29, 2016), http://www.standard.net/Courts/2016/04/28/Malpractice-lawsuit-against-Salt-Lake-City-firm-ends-awards-Ogden-woman-4-7M, accessed August 10, 2016.

5. The law firm was (and still is) known for its advertising slogan, "One Call, That's All," on television and radio, https://www.craigswapp.com/one-call-thats-all/, accessed August 10, 2016.

6. Oregon Revised Statute sec. 12.110(1) (2016).

7. Washington Revised Code sec. 4.16.080(2) (2016).

8. Oregon Revised Statute sec. 12.220 (2016).

9. *Reece and Long v. Clifford Law Offices et al.*, 2015 Ill App (1st) 1140810-I in Appellate Court of Illinois First Judicial District (March 30, 2015), http://www.illinoiscourts.gov/r23_orders/AppellateCourt/2015/1stDistrict/1140810_R23.pdf, accessed September 30, 2016.

10. *Res ipsa loquitur* essentially means that the event was such that it could only be a result of negligence, and hence the plaintiff in a case such as this one would not need to present evidence as to exactly what caused the elevator malfunction.

11. See 735 ILCS 5/13-202.

12. Whereas the statute of limitations for personal injury in Illinois is two years, it is six years for legal malpractice; see 735 ILCS 5/13-214.3.

13. The suit included several other specific allegations of negligence by CLO.

14. With regard to the fraudulent concealment claim, the trial court found that Reece and Long had failed to plead "detrimental reliance," which under Illinois law is required in order to sustain a claim of fraudulent concealment.

15. The appellate decision describes these two claims as having been "forfeited" because of the inadequacy of the appellate brief.

16. The progress of the case can be ascertained from the case docket, https://w3.courtlink.lexisnexis.com/cookcounty/Finddock.asp?DocketKey=CABFoLoAAGJCFoLD, accessed April 12, 2017.

17. The description of this case is based on documents found on Westlaw, including the original complaint (2013 WL 11249575), an expert affidavit (2015 WL 10376778), the trial

order decision dismissing the case (2015 WL 9921333), and the Minnesota Court of Appeals decision upholding that dismissal (2016 WL 4068931).

18. Minnesota Statute sec. 519.11, subd. 2: "Antenuptial or postnuptial contracts or settlements shall be in writing, executed in the presence of two witnesses and acknowledged by the parties, executing the same before any officer or person authorized to administer an oath under the laws of this state."

19. Minnesota Statute sec. 541.05, subd. 1(5). As will be discussed in Chapter 3, there is no legal claim of negligence in the absence of damages.

20. Although there were claims in addition to negligence, the trial court held that everything related back to the single incident of alleged negligence, and hence the applicable standard was that for legal malpractice.

21. *Antone v. Mirviss*, 720 N.W.2d 331, 335 (Minn. 2006).

22. No decision by the Minnesota Supreme Court had been released by the time this book was completed.

23. Mike Mossdale, "Legal Malpractice Case Raises Exposure Fears," *Minnesota Lawyer* (March 14, 2017), http://minnlawyer.com/2017/03/14/legal-malpractice-case-raises-exposure-fears/, accessed April 12, 2017. See also webcast of the oral argument before the Minnesota Supreme Court, http://www.mncourts.gov/SupremeCourt/OralArgumentWebcasts/ArgumentDetail.aspx?cn=A15-2052, accessed April 12, 2017.

24. *Vincent v. DeVries*, Supreme Court of Vermont, 2013 VT 34 (No. 2012-026, October term, 2012), http://www.legalmalpracticeillinois.com/2013/05/; supreme-court-of-vermont-reverses-award.html.

25. Appeals of trial court decisions go directly to the Vermont Supreme Court because Vermont does not have an intermediate appellate court.

26. See *Beal and Bar Plan Mutual Insurance Company v. Blinn* (Case No. 27D03-0705-PL-197), Indiana Court of Appeals, http://www.in.gov/judiciary/opinions/pdf/05071403par.pdf, accessed August 10, 2016; Jennifer Nelson, "Court of Appeals Allows Malpractice Case to Continue," *Indiana Lawyer* (May 7, 2014), http://www.theindianalawyer.com/court-of-appeals-allows-legal-malpractice-case-to-continue/PARAMS/article/34111, accessed August 10, 2016.

27. *Blinn v. Kammen*, 27A04-1008-PL-532 (Ind. Ct. App. June 30, 2011).

28. As part of an unsuccessful settlement strategy, the law firm was eventually dismissed from the suit; see http://www.price-law.com/news-blog/voluntary-dismissal-as-settlement-strategy-not-saved-by-journeys-account-statute/, accessed August 10, 2016.

29. This issue is discussed in more detail in Chapter 3. Other issues included the expert witness testimony and an assertion by the insurance company for Beal's law firm that its policy did not cover the claims against Beal.

30. By the time of the decision, Beal had actually resigned from the Indiana bar. In December 2014, Beal was arrested on charges of forgery and check fraud; see Karla Bowsher, "Beal Turns Himself in on Warrant," *Marion Chronicle-Tribune*, December 16, 2014, http://www.chronicle-tribune.com/news/beal-turns-himself-in-on-warrant/article_3a1a12d8–84c9–11e4-b2da-bfca2fe7163d.html, accessed August 10, 2016.

31. Daniel J. Sernovitz, "Fairfield Investment Co. Sues Wilkes Artis over Allegedly Flawed Tax Credit Advice," *Washington Business Journal*, February 24, 2015, http://www.bizjournals

.com/washington/breaking_ground/2015/02/fairfield-investment-co-suing-wilkes-artis.html, accessed June 13, 2016; Daniel J. Sernovitz, "Wilkes Artis, Fairfield Settle Suit over Claims of Flawed Tax Credit Advice," *Washington Business Journal,* March 17, 2016, http://www.bizjournals.com/washington/breaking_ground/2016/03/wilkes-artis-fairfield-settle-suit-over-allegedly.html, accessed June 13, 2016.

32. *Fairfield Investment Company v. Wilkes Artis Chartered et al.*, US District Court, District of Maryland, Docket 8:15-cv-00428-PJM.

33. Martha Neil, "Ex-Bull Scottie Pippen Blames Law Firm for Bad Investments, Seeks $8M at Trial," *ABA Journal* (June 9, 2010), http://www.abajournal.com/news/article/ex-bull_scottie_pippen_blames_law_firm_for_bad_investments/; Martha Neil, "Scottie Pippen Scores $2 M Verdict in Law Firm Malpractice Case," *ABA Journal* (June 30, 2010), http://www.abajournal.com/news/article/scottie_pippen_scores_2m_verdict_in_law_firm_malpractice_case/, accessed June 13, 2016; "Attorney Malpractice—Ex-Bull Blames His Counsel for Investment Losses," *Cook County Jury Verdict Reporter* (September 3, 2010).

34. See William Lynch Schaller, "Scottie Pippen's Airball: On the Role of Fiduciary Duty Law in Illinois Professional Liability Cases," *John Marshall Law Review* 48, no. 3 (2015): 799–800.

35. *Pippen v. Pedersen & Houpt,* 2013 Ill App (1st), http://www.illinoiscourts.gov/opinions/AppellateCourt/2013/1stDistrict/1111371.pdf, accessed June 13, 2016.

36. See *Frederick Dennerline et al. v. Jim Atterholt, Insurance Commissioner of the State of Indiana,* Appeals Court of Indiana, http://www.in.gov/judiciary/opinions/pdf/05160803tac.pdf, accessed June 13, 2016; Jason R. Reese, "Legal Malpractice Verdict against Law Firm," *Legal Examiner* (November 3, 2006), http://indianapolis.legalexaminer.com/miscellaneous/legal-malpractice-verdict-against-law-firm/, accessed June 13, 2016; Michael W., "Fillenwarth Dennerline Appeals Jury Verdict," *Indianapolis Business Journal* (August 21, 2008), http://www.ibj.com/articles/10149-fillenwarth-dennerline, accessed June 13, 2016.

37. *Dennerline v. Atterholt,* 5.

38. Two former ICIT executives were sentenced to prison for using monies in the plan for personal use and then seeking to conceal shortfalls by listing $2.9 million in bogus precious stones on ICIT's balance sheet.

39. An insurer who declines an offer by the plaintiff to settle a liability claim within the limits of the insured's policy can be subject to a suit for bad faith (including in some states punitive damages) if the case goes to trial and results in an award exceeding the policy limit; see Douglas Richmond, "An Overview of Bad Faith Law," *Seton Hall Law Review* 25 (1994): 103–117.

40. Michael W. Hoskins, "Settlement May Be Largest of Its Kind: State Agency Resolves Federal Lawsuit That Began with Legal Malpractice Claim," *Indiana Lawyer* (January 1, 2008), http://www.theindianalawyer.com/settlement-may-be-largest-of-its-kind-state-agency-resolves-federal-lawsuit-that-began-with-legal-malpractice-claim/PARAMS/article/23175, accessed June 13, 2016.

41. Michael W., "Insurer Settles State Lawsuit for $16.5M," *Indianapolis Business Journal* (October 13, 2008), http://www.ibj.com/articles/print/10276-insurer-settles-state-lawsuit-for-16-5m, accessed June 13, 2016.

42. *Karadsheh v. Kempski* (Mil,W No. 13-85867), http://courts.mi.gov/opinions_orders/businesscourtssearch/BusinessCourtDocuments/C17-2012-05222-NMB%20(July%2017,%202014).pdf#search=%22breach%22, accessed June 14, 2016; see also Douglas Levy, "$1.5 M Verdict in Legal Malpractice Case," *Daily Record Newswire,* http://www.legalnews.com/detroit/1399417, accessed June 14, 2016.

43. *Takahashi v. Snell & Wilmer,* Court of Appeals of California, 4th District No. G041728 (January 12, 2011).

44. His legal counsel explained to the court that his client suffered from personality disorders, was bipolar, suffered from attention deficit disorder, and could be abusive; his counsel reported that he had in fact consulted a psychiatrist about his client's aberrant behavior.

45. This was allowed in the context of a jury instruction Snell & Wilmer requested, to which Takahashi's counsel objected: "You may consider the ability of each party to provide evidence. If a party provided weaker evidence when it could have provided stronger evidence, you may distrust the weaker evidence."

CHAPTER 3. PRELIMINARY ISSUES

1. See Neil Vidmar, *Medical Malpractice and the American Jury: Confronting the Myths about Jury Incompetence, Deep Pockets, and Outrageous Damage Awards* (Ann Arbor: University of Michigan Press, 1995). Although there are many exceptions, a substantial proportion of medical malpractice cases, especially involving serious injury or death, involve multiple defendants: for example, the main surgeon, one or more assisting surgeons, one or more nurses in the operating room, and the hospital itself. In such cases, some of the defendants may admit liability and settle with the plaintiff whereas the remaining defendant(s) dispute the claim and proceed to trial. In contrast, most legal malpractice cases involve a single defendant, either an individual practitioner or a law firm; the exceptions where there are multiple defendants are usually very large cases in situations where multiple firms were representing a single client.

2. This is true in England, Scotland, Ireland, Canada, and Australia; a notable country missing is New Zealand, where there is no such requirement. There is also no insurance requirement for advocates in India; see Herbert M. Kritzer, "Lawyers' Professional Liability: Comparative Perspectives," *International Journal of the Legal Profession* 24, no. 2 (2017): 82–83.

3. See Bruno Nascimbene, *The Legal Profession in the European Union* (Alphen aan den Rijn, Netherlands: Walter Kluwer, 2009). The Council of Bars and Law Societies of Europe has established a set of "minimum standards for European lawyers' professional indemnity insurance"; see http://www.ccbe.org/fileadmin/user_upload/NTCdocument/minimum_standards_on1_1203412931.pdf, accessed April 25, 2016.

4. See https://www.osbplf.org/coverage/overview.html, accessed February 24, 2016.

5. See https://www.osbplf.org/, accessed April 10, 2015.

6. Carol Bernick to Herbert Kritzer, e-mail, April 25, 2016.

7. ABA Center for Professional Responsibility, Survey of Lawyers' Funds for Client Protection, 2011–2013 (Chicago, IL: American Bar Association, 2014), 155, http://www.american

bar.org/content/dam/aba/administrative/professional_responsibility/aba_2014_lfcp_survey.authcheckdam.pdf, accessed February 24, 2016.

8. See Nicole A. Cunitz, "Mandatory Malpractice Insurance for Lawyers: Is There a Possibility of Public Protection without Compulsion?" *Georgetown Journal of Legal Ethics* 8, no. 3 (Spring 1995), 652–657; Committee on Professional Responsibility, "Mandatory Legal Malpractice Insurance," *Record of the Association of the Bar of the City of New York* 50, no. 4 (1995): 374–375; Jerome B. Schultz, "Ensured Insurance: Bars Look at Mandatory Coverage," *Bar Leader* 12 (January–February): 19.

9. See Clay R. Williams, "LLCs, LLPs, and S.C.S: The Rules for Lawyers Have Changed," *Wisconsin Lawyer* 70, no. 5 (May 1997), http://www.wisbar.org/NewsPublications/WisconsinLawyer/Pages/Article.aspx?Volume=70&Issue=5&ArticleID=22718, accessed April 10, 2015.

10. At one time Texas had a general statutory requirement that LLPs of all types carry a minimum of $100,000 of liability insurance, but that requirement was eliminated in 2011; see "Business Organization: Recent Changes in Texas Law Favor Limited Liability Partnerships," *Blakeley's Texas Law Blog* (January 16, 2012), http://blakeleylawblog.com/San-Antonio-attorney-Brian-Blakeley-Recent-Changes-in-Texas-Law-Favor-Limited-Liability-Partnerships/17, accessed February 24, 2016.

11. See Susan Saab Fortney, "Law as a Profession: Examining the Role of Accountability," *Fordham Urban Law Journal* 40, no. 1 (2012): 188–208.

12. Leslie C. Levin, "Lawyers Going Bare and Clients Going Blind," *Florida Law Review* 68, no. 5 (2016): 1286; the requirement lapsed in 2000 but was then reinstated in 2009.

13. ABA Center for Professional Responsibility, Survey of Lawyers' Funds, 155; see also "Possible Disclosure Rule for Uninsured Lawyers," *California Bar Journal* (January 2006), http://archive.calbar.ca.gov/Archive.aspx?articleId=73308&categoryId=73304&month=1&year=2006, accessed April 12, 2015.

14. South Dakota Rules of Professional Conduct, Rule 1.4(c) and Rule 1.5.

15. Levin, "Lawyers Going Bare and Clients Going Blind," 1286.

16. David J. Beck, Texas Bar Task Force on Insurance Disclosure Memorandum, June 11, 2008, 3, http://www.texasbar.com/pliflashdrive/material/3_TaskForce_Report_June08.pdf, accessed April 11, 2015. A later report put the figure at 6 percent; see Levin, "Lawyers Going Bare and Clients Going Blind," 1299.

17. Chuck Herring, "Pro/Con Professional Liability Insurance Disclosure. Pro: Disclosure *Should* Be Required," *Texas Bar Journal* 72, no. 10 (November 2009): 823n2.

18. The percentage "going bare" in California appears to have declined from 20 years prior to the 2006 report; see Debra Cassens Moss, "Going Bare: Practicing without Malpractice Insurance," *ABA Journal* 73, no. 12 (December 1987): 82.

19. Levin, "Lawyers Going Bare and Clients Going Blind," 1301–1302.

20. Bridget C. Gernander, clerk of the Appellate Courts, to Herbert Kritzer, e-mail, June 1, 2012.

21. James Grogan to Herbert Kritzer, e-mail, August 16, 2016.

22. The Illinois data provided by James Grogan show that whereas 41.1 percent of solo private practitioners practice without insurance, this figure drops to 9.3 percent of lawyers

in firms of 2 to 10 lawyers, 3.3 percent for lawyers in firms of 11 to 100 lawyers, and 2.7 percent for lawyers in firms of more than 100 lawyers.

23. Levin, "Lawyers Going Bare and Clients Going Blind," 1288–1296.

24. Based on a survey she conducted of solo and small-firm lawyers in Connecticut, Levin reported a fairly low level of concern about the threat of a malpractice suit; see Levin, "Regulation at the Margins," 595–600.

25. Levin, "Lawyers Going Bare and Clients Going Blind," 1293.

26. See Levin, "Regulation at the Margins," 565–595.

27. See nabrico.com, accessed February 26, 2016. There are also NABRICO affiliates in Canada and Ireland.

28. Bar Plan Mutual Annual Report 2014, http://www.thebarplan.com/wp-content/uploads/2014-The-Bar-Plan-Annual-Report.pdf, accessed February 26, 2016.

29. A list of insurers, both mutual and commercial, can be found at http://apps.americanbar.org/legalservices/lpl/directory/carriers/, accessed February 26, 2016; this list is probably somewhat out of date.

30. "OneBeacon Sells Lawyers Liability Business to Argo," *Insurance Journal* (December 17, 2014), http://www.insurancejournal.com/news/national/2014/12/17/350379.htm, accessed February 26, 2016.

31. Vin Gurrieri, "OneBeacon Hit with $34M Verdict over Dish Malpractice Case," *Law 360* (October 20, 2014), http://www.law360.com/articles/588260/corrected-onebeacon-hit-with-34m-verdict-over-dish-malpractice-case, accessed February 26, 2016.

32. See http://www.thehartford.com/management-professional-liability-insurance/lawyers, accessed February 26, 2016.

33. See http://www.lawyersmutual.com/, accessed February 26, 2016.

34. See http://targetproins.com/target-insurance-programs/lawyers-insurance-program-landing-page/lawyers-the-hartford/, accessed February 26, 2016.

35. See http://wilmic.com/insurance-services/about-our-insurance/, accessed February 26, 2016.

36. See https://www.mlmins.com/insurance/insurance-overview, accessed February 26, 2016.

37. The reason criminal defense tends to be low risk is discussed later in this chapter.

38. See http://targetproins.com/target-insurance-programs/lawyers-insurance-program-landing-page/lawyers-the-hartford/, accessed February 26, 2016.

39. See https://www.osbplf.org/coverage/overview.html, accessed February 26, 2016.

40. Levin, "Regulation at the Margins," 559.

41. This section draws heavily on Tom Baker and Rick Swedloff, "Liability Insurer Data as a Window on Lawyers' Professional Liability," *UC Irvine Law Review* 5, no. 6 (2015): 1273–1316.

42. Id., 1278. Actually, several current ALAS members have fewer than 35 lawyers; presumably they either became members before the 35-lawyer minimum was imposed or at one time had more than 35 lawyers.

43. As of the 2014 report, four of those firms are based in Oregon; even with the insurance through ALAS those firms must also purchase the required LPL insurance from PLF

for their Oregon lawyers. In August 2017, ALAS's website listed three Oregon firms. At that time the total number of firms had declined slightly to 214, but the number of lawyers had increased to 62,000; http://www.alas.com/public/our_firms.aspx, accessed August 25, 2017.

44. Baker and Swedloff, "Liability Insurer Data," 1284.

45. Aon places insurance for the BAR, and Marsh does the same for MPC; id., 1287n44.

46. Id., 1282–1283.

47. A syndicate need not be assembled by a broker; it might be that a single insurer would front the entire layer but find one or more other insurers to take on a quota share of the risk. It is also not necessary that each quota share in a layer be equal.

48. As is true of any business, lawyers could face premises liability for injuries that occurred at their office facility or liability arising from traffic accidents when driving in the course of their work; we exclude these and similar types of liability from our discussion.

49. Ronald E. Mallen and Jeffrey M. Smith with Allison D. Rhodes, *Legal Malpractice, 2016 Edition: Liability, Prevention, Litigation, Insurance* (St. Paul, MN: Thomson Reuters, 2016).

50. Vincent R. Johnson, *Legal Malpractice Law in a Nutshell* (St. Paul, MN: West, 2011), 61.

51. Expert testimony is not required when the breach is something where "jurors' common knowledge and experience can adequately establish the standard of care" (e.g., missing a deadline); Douglas R. Richmond, "Why Legal Ethics Rules Are Relevant to Lawyer Liability," *St. Mary's Law Journal* 38, no. 4 (2007): 934.

52. Johnson, *Legal Malpractice Law in a Nutshell,* 104.

53. The exceptions typically relate to witnessing traumatic injury of a close family member or personally coming extremely close to experiencing a significant personal injury.

54. Johnson, *Legal Malpractice Law in a Nutshell,* 239.

55. Susan Saab Fortney and Vincent R. Johnson, *Legal Malpractice Law: Problems and Prevention* (St. Paul, MN: Thomson/West, 2008), 183.

56. Johnson, *Legal Malpractice Law in a Nutshell,* 126.

57. *Gibson v. Ellis,* 126 S.W.3d 324, 330 (Tex. App.-Dallas, 2004), quoted in Richmond, "Why Legal Ethics Rules Are Relevant to Lawyer Liability," 931.

58. Fortney and Johnson, *Legal Malpractice Law,* 105.

59. Mallen and Smith with Rhodes, *Legal Malpractice, 2016 Edition*, sec. 8:7.

60. The statute of limitations for a contract claim could also be shorter than for a negligence claim.

61. Douglas R. Richmond, "Fraud and Misrepresentation Claims against Lawyers." *Nevada Law Journal* 16, no. 1 (2015): 57–105.

62. It is unusual in a personal injury claim to seek compensation beyond the funds available from the tortfeasor's insurance; see Tom Baker, "Blood Money, New Money, and the Moral Economy of Tort Law in Action," *Law & Society Review* 33, no. 2 (2001): 275–319.

63. The specific elements of negligent misrepresentation vary from jurisdiction to jurisdiction; see Fortney and Johnson, *Legal Malpractice Law,* 156–160.

64. See https://en.wikipedia.org/wiki/Enron_scandal, accessed August 24, 2016.

65. In many instances it might be that the nature of the consequences of medical negligence is temporary and so limited (e.g., pain extended for an extra day or two, or hospitalization extended by a few days) that it is uneconomical to pursue a claim.

66. Punitive damages are rare in either medical liability claims or LPL claims in the absence of intentional conduct.

67. Based on our analysis, this kind of expert testimony appears to be required in ten jurisdictions: Colorado, District of Columbia, Kansas, Minnesota, Mississippi, Nebraska, New Hampshire, Texas, Vermont, and Virginia. There were a substantial number of other jurisdictions where such testimony might be required, but we were not able to reach a clear conclusion. In at least some jurisdictions, Texas for example, it is sufficient for the plaintiff in this kind of case to prove that it was "more likely than not" that the plaintiff would have won the underlying case at trial.

68. Johnson, *Legal Malpractice Law in a Nutshell,* 275–295.

69. We understand the rule to be a damages rule when the case law refers to knowledge of "all necessary elements," "suffers injury," or "the harm occurred."

70. Johnson, *Legal Malpractice Law in a Nutshell,* 272–275; see also Christopher Scott Maravilla, "Monday Morning Lawyering: Proximate Cause and the Requirement of Actual Innocence in a Criminal Defense Malpractice Action," *Widener Law Journal* 16, no. 1 (2006): 131–140.

71. Johnson, *Legal Malpractice Law in a Nutshell,* 274.

72. Id., 274–275.

73. David B. Wilkins, "Who Should Regulate Lawyers?" *Harvard Law Review* 105, no. 4 (1992): 805–809.

74. American Bar Association, "Preamble and Scope," *Model Rules of Professional Conduct* (2002), sec. 20, http://www.americanbar.org/groups/professional_responsibility/publications/model_rules_of_professional_conduct/model_rules_of_professional_conduct_preamble_scope.html, accessed April 27, 2017.

75. Richmond, "Why Legal Ethics Rules Are Relevant to Lawyer Liability," 937. There might be some very specific exceptions to this; see Mallen and Smith with Rhodes, *Legal Malpractice, 2016 Edition,* sec. 20:11n9.

76. Mallen and Smith with Rhodes, *Legal Malpractice, 2016 Edition,* sec. 20:12.

77. Marc R. Greenough, "The Inadmissibility of Professional Ethical Standards in Legal Malpractice Actions after *Hizey v. Carpenter,*" *Washington Law Review* 68, no. 2 (1993): 398–399. Regarding the last category, Greenough identifies only one state taking that approach, Washington.

78. An exception is civil fraud, which generally requires "clear and convincing evidence"; see Hal R. Lieberman, "'Dunn': Collateral Estoppel and Attorney Discipline," *New York Law Journal* (June 16, 2015), http://nylegalethics.attorney/dunn-collateral-estoppel-and-attorney-discipline/, accessed May 2, 2017. Lieberman also points out that, although New York's attorney disciplinary system uses a "preponderance of evidence" standard, panels in most districts ("departments") had not applied the doctrine of collateral estoppel except in applying findings from ethics panels in other states.

79. Lester Brickman and John M. Bibona, "Collateral Estoppel as a Basis for Attorney Discipline: The Next Step," *Georgetown Journal of Legal Ethics* 5, no. 1 (1991): 3.

80. We did find some indication that in some jurisdictions non-LPL cases involving nonjury matters, findings of a disciplinary panel can preclude the disciplined lawyer from

relitigating issues regarding those findings. See *Feng Li v. Peng,* 516 B.R. 26 (2014 USDC-NJ); *A to Z Associates et al. v. Cooper,* 613 N.Y.S.2d 512 (1993); *A to Z Associates et al. v. Cooper,* 215 A.D.2d 161 (1995); *Culver v. Maryland Insurance Commissioner,* 931 A.2d 537 (2007).

81. See *Kuehn v. Garcia,* 608 F.2d 1143, 1147 (1979).

82. Only judgments of criminal convictions and judgments concerning certain other matters pertaining to family issues are admissible; other types of court judgments and decisions of administrative tribunals are deemed hearsay.

83. *Roy v. Diamond,* 16 S.W.3d 783 (Tenn. App. 1999).

84. See Donald F. Paine, "Are Judgments Hearsay?" *Tennessee Bar Journal* 40, no. 11 (November 2004): 19.

85. *Roy v. Diamond,* 791 (emphasis in the original).

86. There are some circumstances in which the lawyer representing a claimant in an LPL claim is supposed to report unethical behavior to the disciplinary body. Specifically, under MRPC 8.3(a), "A lawyer who knows that another lawyer has committed a violation of the Rules of Professional Conduct that raises a substantial question as to that lawyer's honesty, trustworthiness, or fitness as a lawyer in other respects, shall inform the appropriate professional authority." Although the rule does not specify when the violation must be reported (which would appear to allow the claimant's lawyer to wait until the LPL claim has been resolved before reporting), failing to report is itself a violation of the rules and could subject the nonreporting lawyer to discipline. This happened in a case in Illinois, but in that case the nonreporting lawyer, who was suspended for one year, might have used the threat of reporting to leverage a larger settlement with the defendant lawyer; see *In re Himmel,* 533 N.E.2d 790 (Ill. 1998).

87. Jerome E. Carlin, *Lawyers' Ethics: A Survey of the New York City Bar* (New York: Russell Sage Foundation, 1966), 119–132; Bruce L. Arnold and John Hagan, "Careers of Misconduct: The Structure of Prosecution of Professional Deviance among Lawyers," *American Sociological Review* 57, no. 6 (December 1992): 774; Leslie C. Levin, "The Ethical World of Solo and Small-Firm Practitioners," *Houston Law Review* 41, no. 2 (2004): 309–392; Richard L. Abel, *American Lawyers* (New York: Oxford University Press, 1989), 144–145; Richard L. Abel, *Lawyers in the Dock: Learning from Attorney Disciplinary Proceedings* (New York: Oxford University Press, 2008), 54–56. See also Richard L. Abel, *Lawyers on Trial: Understanding Ethical Misconduct* (New York: Oxford University Press, 2011).

88. See Lisa G. Lerman, "Scenes from a Law Firm," *Rutgers Law Review* 50, no. 4 (1998): 2153–2188; Lisa Lerman, "Blue-Chip Bilking: Regulation of Billing Expense Fraud by Lawyers," *Georgetown Journal of Legal Ethics* 12, no. 2 (1999): 205–365.

89. Although both insurance markets include a mix of commercial and mutual insurers, there are differences in the two markets. Specifically, there is no bifurcation in terms of who is insured in the MPL market as there is in the LPL market. A second difference is that some large medical providers self-insure; there is nothing equivalent for legal professionals.

90. American Medical Association Advocacy Resource Center, "State Laws Mandating Minimum Levels of Professional Liability Insurance," prepared for the 2015 Medical Group Management Association Annual Conference, Nashville, Tennessee, October 11–15; http://

s36.a2zinc.net/clients/mgma/MGMA15/Custom/Handout/Speakero_Session907_5.pdf, accessed August 18, 2016.

91. Charles Silver, David A. Hyman, Bernard S. Black, and Myungho Paik. "Policy Limits, Payouts, and Blood Money: Medical Malpractice Settlements in the Shadow of Insurance," *UC Irvine Law Review* 5, no. 3 (2015): 565–567.

92. Data from medical malpractice claims in Illinois that involved serious injuries and either payment of at least $25,000 in indemnity or $5,000 in defense cost show that 33.2 percent of such cases involved more than one defendant; David Hyman to Herbert Kritzer, e-mail, August 22, 2016.

93. Vidmar, *Medical Malpractice and the American Jury*, 33.

94. Michelle M. Mello and David M. Studdert, "Deconstructing Negligence: The Role of Individual and System Factors in Causing Medical Injuries," *Georgetown Law Journal* 96, no. 2 (2008): 605.

95. Computed from David A. Hyman, Mohammad Rahmati, Bernard S. Black, and Charles Silver, "Medical Malpractice Litigation and the Market for Plaintiff-Side Representation: Evidence from Illinois," *Journal of Empirical Legal Studies* 13, no. 4 (2016): 608.

96. See Herbert M. Kritzer, *Risks, Reputations, and Rewards: Contingency Fee Legal Practice in the United States* (Stanford, CA: Stanford University Press, 2004), 86–87.

97. See Neil Vidmar, Kara MacKillop, and Paul Lee, "Million Dollar Medical Malpractice Cases in Florida: Post-Verdicts and Pre-Suit Settlements," *Vanderbilt Law Review* 59, no. 4 (2006): 1360–1378.

98. See https://www.npdb.hrsa.gov/, accessed August 19, 2016.

99. We suspect LPL lawsuits are more likely to end with adjudicated outcomes short of trial (i.e., summary judgment) than are MPL lawsuits, perhaps reflecting the very high percentage of LPL claims prosecuted by lawyers lacking substantial experience with such claims. However, this supposition is based on impression rather than hard evidence.

100. Christopher T. Robertson and David V. Yokum, "The Effect of Blinded Experts on Juror Verdicts," *Journal of Empirical Legal Studies* 9, no. 4 (2012): 777 (authors' computation from Table 3).

101. In cases involving only a single claim, only 37.9 percent resulted in a payment to the claimant.

102. See Vidmar, *Medical Malpractice and the American Jury*, 33.

103. The difference was statistically significant ($p = .040$).

CHAPTER 4. CLAIMS

1. For a summary of this research, see Tom Baker, *The Medical Malpractice Myth* (Chicago, IL: University of Chicago Press, 2005), 24–33.

2. Specifically, we use Consumer Price Index, "Detailed Report," Table 24: Historical Consumer Price Index for All Urban Consumers, http://www.bls.gov/cpi/#tables, accessed January 12, 2016.

3. Of the 14 members of the National Association of Bar-Related Insurance Companies (NABRICO), 11 contributed to the 2008–2011 study; 8 commercial insurance companies contributed, but we have no information on the number of commercial companies writing lawyers' professional liability insurance during the period covered by the study. We sought to determine what proportion of the claims covered in the 2008–2011 report came from NABRICO companies, but SCLPL would not provide that information. Two of the people we contacted in seeking this information expressed the view that more of the cases came from the NABRICO companies than from the commercial companies.

4. Some of the insurers that service large firms, such as CNA, have participated. It would be nice to be able to report what percentage of the market for legal malpractice insurance the participants have, but that information is not readily ascertainable.

5. The specific participating companies vary from report to report.

6. Standing Committee on Lawyers' Professional Liability (SCLPL), "Profile of Legal Malpractice Claims, 2008–2011" (Chicago, IL: American Bar Association, 2012) (hereafter SCLPL 2008–2011).

7. Tom Baker and Rick Swedloff, "Liability Insurer Data as a Window on Lawyers' Professional Liability," *UC Irvine Law Review* 6 (2016), 5, 1287–1300.

8. We sought to locate reports from the remaining bar-related insurers, but as best as we can tell, none of the others publish reports with data about claims experience.

9. See https://www.mlmins.com/ (hereafter MLMINS); MLMINS writes insurance in 15 states, mostly in the Midwest.

10. Wisconsin Lawyers Mutual Insurance Company (WILMIC), "Annual Report," 2013, https://www.wilmic.com/data/AnnualReport.pdf, accessed April 21, 2015 (hereinafter WILMIC, 2013 Report).

11. Lawyers Mutual Insurance Company of North Carolina (LMICNC), claims figures, http://www.lawyersmutualnc.com/annual-report/2013/year-in-review/claims-charts, accessed April 21, 2015 (hereinafter LMICNC).

12. Lawyers Mutual Insurance Company of Kentucky (LMICK), "Annual Report," 2013, http://www.lmick.com/_resources/documents/financials/2013_annual_report.pdf, accessed April 21, 2015 (hereinafter LMICK, 2013 Report).

13. Bar Plan Mutual Insurance Company (of Missouri) (BPMIC), "Annual Report," 2013, http://www.thebarplan.com/wp-content/uploads/the-bar-plan-2013-annual-report.pdf, accessed April 22, 2015 (hereinafter BPMIC, 2013 Report). As of 2013, BPMIC wrote legal malpractice insurance in Missouri, Kansas, New Mexico, Indiana, and Tennessee

14. Oregon State Bar Professional Liability Fund (PLF), "Annual Report," 2013, https://www.osbplf.org/assets/documents/annual_reports/2013%20Annual%20Report%20FINAL.pdf (hereinafter OSBPLF, 2013 Report).

15. Douglas Richmond, Mark J. Peterson, and Matthew K. Corbin, "The Aon Claims Experience," *Quality Assurance Review* (Summer 2015).

16. The reports carry the title "[Year] Missouri Legal Malpractice Insurance Report," http://insurance.mo.gov/reports/legmal/, accessed April 23, 2015.

17. BPMIC, 2013 Report, 93; Bar Plan Mutual Insurance Company (of Missouri) (BPMIC), "Annual Report," 2009, 89.

18. Rachel Crowe, Missouri Department of Insurance, Division of Financial Institutions and Professional Regulation, to Herbert Kritzer, April 29, 2015. Note that the annual range figures omit 1987, when BPMIC was just getting started; that year BPMIC constituted only 37.6 percent of claims, but the next year the percentage increased to 82.9 percent.

19. The dataset we obtained from the Florida Office of Insurance Regulation (FLOIR) contained information on 9,651 claims; 51 of those claims had been resolved in the early months of 2015, and we have excluded them from our analyses.

20. See Baker, *Medical Malpractice Myth*, 24–33.

21. We use claims per 1,000 lawyers in the figures even though, as we note when discussing specific insurers, some of the sources report claims per 100 basis; we do this because some sources report on this basis and have fewer than 10 claims per 1,000.

22. WILMIC, 2013 Report, 14. LMICK, 2013 Report, 2.

23. Brian Anderson, claims counsel, WILMIC to Herbert Kritzer, telephone conversation, April 21, 2015.

24. Carol Bernick to Herbert Kritzer, e-mail, February 18, 2015.

25. Carol Bernick to Herbert Kritzer, e-mail, April 6, 2015.

26. Carol Bernick to Herbert Kritzer, e-mail, April 20, 2015.

27. All Canadian provinces require LLP insurance, but for only three were there published reports showing claim rate information.

28. In Oregon there is some reduction of premiums for new practitioners during their first three years of practice, but not for part-time practitioners; Carol Bernick to Herbert Kritzer, e-mail, August, 17, 2016.

29. LawPRO, "Annual Report," 2014, 13 (based on claims reported), http://www.lawpro.ca/annual_reports/default.asp.

30. Law Society of British Columbia, "2014 Report on Performance," 14 (this report refers to "insurance reports," meaning reports to the insurer that "the legal services delivered may have failed to meet acceptable standards"), https://www.lawsociety.bc.ca/docs/publications/ar/2014-annualreport.pdf.

31. Alberta Lawyers Insurance Association "Annual Report," 2014, 9 (based on "claims reports"), http://lawsociety.ab.ca/files/financial/annual_report_ALIA_ALIEX_2014/2014_AR.html.

32. Attorneys' Liability Assurance Society (ALAS), *2014 Annual Report* (Chicago: ALAS, 2015), 11.

33. Baker and Swedloff, "Liability Insurance," 1304.

34. Douglas Richmond to Herbert Kritzer, e-mail, June 26, 2015.

35. We draw in part on the table prepared by Baker and Swedloff, "Liability Insurance," 1308, in generating this figure. We have collapsed the categories of "corporate/business organization" and "business transactions/commercial" into the category we have labeled "corporate/commercial." The other areas of practice identified in the SCLPL reports are labor law; workers' compensation; patent, trademark, copyright; taxation; civil rights discrimination; immigration/naturalization; construction (building contracts); local government; government contracts/claims; securities (SEC); consumer claims; natural resources; environment law; admiralty; antitrust; and international law.

36. BPMIC, 2013 Report. The pages of the report are unnumbered, but the quote can be found on the second page of the report, and the statistics can be found on the sixth page.

37. PLF labels this category "estates, trusts, and probate."

38. PLF describes this category as "workers' compensation and admiralty." Although at first this might appear to be a strange combination, we were told that the admiralty cases are actually largely Jones Act matters; the Jones Act effectively functions as the workers' compensation program for sailors injured in US waters. Unlike standard workers' compensation, it does operate under negligence rules and provides a right of trial by jury.

39. ALAS, *2014 Annual Report*, 12, http://www.alas.com/public/annualreport2014.pdf, accessed June 21, 2015.

40. For ALAS and Aon, the loss figures include both indemnity paid to the claimant and costs of defense; the loss figures for a given time also include actual expenditures and amounts held in reserve in connection with pending claims. One difference between ALAS and Aon is that ALAS does not include amounts covered by an insured's self-insured retention (deductible) whereas Aon does.

41. An article in a 2016 ALAS publication reported that between 1979 and 2011, the ratio of loss in corporate matters to losses in litigation matters was 2.76 to 1 but had shifted to 0.75 to 1 for 2012 to 2015, with the leading cause of loss in litigation being mistakes; see Joan A. Burlingame and Daniel W. Smith, "Claim Trends from 2011 to 2015," *ALAS Loss Prevention Journal* 27, no. 2 (Summer 2016): 7.

42. Figure 4.5 is based on data from SCLPL 2012–2015, 14.

43. Unfortunately, the American Bar Foundation discontinued the statistical reports after 2005.

44. This is also true for Oregon's PLF, although it is possible that large firms do not bother to file a claim with PLF because PLF only covers the first $300,000, and instead go straight to the insurer that covers the bulk of any claim. PLF does not record or report information on the firm size in its claims management system.

45. One other possibility is that the method employed by the American Bar Foundation, analyzing information in Martindale-Hubbell (a long-standing directory of lawyers) to determine the practice size for each lawyer, might count as solo practitioners a significant number of lawyers in small firms of two to five lawyers; it might be the case that firms were not identified for lawyers practicing with only a small number of other lawyers.

46. We note also that the contents of the "other" category differ depending on the size practice, with workers' compensation constituting about a third of the "other" claims for practices of five or fewer lawyers but only a sixth for the largest category. Intellectual property is about 10 percent of "other" claims for the two larger categories but only 1 or 2 percent for the two smaller categories. Tax goes from 5 percent for solo practitioners to 14 percent for firms with more than 30 lawyers.

47. Thomas L. Brown and Thomas P. Sukowicz, "Attorney Liability Risk Management," in *Attorneys' Legal Liability* (Springfield: Illinois Institute for Continuing Legal Education, 2014), 16–19, https://www.iicle.com/links/AttorneysLegalLiability12-Ch16.pdf, accessed April 23, 2015.

48. Daniel W. Smith and Robert L. Denby, "Recent Trends in Lawyer Liability: An Examination of Significant Claims in Fiscal 2011," *ALAS Loss Prevention Journal* 23, no. 2 (Summer 2012): 11.

49. Douglas Richmond, "The Law Firm Liability Terrain and the Aon Claims Experience," prepared for the Law Firm General Counsel Roundtable, May 2015, Slide 2. An earlier version of this can be found at American Bar Association, *The Law Firm Liability Terrain: Publicly Reported Settlements and Verdicts,* December 29, 2014, http://www.americanbar.org/content/dam/aba/administrative/tips/webinars/lawfirmliabilityterrainrichmond.authcheckdam.pdf, accessed June 28, 2015.

50. Id., Slide 3.

51. WILMIC 2013 Report, 14.

52. Todd C. Scott, "Who Has the Most Malpractice? Hint: It's Not the New Lawyers," *View* 29, no. 2 (April 2013): 1, https://www.mlmins.com/LibraryContent/April%202013%20Newsletter.pdf, accessed June 21, 2013.

53. William H. Gates, "Lawyers' Malpractice: Some Recent Data about a Growing Problem," *Mercer Law Review* 37, no. 2 (1986): 559–567.

54. Barbara Curran, Katherine Rosich, Clara N. Carson, and Mark C. Puccetti, *The Lawyer Statistical Report: A Statistical Profile of the U.S. Legal Profession in the 1980s* (Chicago, IL: American Bar Foundation, 1985), 28.

55. A study of disciplinary proceedings in California reported that "those disciplined are disproportionately male, between the ages of 35–45, in practice just over ten years, and practicing in Los Angeles or Orange Counties"; Robert Fellmuth, Sixth Progress Report of the State Bar Discipline Monitor (San Diego, CA: Center for Public Interest Law, University of San Diego, 1990), 89–90. Another study reported that "a disproportionate number of disciplined attorneys have been in practice more than 25 years" and that "disciplined attorneys on average are older than attorneys generally"; Patricia W. Hatamyar and Kevin M. Simmons, "Are Women More Ethical Lawyers? An Empirical Study," *Florida State University Law Review* 31, no. 4 (2004): 832. However, a study of disciplinary proceedings before one of the provincial law societies in Canada found that the likelihood of disciplinary proceedings declined with experience; see Bruce L. Arnold and John Hagan, "Careers of Misconduct: The Structure of Prosecution of Professional Deviance among Lawyers," *American Sociological Review* 57, no. 6 (1992): 777.

56. Here again we omit from the computation the "other" category in the Missouri data because SCLPL does not report that category; that category accounts for about 15 percent of all the Missouri claims.

57. The figures for Missouri omit cases in which the alleged error was coded as "other"; this was done to ensure comparability with the SCLPL figures, which do not include an "other" category.

58. Given the substantial number of cases represented in Figure 4.6, the variation is statistically significant regardless of whether plaintiffs' personal injuries are included (chi square = 1166.03, $p < .001$, df = 20, n = 4,418) or excluded (chi square = 73.92, $p < .001$, df = 16, n = 2,905).

59. Austin Sarat and William L. F. Felstiner. *Divorce Lawyers and Their Clients: Power and Meaning in the Legal Process* (New York: Oxford University Press, 1995); Roy B. Flemming, "The Client Game: Defense Attorney Perspectives on Their Relations with Criminal Clients," *American Bar Foundation Research Journal* 1 (Spring 1986): 253–277.

60. Richmond, Peterson, and Corbin, "Aon Claims Experience," 6–17. The report actually includes a sixth basis for claims, "impaired lawyer"; however, there were only 4 such cases out of a total of 5,941, and they were omitted from the analysis presented here.

61. See John P. Heinz, "The Power of Lawyers," *Georgia Law Review* 17, no. 4 (Summer 1983): 891–911; Herbert M. Kritzer, "The Dimensions of Lawyer-Client Relations: Notes toward a Theory and a Field Study," *American Bar Foundation Research Journal* 1984, no. 2 (Spring 1984): 409–428. See also David B. Wilkins, "Who Should Regulate Lawyers," *Harvard Law Review* 105, no. 4 (1992): 799–888.

CHAPTER 5. RESOLVING CLAIMS

1. This is less than a perfect solution: it appears that information on loss expense is not complete because there are some claims in all disposition categories, including trials and appeals, in which the loss expense appears as 0.

2. The dashed lines were produced using the LOWESS procedure; see William S. Cleveland, "Robust Locally Weighted Regression and Smoothing Scatterplots," *Journal of the American Statistical Association* 74 (1979): 829–836, or William S. Cleveland, "Lowess: A Program for Smoothing Scatterplots by Robust Locally Weighted Regression," *American Statistician* 35, no. 1 (1981): 54.

3. The study is reported in Herbert M. Kritzer, *Risks, Reputations, and Rewards: Contingency Fee Legal Practice in the United States* (Stanford, CA: Stanford University Press, 2004).

4. Wisconsin Statutes 893.80(1)(b). The appeal also argued that because the service was by mail, the response time should have been three days longer under provisions of Wisconsin Statutes 801.15(5)(a), but the appeals court did not rule on that issue.

5. Oregon State Bar Professional Liability Fund, *2014 Annual Report* (2015), 4.

6. In 15.3 percent of the claims in which there was a dispute over the fee, there were no other allegations against the lawyer. Only 3.9 percent of the fee-only claims resulted in a payment to the claimant.

7. Four areas with fewer than 10 cases were omitted from Figure 5.6 but were included in the calculation of the chi square statistic: international law, environmental law, admiralty law, and antitrust.

8. Although the Oregon data include information on the nature of the alleged error, the multiple response nature of that information precludes a meaningful examination of variation in success that might be dependent on the nature of the error.

9. The SCLPL reports show payment amounts in a set of four categories: $1 to $10,000, $10,001 to $50,000, $50,001 to $100,000, and $100,001 or more; later reports break down the latter category further, but that does not affect our estimate of the median. We obtained

an estimate of the inflation-adjusted median by using the method for estimating medians from grouped data described by H. M. Blalock, *Social Statistics,* 2nd rev. ed. (New York: McGraw Hill, 1979), 63–66; we then applied the inflation adjustment to the estimated median.

10. One insurer told us that his company had encountered having to pay an overlimits amount in Alaska, where there is a two-way fee-shifting rule; in such cases the insurer had to pay an additional amount to cover the fee shift to the plaintiff's lawyer.

11. Actually, three of those cases were, for various reasons, in excess of the policy limit.

12. David A. Hyman, Bernard Black, and Charles Silver, "Settlement at Policy Limits and the Duty to Settle: Evidence from Texas," *Journal of Empirical Legal Studies* 8, no. 1 (2011): 48–84. For a slightly updated analysis, see Charles Silver, David A. Hyman, Bernard S. Black, and Myungho Paik, "Policy Limits, Payouts, and Blood Money: Medical Malpractice Settlements in the Shadow of Insurance," *UC Irvine Law Review* 5 (2015): 559–586.

13. Debra Cassens Weiss, "This Big Law Firm Is Found Liable for Nearly $200M in Malpractice Trial," *ABA Journal* (November 19, 2015 [online]), http://www.abajournal.com/news/article/jurors_found_this_big_law_firm_liable_for_nearly_200m_in_malpractice_trial, accessed January 17, 2016. Several months after the verdict, and after post-trial mediation ordered by the trial judge, the parties settled for an undisclosed amount; see Michelle Casady, "Settlement Reached In $200M Andrews Kurth Malpractice Suit," https://www.law360.com/articles/759999/settlement-reached-in-200m-andrews-kurth-malpractice-suit, accessed April 17, 2017.

14. Douglas Richmond, "The Law Firm Liability Terrain and the Aon Claims Experience," prepared for the Law Firm General Counsel Roundtable, May 2015, Slides 2 and 3. An earlier version of this can be found at *The Law Firm Liability Terrain: Publicly Reported Settlements and Verdicts,* American Bar Association (December 29, 2014), http://www.americanbar.org/content/dam/aba/administrative/tips/webinars/LawFirmLiabilityTerrainRichmond.authcheckdam.pdf, accessed June 28, 2015.

15. We hedge regarding premiums because it might be that the premiums are largely influenced by what those who have study premiums for medical malpractice have described as an underwriting cycle, which reflects investment returns; see Tom Baker, *The Medical Malpractice Myth* (Chicago, IL: University of Chicago Press, 2005), 51–58.

16. There is a way to estimate a mean based on grouped data, but that is problematic when there is a top, open-ended category as there is in the SCLPL reports because it requires one to make a guess as to what the midpoint is for that category, and there is no way of doing so without knowing the maximum value; it is also problematic because the estimation process essentially assumes that the midpoint of each category roughly approximates the mean of that category, which is unlikely if there are a small number of very extreme values in the open-ended category.

17. ALAS, *2014 Annual Report,* 12.

18. For Florida, we have restricted the computation to the years when all claims had to be reported to FLOIR.

19. All of our figures for Aon come from Douglas Richmond, Mark J. Peterson, and Matthew K. Corbin, "The Aon Claims Experience," *Quality Assurance Review* (Summer 2015).

20. The requirement to report all claims ended in 1997; after that only claims with payment to a claimant or incurring at least $5,000 in adjustment expense had to be reported.

21. Except for securities-related claims, all of the seventy-fifth percentiles in Oregon are less than $50,000, and for 6 of those 10 areas, the third quartile is less than $30,000; the third quartile for securities is $128,000. Except for securities, all of the first quartiles are less than $6,500, and the majority are less than half that figure.

22. The percentages omit damages arising from the "Other" category of errors.

23. Figures 5.17 and 5.18 omit the category Aon labeled "Governmental Relations/Lobbying." These constitute only 1.6 percent of claims with some incurred loss. We omitted them because we were informed that all of the paid claims arose from the Abramoff lobbying scandal; Douglas Richmond to Herbert Kritzer, e-mail, February 13, 2016. The median for this category was $1.6 million and the mean was $4.06 million, both of which substantially exceeded the categories with the next highest median or mean.

24. Computed from *ALAS 2014 Annual Report*, 23.

25. Id., 3.

26. Richmond, "Aon's Claim Experience," 3.

27. This is a rough average based on the annual number of claims between 2009 and 2014;*ALAS 2014 Annual Report*, 11.

28. Leslie C. Levin, "Lawyers Going Bare and Clients Going Blind," *Florida Law Review* 68, no. 5 (2016): 1311.

29. US Census Department, "Professional, Scientific, and Technical Services: Subject Series—Misc. Subjects: Receipts/Revenue by Class of Customer for Selected Kind of Business for the United States 2007," Table EC0754SXSB02.

CHAPTER 6. LEGAL MALPRACTICE TRIALS

1. Paula Hannaford-Agor, Scott Graves, and Shelley Spacek Miller, *The Landscape of Civil Litigation in State Courts* (Williamsburg, VA: National Center for State Courts, 2015), 22. This figure does not count default, summary, or unspecified judgments.

2. See, for example, Neil Vidmar, *Medical Malpractice and the American Jury: Confronting the Myths about Jury Incompetence, Deep Pockets, and Outrageous Damage Awards* (Ann Arbor: University of Michigan Press, 1995); Stephen Daniels and Joanne Martin, *Civil Juries and the Politics of Reform* (Evanston, IL: Northwestern University Press, 1995), 92–151; Thomas H. Cohen, *Medical Malpractice Trials and Verdicts in Large Counties, 2001* (Washington, DC: Bureau of Justice Statistics, 2004).

3. Information study designs and selected results from these studies can be found in Carol J. DeFrances and Marika F. X. Litras, *Civil Trial Cases and Verdicts in Large Counties, 1996* (Washington, DC: Bureau of Justice Statistics, 1999); Thomas H. Cohen, *Contract Trials and Verdicts in Large Counties, 2001* (Washington, DC: Bureau of Justice Statistics, 2005); Lynn Langton and Thomas H. Cohen, *Civil Bench and Jury Trials in State Courts, 2005* (Washington, DC: Bureau of Justice Statistics, 2008).

4. Hannaford-Agor, Graves, and Miller, *Landscape of Civil Litigation;* http://www.ncsc.org/~/media/Files/PDF/Research/CivilJusticeReport-2015.ashx, accessed January 12, 2015.

5. A fourth court had such a coding category; however, we were told that the information from that court was suspect, and hence we omit any reference to it.

6. Paula Hannaford-Agor and Scott Graves to Herbert Kritzer, e-mails, January 24–28, 2016.

7. This reporter, now published by Law Bulletin (see https://www.lawbulletin.com/legal/jury-verdict, accessed May 2, 2015), started life in the late 1950s as the *Cook County Jury Verdict Reporter* (CCJVR). In 1973 the coverage of the publication was extended to the rest of Illinois; the coverage for downstate counties is likely to be less complete than for the counties around Chicago. Importantly, the coverage of bench trials is minimal (John Kirkton to Herbert Kritzer, e-mail, May 8). Most of the trials reported in *IJVR* were jury trials; only 7 of the 105 cases involved bench trials. This reporter is the source for the earliest systematic studies of jury verdicts conducted by the RAND Institute of Civil Justice.

8. As a point of comparison, *IJVR*'s database included 3,802 verdicts in medical malpractice cases during the same period; John Kirkton to Herbert Kritzer, e-mail, February 11, 2015. The legal malpractice verdicts we received included the abuse of process case brought by Lexecon against the Milberg law firm and several of its former partners (e.g., William Lerach), plus one case that did not actually produce a verdict but settled after the jury deadlocked. We have not included those cases among the 103, and they are not included in the analysis we present.

9. The latest report posted on the Administrative Office of the Court website as this book was written was for 2014, and the earliest is for 2004; see http://www.judiciary.state.nj.us/quant/index.htm, accessed May 1, 2015.

10. These reports were at http://www.txcourts.gov/statistics/annual-statistical-reports.aspx, accessed February 20, 2016.

11. Standing Committee on Lawyers' Professional Liability (SCLPL), *Profile of Legal Malpractice Claims, 2012–2015* (Chicago, IL: American Bar Association, 2016), 17; SCLPL, *Profile of Legal Malpractice Claims, 2000–2003* (Chicago, IL: American Bar Association, 2005), 8.

12. Oregon State Bar Professional Liability Fund (PLF), *Annual Report*, 4, https://www.osbplf.org/assets/documents/annual_reports/2013%20Annual%20Report%20final.pdf, accessed January 27, 2016.

13. The disposition codes used by Missouri Department of Insurance, Financial Institutions, and Professional Regulation (DIFP) did not allow us to identify which cases were tried. DIFP's reporting form combines trials and hearings, which would include summary judgment hearings or hearings regarding other dispositive motions.

14. In only 15 of the 109 cases did the claim indicate that the plaintiff had obtained some recovery.

15. Attorneys' Liability Assurance Society (ALAS), *2014 Annual Report*, 11–12.

16. Authors' analysis of Florida data; excluding directed verdicts the percentage would be 4.0 percent.

17. Hannaford-Agor, Graves, and Miller, *Landscape of Civil Litigation.*

18. Harris County (Texas) District Court also reported some numbers related to legal malpractice; however, the figures from the county seemed problematic, and we have excluded them from this discussion.

19. Paula Hannaford-Agor to Herbert Kritzer, e-mail, January 12, 2016.

20. Nicole Waters to Herbert Kritzer, e-mail, May 5, 2015. The states included are Florida, Kansas, Michigan, Minnesota, Missouri, New Jersey, New York, Ohio, Tennessee, Texas, Utah, Washington, and Wisconsin.

21. These two years are the first and the most recent years posted on the Administrative Office of the Court website, http://www.judiciary.state.nj.us/quant/index.htm, accessed May 1, 2015.

22. In fact, the federal figures overstate for a second reason: the federal statistics refer to cases that start trial, and they do not discount for cases settled during trial. Specifically reported is the "procedural progress of a case at termination"; see Herbert M. Kritzer, *The Trials and Tribulations of Counting Trials, DePaul Law Review* 63 (2013): 415, 421.

23. See George L. Priest and Benjamin Klein, "The Selection of Disputes for Litigation," *Journal of Legal Studies* 13, no. 1 (1984): 1–55. A body of research has grown up in responses to Priest and Klein's, at least some of which points out substantial variation in the outcome of trials depending on the kind of case involved. See Donald Wittman, "Is the Selection of Cases for Trial Biased?" *Journal of Legal Studies* 14, no. 1 (1985): 185–214; Donald Wittman, "Dispute Resolution, Bargaining, and the Selection of Cases for Trial: A Study of the Generation of Biased and Unbiased Data," *Journal of Legal Studies* 17, no. 2 (1988): 313–352; Luke Froeb, "The Adverse Selection of Cases for Trial," *International Review of Law & Economics* 13, no. 3 (1993): 317–324; Joni Hersch, "Demand for a Jury Trial and the Selection of Cases for Trial," *Journal of Legal Studies* 35, no. 1 (2005): 119–142; Keith N. Hylton and Haizhen Lin, "Trial Selection Theory and Evidence: A Review," in *Encyclopedia of Law and Economics: Procedural Law and Economics,* vol. 10, ed. Chris Sanchirico (Northampton, MA: Edward Elgar, 2009); Robert E. Thomas, "The Trial Selection Hypothesis without the 50 Percent Rule: Some Experimental Evidence," *Journal of Legal Studies* 24, no. 1 (1995): 209–228; Joel Waldfogel, "The Selection Hypothesis and the Relationship between Trial and Plaintiff Victory," *Journal of Political Economy* 103, no. 3 (1995): 229–260. One issue here is that for some types of cases that get to trial, the issue is not one of liability but of damages, over whether there are specific kinds of damages or over the proper amount of damages; a good example of the latter is rear-end collision cases; see Samuel R. Gross and Kent D. Syverud, "Getting to No: A Study of Settlement Negotiations and the Selection of Cases for Trial," *Michigan Law Review* 90, no. 2 (1991): 319–393.

24. Daniel Kessler, Thomas Meites, and Geoffrey Miller, "Explaining Deviations from the Fifty-Percent Rule: A Multimodal Approach to the Selection of Cases for Litigation," *Journal of Legal Studies* 25 (1996): 233–259.

25. See Neil Vidmar, "Are Juries Competent to Decide Liability in Tort Cases Involving Scientific/Medical Issues? Some Data from Medical Malpractice," *Emory Law Journal* 43, no. 3 (1994): 885–911. National studies covering trials in 2001 and 2005 found that plaintiffs prevailed in 27.1 percent of trials in 2001; Cohen, *Medical Malpractice Trials and Verdicts in Large Counties.* This figure was 22.7 percent in 2005; Thomas H. Cohen, *Tort Bench and Jury Trials in State Courts, 2005* (Washington, DC: Bureau of Justice Statistics, 2009). An

interesting question is why the win rate is so low. There are at least three possible explanations, all probably partial explanations at best. First, a significant number of medical malpractice cases are handled by plaintiffs' lawyers lacking adequate experience or expertise to handle such cases effectively; see Stephen Daniels, Mary Grossman, and Joy Malby Bertrand, "Why Kill All the Lawyers? Repeat Players and Strategic Advantage in Medical Malpractice Claims," American Bar Foundation Working Paper (Chicago, IL: American Bar Foundation, 1992); David A. Hyman, Mohammad Rahmati, Bernard S. Black, and Charles Silver, "Medical Malpractice Litigation and the Market for Plaintiff-Side Representation: Evidence from Illinois," *Journal of Empirical Legal Studies* 13, no. 4 (2016): 603–636. A second explanation is that jurors are biased in favor of physician defendants; one mock jury study using a hypothetical medical malpractice case designed to involve negligence found that fewer than half of the mock jurors found the physician negligent; see Christopher T. Robertson and David V. Yokum, "The Effect of Blinded Experts on Juror Verdicts," *Journal of Empirical Legal Studies* 9, no. 4 (2012): 777. A third explanation is that many medical malpractice cases involve multiple defendants (e.g., surgeon, anesthesiologist, hospital); in a fraction of those cases some of those defendants settle—probably those with the weaker defense, and the case goes to trial against the remaining defendants—probably those with the stronger defense; see Vidmar, *Medical Malpractice and the American Jury*, 33. However, in Chapter 3 we used data from Missouri to test this experiment but failed to find support for it.

26. There is a statistically significant difference in the likelihood of a plaintiff victory depending on whether the claim was reported in the early version of the reporting form or on the later form, which came into use around 1995: 14 percent for the early form and 30 percent for the later form (chi square = 7.17, p = .007). We do not know whether this reflected genuine change in the pattern of trial outcomes or differences in how the two versions of the reporting form were completed.

27. The figures reported to the Florida Office of Insurance Regulation (FLOIR) by the insurers are the amounts ultimately paid, not the amount of the original verdict award.

28. In nominal, unadjusted dollars, the range was $2,000 to $3.5 million.

29. The first and third quartiles were $23,368 and $401,224, respectively.

30. In the 2005 study, the codes separated out "hospital" (n = 38) and "other health" malpractice (n = 33); lumping these with the 2005 "physician" malpractice cases reduces the plaintiff success rate for this category from 23.2 percent to 22.8 percent.

31. Adjusting all awards to 2010 dollars, the four percentages were 15.5, 41.3, 7.7, and 21.7 for lawyers, physicians, dentists, and other, respectively.

32. Similar information is provided for defendants, but that information is not relevant for our purposes.

33. This difference borders on achieving statistical significance; Kruskal-Wallace test, chi square = 3.42 (df = 1), p = .0643.

34. We include among the 67 cases coded as individuals 2 cases we actually coded as both individual and business because those involved individually owned businesses.

35. The difference in awards to individuals and businesses is statistically significant according to both a Wilcoxon test (z = 2.147, p = .0318) and a medians test (chi square = 4.49, p = .030).

36. The percentage drops slightly to 33 percent in terms of nominal dollars.

37. The 50 percent holds for business plaintiffs regardless of whether one looks at 2010 or nominal dollars. For individuals, the figures are 22 percent for nominal dollars and 28 percent for inflation-adjusted 2010 dollars. This difference is statistically significant for nominal dollars (chi square = 4.78, p = .029) but significant only under a one-tailed hypothesis for inflation-adjusted dollars (chi square = 2.92. p = .088).

38. Tort defense made up 11 percent of business cases, but that was only a total of four cases.

39. Originally we had a separate category for client communication issues, but only four cases fell into that category; consequently we combined that category with the "Other or Unclear" category.

40. We also cross-tabulated area of practice with alleged error. This produces a table with 140 cells, across which are spread the 103 trials; the majority of cells is zero, and only one stands out: consistent with what was reported in Chapter 6, the alleged error in 10 of the 20 cases brought by plaintiffs alleging malpractice in a tort-related action involved deadline issues.

41. No information is available on the outcomes of trials or the amount of awards in claims against law firms that insure through Aon.

42. ALAS, *2014 Annual Report*, 11–12.

43. See, for example, Benjamin H. Barton, *The Lawyer-Judge Bias in the American Legal System* (New York: Cambridge University Press, 2011), 161–187.

44. Herbert M. Kritzer and Neil Vidmar, "Lawyers on Trial: Juror Hostility to Defendants in Legal Malpractice Cases," *Hofstra Law Review* 44, no. 2 (1975): 375–399.

45. This case was based on a trial observed by the first author as part of a study of insurance defense practice; see Herbert M. Kritzer, "The Commodification of Insurance Defense Practice," *Vanderbilt Law Review* 59, no. 6 (2006): 2053–2094.

46. This case was based on a case used in a prior study that tested the impact of the lawyers suggesting specific amounts of damages; see Leslie Ellis, "Don't Find My Client Liable, but If You Do . . . : Defense Recommendations, Liability Verdicts, and General Damage Awards," Ph.D. diss., University of Illinois at Chicago, 2002.

47. This case was based on a case used in a prior study that tested the impact on jurors of being told that one or both experts had not been informed for which side the expert was testifying; see Robertson and Yokum, "Effect of Blinded Experts on Juror Verdicts," 765–794.

48. Because the outcome was the reverse of what was hypothesized, a test of statistical significance was inappropriate.

49. Because of the skew in the responses, several different tests of significance were employed: t-test for difference of means on the original values, t-test for difference of means on the logarithms of the original values, and the Wilcoxon rank sum test. The difference of medians test was also applied. The results for this fourth test were highly dependent on how observations falling exactly at the median were treated and hence were not particularly informative.

CHAPTER 7. PROCESSING LAWYERS' PROFESSIONAL LIABILITY CLAIMS

1. For this reason, some of the quotes we give are our reconstructions rather than quotes taken from actual transcripts.

2. Only one of the lawyers with whom we spoke was female (as was one of the insurance company people). From all the evidence we could find, few women handle legal malpractice claims on behalf of plaintiffs; women might be more common on the defense side. I asked our one woman respondent why she thought so few women handled plaintiffs' legal malpractice, and the primary reason she cited was risk aversion.

3. We also ran the Google search adding the keyword "Minnesota," which produced more than 6,000 hits. When we looked through the first 100 hits, we found only 3 for Minnesota lawyers handling plaintiffs' legal malpractice. One hit supposedly was a listing of legal malpractice attorneys in Red Wing, Minnesota, but we looked at the first 5 listed and could find no evidence that they handled legal malpractice cases.

4. See http://members.calbar.ca.gov/search/demographics.aspx, accessed May 6, 2015; the exact number on that day was 183,985.

5. Accessed March 11, 2015; three lawyers' websites indicated that they handled both plaintiff and defense legal malpractice cases, for one it was unclear, and one worked primarily as an expert witness. Only 4 of the lawyers specializing in plaintiffs' legal malpractice were women; 22 of 69 specializing on the defense side were women. There are two national organizations with which some legal malpractice specialists might be associated, the Association of Professional Responsibility Lawyers and the American Board of Professional Liability Attorneys; we suspect that lawyers focused on the plaintiffs' side of legal malpractice constitute a small proportion of members of these groups.

6. Two of the lawyers were in firms with more than 50 lawyers. These lawyers were both among a small group within their firms that handled plaintiffs' work (i.e., personal injury and other torts); most of the other lawyers in these firms had nonlitigation practices.

7. One lawyer with whom we spoke who had handled only a single legal malpractice case reported that the word got around that he had taken such a case, and he still gets calls from persons seeking a lawyer to handle legal malpractice claims. Both the case he handled (which he won but could not collect on because the lawyer-defendant was uninsured, something he did not discover until late in the process) and most of the subsequent calls were from persons convicted of crimes but later exonerated.

8. Regarding the selectivity in accepting medical malpractice cases, see Herbert M. Kritzer, *Risks, Reputations, and Rewards: Contingency Fee Legal Practice in the United States* (Stanford, CA: Stanford University Press, 2004), 87–88; Stephen Dietz, C. Bruce Baird, and Lawrence Berul, "The Medical Malpractice Legal System," in *Appendix: Report of the Secretary's Commission on Medical Malpractice* (Washington, DC: Department of Health Education, and Welfare [OS 73-89], 1973), 95–101; Stephen Daniels and Joanne Martin, "The Texas Two-Step: Evidence on the Link between Damage Caps and Access to the Civil Justice System," *DePaul Law Review* 55, no. 2 (2006): 657; Stephen Daniels and Joanne Martin, *Tort Reform, Plaintiffs' Lawyers, and Access to Justice* (Lawrence: University Press of Kansas, 2015), 158–160. Importantly, given the heavy reliance on referrals from other lawyers, many of the contacts involve issues in a sense prescreened by someone with at least a modicum of expertise.

9. Also, given the actual innocence requirement, it is likely that many criminal defense practitioners choose not to carry LPL insurance, another factor that discourages knowledgeable lawyers from accepting LPL cases.

10. Potential claims related to child custody or visitation were problematic because of the absence of an economic element.

11. This kind of concern is by no means unique to lawyers handling LPL cases; see Kritzer, *Risks, Reputations, and Rewards*, 86.

12. This is a common perception of plaintiffs' lawyers; see id., 130–131. Whether it is actually true, given the pressures from insurance companies on the defense lawyers they retain to limit costs, is unclear; see Herbert M. Kritzer, "The Commodification of Insurance Defense Practice," *Vanderbilt Law Review* 59, no. 6 (2006): 2070–2076.

13. Unfortunately, we do not have hard evidence on this point because none of the datasets we have located provide information on the lawyer representing the claimant.

14. One insurer estimated that in about 20 percent of actual claims the company was dealing with an unrepresented claimant.

15. An expert will also be consulted if there is a dispute regarding whether negligence occurred. One insurer reported that such consultations occurred in 30 percent of the files the company opened.

16. Some cases get into suit even if there are not major issues regarding merit. A lawsuit might be filed if the statute of limitations is about to run out. As suggested by the comments of some of the plaintiffs' lawyers with whom we spoke, some plaintiffs' lawyers might have a practice of more or less automatically filing suit without first seeking to settle the case. One insurer reported that in 10 percent of the files the company opened, the first notice it had of the claim was when its insured forwarded the summons the insured had received.

17. This might be something of an overstatement with regard to legal malpractice claims because this insurer's policies also cover some expenses in disciplinary matters, and almost a quarter of the files opened are "ethics" only.

18. We asked the person who made this point whether claims more frequently involved nonspecialists (i.e., general practitioners) than specialists. We were told that the claim rate is about the same, but if frequency for specialists is less, it is likely that the claims that do occur involve more in potential damages.

19. This is an issue generally in the relationship between insured and insurer, particularly when there is the potential of a verdict exceeding the amount of coverage; see Herbert M. Kritzer, "Betwixt and Between: The Ethical Dilemmas of Insurance Defense Practice," in *Lawyers in Practice: Ethical Decision Making in Context*, ed. Leslie C. Levin and Lynn Mather (Chicago, IL: University of Chicago Press, 2012), 142–145.

20. See Ellen S. Pryor and Charles Silver, "Defense Lawyers' Professional Responsibilities: Part I—Excess Exposure Cases," *Texas Law Review* 78, no. 3 (2001): 623–624.

21. National Association of Bar Related Insurance Companies, http://www.nabrico.com.

22. Summary judgment can also be a pivotal point if there is an issue of whether the lawyer-defendant had any duty toward the claimant, as in cases where heirs or beneficiaries of trusts claim that the lawyer made errors in writing the will or creating the trust.

23. A study of 2,735 medical malpractice claims closed in Wisconsin between 1976 and 1988 found that 728 distinct attorneys appeared, 625 (86 percent) of whom appeared five or fewer times; however, those 625 attorneys accounted for only 42 percent of the closed claims. That is, 58 percent of the claims were handled by attorneys with six or more appearances

in the dataset; 40 percent of the claims were handled by lawyers with more than 10 appearances, and 21 percent by lawyers with more than 30 appearances. See Stephen Daniels, Mary Grossman, and Joy Malby Bertrand, "Why Kill All the Lawyers? Repeat Players and Strategic Advantage in Medical Malpractice Claims," working paper (Chicago, IL: American Bar Foundation, 1992), Table 1b. Drawing on data reported to the Illinois Department of Insurance on every medical malpractice claim closed in Illinois between 2000 and 2010, Hyman et al. report that the 8.5 percent of firms that had recovered a total of $5 million or more accounted for 37.4 percent of all cases (45.0 percent if pro se cases are omitted) and 73.4 percent of the total amount recovered over the period; see David A. Hyman, Mohammad Rahmati, Bernard S. Black, and Charles Silver, "Medical Malpractice Litigation and the Market for Plaintiff-Side Representation: Evidence from Illinois," *Journal of Empirical Legal Studies* 13, no. 4 (2016): 608.

CHAPTER 8. IMPROVING ACCESS TO JUSTICE FOR THOSE HARMED BY THE ACTIONS OF THEIR LAWYERS

1. See John P. Heinz and Edward O. Laumann, *Chicago Lawyers: The Social Structure of the Bar* (New York: Russell Sage Foundation, 1982).

2. We believe that it is also probably likely that in many incidents of legal negligence, the lawyer can repair the problem and thus avoid the client experiencing harm. This also contrasts with medical negligence, in which any but the most minimal error is likely to result in some harm even if that is only a few extra days of hospitalization or a few days of discomfort or pain.

3. See Benjamin H. Baron, *The Lawyer-Judge Bias in the American Legal System* (New York: Cambridge University Press, 2011), 163. Barton attributes this in part to the role lawyers play in judges getting and keeping their positions and in part to the training and experience judges share with the lawyers who come before them, either as representatives or as litigants. See also Lawrence W. Kessler, "The Unchanging Face of Legal Malpractice: How the 'Captured' Regulators of the Bar Protect Attorneys," *Marquette Law Review* 86 (2002): 457–499.

4. A research assistant produced a list of 47 articles in bar journals, law reviews, and other periodicals aimed at the legal profession that discuss the issue of mandatory insurance. Many of the articles advocate in support of mandatory malpractice insurance.

5. Oregon law authorizes the board of governors of the Oregon State Bar to require all private practitioners to have liability insurance; 2013 ORS sec. 9.080(2)(a). The Oregon State Bar imposed mandatory insurance in 1977 effective July 1, 1978, and created the Professional Liability Fund (PLF) to be the provider of that mandatory insurance; https://www.osbar.org/plf/plf.html, accessed May 11, 2015.

6. In a conversation with a claims manager at one of the mutual companies, we were told the insurers opposed mandatory insurance because it would require them, either directly or indirectly (by required subsidization of a high-risk pool), to insure bad risks.

7. See Herbert M. Kritzer, "Lawyers' Professional Liability: Comparative Perspectives," *International Journal of the Legal Profession* 24, no. 2 (2017): 82–83.

8. Bruno Nascimbene, *The Legal Profession in the European Union* (Alphen aan den Rijn, Netherlands: Walter Kluwer, 2009); some missing information was obtained through e-mail correspondence.

9. Kritzer, "Lawyers' Professional Liability."

10. As discussed in Chapter 4, the annual claim rate in Oregon is about 12 per 100 lawyers, several times higher than that reported by other state bar–affiliated insurers that can be selective in whom they insure. All of the Canadian provinces require LPL insurance, and publicly available data for insurers in three of the provinces show claim rates in the same range as reported by the Oregon State Bar's PLF; see Kritzer, "Lawyers' Professional Liability," 77.

11. An effort to find examples of disciplinary consequences for nonpayment of a malpractice judgment found a small number of cases in which that nonpayment might have contributed to a decision to impose discipline, but no cases in which nonpayment alone resulted in discipline.

12. The model rules can be found at http://www.americanbar.org/groups/professional_responsibility/publications/model_rules_of_professional_conduct/model_rules_of_professional_conduct_table_of_contents.html, accessed October 23, 2016.

13. Tim Burke, Minnesota Office of Lawyers Professional Responsibility, phone conversation with Herbert Kritzer, October 19, 2016.

14. See http://www.legalombudsman.org.uk/, accessed May 11, 2015.

15. Adam Sampson, "Don't Be Afraid to Complain about Your Lawyer, Says Legal Ombudsman," *Guardian*, October 15, 2012, http://www.theguardian.com/law/2012/oct/15/legal-ombudsman-complaints-lawyer, accessed May 11, 2015.

16. This is referred to as a complaint dealing with a "reserved activity," Scheme Rules 10, January 28, 2015, http://www.legalombudsman.org.uk/downloads/documents/publications/scheme-rules.pdf, accessed May 11, 2015.

17. See Andrew Boon, "Understanding Lawyer Default in England and Wales: An Analysis of Insurance and Complaints Data," *International Journal of the Legal Profession* 24, no. 2 (2017): 97.

18. American Bar Association, Standing Committee on Lawyers' Professional Liability (SCLPL), *Profile of Legal Malpractice Claims, 2012–2015* (Chicago, IL: American Bar Foundation, 2012), 20.

19. In 2010 dollars, the corresponding percentages are 85.6 and 72.3, respectively.

20. See http://www.financial-ombudsman.org.uk/, accessed May 11, 2015. Studies of the Financial Ombudsman Service (FOS) can be found in Sharon Gilad, "Accountability or Expectations Management? The Role of the Ombudsman in Financial Regulation," *Law & Policy* 30, no. 2 (2008): 227–253; or Daniel Schwarcz, "Redesigning Consumer Dispute Resolution: A Case Study of the British and American Approaches to Insurance Claims Conflict," *Tulane.Law Review* 83, no. 3 (2009): 755–812. A Google search for "financial services ombudsman" reveals that similar services exist in Ireland, Australia, Canada, and New Zealand (and probably in several non-English-speaking countries as well).

21. See Schwarcz, "Redesigning Consumer Dispute Resolution," 770–779, for a good description of the FOS process for dealing with complaints it receives.

22. See http://www.financial-ombudsman.org.uk/publications/factsheets/compensation-over-100000.pdf, accessed May 11, 2015.

23. Schwarcz, "Redesigning Consumer Dispute Resolution," 773.

24. The FOS actually serves the whole of the United Kingdom, with a population of 64 million.

25. See Sampson, "Don't Be Afraid to Complain about Your Lawyer, Says Legal Ombudsman."

26. See http://www.financial-ombudsman.org.uk/publications/ar14/about.html#product, accessed May 11, 2015.

27. *Pro hoc vice,* Latin for "for or on this occasion only," is the method by which lawyers not licensed in state are admitted for the purpose of appearing in court for a specific case in a jurisdiction where the lawyer is not admitted to practice.

28. Schwarcz, "Redesigning Consumer Dispute Resolution," 770. The banking industry (including the British equivalent of what once were called savings and loan associations in the United States) also set up ombudsman services; see Philip Rawlings and Chris Willett, "Ombudsman Schemes in the United Kingdom's Financial Sector: The Insurance Ombudsman, the Banking Ombudsman, and the Building Societies Ombudsman," *Journal of Consumer Policy* 17, no. 3 (1994): 307–333.

29. Walter Merrick, head of FOS, conversation with Herbert Kritzer at FOS office, January 9, 2006.

30. Schwarcz, "Redesigning Consumer Dispute Resolution," 782. Schwarcz points out that another disincentive for a consumer is the risk of having to pay the defendant's legal fees in an unsuccessful court action.

31. See https://www.vcat.vic.gov.au/adv/disputes/legal-practice, accessed April 11, 2016.

32. See https://www.vcat.vic.gov.au/system/files/2014–2015_vcat_annual_report.pdf, p. 35; accessed April 11, 2016.

33. Kritzer, "Lawyers' Professional Liability."

34. Nienke Doombos and Leny E. de Groot-van Leeuwen, "From Complaint to Compensation: Access to Justice in Dutch Legal Malpractice Cases," paper presented at Workshop on Consumer Redress When Lawyers Are Negligent, International Institute for Sociology of Law, Oñati, Spain, July 9–10, 2015, 19.

35. Kritzer, "Lawyers' Professional Liability."

36. Id.

37. See Susanne Di Pietro and Teresa W. Carns, "Alaska's English Rule: Attorneys' Fee Shifting in Civil Cases," *Alaska Law Review* 13, no. 1 (1996): 33–93.

38. See Susan M. Olson, "How Much Access to Justice from State 'Equal Access to Justice Acts'?" *Chicago-Kent Law Review* 71, no. 2 (1994): 547–582; Susan Gluck Mezey and Susan M. Olson, "Fee Shifting and Public Policy: The Equal Access to Justice Act," *Judicature* 77, no. 1 (1993): 13–20; Robert V. Percival and Geoffrey P. Miller, "The Role of Attorney Fee Shifting in Public Interest Litigation," *Law & Contemporary Problems* 47, no. 1 (1984): 233–248.

39. *Saffer v. Willoughby,* 670 A.2d 527, 534 (NJ 1996).

40. See Charles Silver, "Unloading the Lodestar: Toward a New Fee Award Procedure," *Texas Law Review* 70, no. 4 (1992): 865–970.

41. *Nix v. Verp* (New Jersey Superior Court, Appellate Division), 2015 WL 10322006 (February 22, 2016); *Geranio v. FEC Mortgage Corp.* (New Jersey Superior Court, Appellate Division), 2009 WL 383348 (February 18, 2009); *Middlebrook and Shapiro, P.C. v. Esdale* (New Jersey Superior Court, Appellate Division), 2008 WL 649181 (March 12, 2008); *Atlantic Research Corporation v. Robertson, Freilich, Bruno & Cohen LLC* (New Jersey Superior Court, Appellate Division), 2011 WL 557947 (February 18, 2011). Despite these decisions, the New Jersey Supreme Court has not definitively decided that a lodestar approach is the proper method of computing fees payable by the losing defendant in a legal malpractice case.

42. Some states might, in certain circumstances, allow noneconomic damages in such cases; see Ronald E. Mallen and Jeffrey M. Smith with Allison D. Rhodes, *Legal Malpractice, 2016 Edition: Liability, Prevention, Litigation, Insurance* (St. Paul, MN: Thomson Reuters, 2016), 21:11.

43. David A. Fischer, "Tort Recovery for Loss of a Chance," *Wake Forest Law Review* 36, no. 3 (2001): 605–655; Joseph H. King, "'Reduction of Likelihood' Reformulation and Other Retrofitting of the Loss-of-a-Chance Doctrine," *University of Memphis Law Review* 28, no. 2 (1998): 491–560.

44. Ellen M. Burlick, *A Concise Restatement of Torts*, 2nd ed. (St. Paul, MN: American Law Institute Publishers, 2010), 199–201.

45. See Fischer, "Tort Recovery for Loss of a Chance"; Marcia M. Boumil and Paul A. Hattis, *Medical Liability*, 3rd ed. (St. Paul, MN: West, 2011): 155–159.

46. Jonathan P. Kieffer, "The Case for Across-the-Board Application of the Loss-of-Chance Doctrine," *Defense Counsel Journal* 64, no. 4 (October 1997): 568–580.

47. See Benjamin H. Barton, "Do Judges Systematically Favor the Interests of the Legal Profession?" *Alabama Law Review* 59, no. 2 (2008): 495–496.

48. Kentucky Stat. sec. 413.245.

49. Louisiana Rev. Stat. sec. 9:5605.

50. Hawaii Rev. Stat. sec. 657-1(1).

51. Wisconsin Stat. sec. 893.53.

52. See Mallen, Smith, and Rhodes, *Legal Malpractice*, sec. 23:10.

53. The lawyer could agree to toll the statute of limitations (i.e., stop the clock).

54. Providing an option of an "assigned risk pool" similar to what exists for auto insurance in states with mandatory auto insurance would raise problems if such a program required contributions from the other insurers because that would essentially require that insurable lawyers subsidize the high-risk lawyers. However, this is essentially what the program in Oregon does, and the cost is not that high.

Index

www.ingramcontent.com/pod-product-compliance
Lightning Source LLC
Chambersburg PA
CBHW031928160726
48298CB00013B/249/J
9780700625857